The Carlsberg Story

Ditlev Tamm

The Carlsberg Story

Founders, Foundations, and Fortunes

English translation by Russell Dees

Springer

Ditlev Tamm
University of Copenhagen
Copenhagen, Denmark

ISBN 978-3-030-52669-6 ISBN 978-3-030-52670-2 (eBook)
https://doi.org/10.1007/978-3-030-52670-2

This Springer imprint is published by the registered company Springer Nature Switzerland AG
The registered company address is: Gewerbestrasse 11, 6330 Cham, Switzerland

Preface

This book tells the story of the Carlsberg Breweries since their foundation in 1847. It is a story of a talented family of brewers and, at the same time, a story of early industrialism. It is a story of beer production and of how science and business met to create a new way of brewing. It is the story of how a Danish brewer started a company that ended up becoming one of the biggest international concerns in its field. It is also the very peculiar story of how a foundation run by academics could also run a big business.

The story of Carlsberg presented here is based on the Danish version of the book *De klogeste og skarpeste—Historien om Carlsbergfondet, bryggeriet og vores øl,* which was published in Danish in 2018. It was written at the initiative of the Carlsberg Foundation's current chairman, Professor Flemming Besenbacher. He had in mind an account of the most recent changes in the Carlsberg Foundation's charter, which paved the way for a new global Carlsberg. That story, however, cannot be properly understood except in the context of the earlier history. This book, therefore, tells the story from the founding of Carlsberg in 1847 until now.

The book is the result of intensive archive studies both at the Carlsberg Foundation and at the Brewery. In addition, there were intensive conversations with relevant people. Apart from Flemming Besenbacher, the following people deserve thanks: Nils Smedegaard Andersen, Carl Bache, Anders Bering, Jens Bigum, Jan Schans Christensen, Claes Gjermansen, Zoran Gojkovic, Jørgen Grønborg, Søren Hansen, Jørn P. Jensen, Povl Krogsgaard Larsen, Flemming Lindeløv, Palle Marcus, Poul Christian

Matthiessen, Birger Lindtner Møller, Niels Kærgaard, Ole Olsen, Walther Paulsen, Niels Petri, Jørgen Buhl Rasmussen, Lars Rebien Sørensen, Majken Schultz, Birgitte Skadhauge, Anne-Marie Skov, Nina Smith, Poul Johan and Lise Svanholm, Jess Søderberg, Søren Theilgaard, quaestor Jens Otto Veile, Carlsberg's attorney Peter Wengler-Jørgensen, and Per Øhrgaard, who have my heartfelt thanks for their generous, in-depth conversations from which this author has learned much. An especially hearty thanks must be given to Thomas Storgaard, who has helped inexhaustibly in the scouring of the archives and by providing many valuable comments while the work was underway.

Thanks also to Carl Bache, Michael Christiansen, Palle Marcus, and P. C. Matthiessen for valuable comments on the translation and to Russell L. Dees, the translator, who did a good job finding the (hopefully) right terms for quite complicated concepts.

The translation was made possible thanks to support from the Carlsberg Foundation and the Konsul George and hustru Emma Jorck's Foundation for which I am grateful.

Copenhagen, Denmark Ditlev Tamm
May 2020

About This Book

The beer industry and the history of beer are fascinating topics. The story told in this book is about how a large and important Danish brewery came into being and the foundation behind it, which has preserved its independence until now. It is about the Carlsberg Foundation and its relation to the Carlsberg Brewery; it is about management, about the way Carlsberg later expanded, about beer and science, about large amounts of money, and about people who have been preoccupied with these things. It is a family story and also the story of how one of Denmark's biggest companies has been owned and run by a foundation governed by scientists and scholars. It is about fortune in both senses of the word. A lot of money has been earned on beer, but some luck is also needed to survive in a highly competitive business world.

Traditionally, beer is something drunk in great quantities in Denmark, and this book begins in the early 19th century with the story of how one particular brewer, J. C. Jacobsen, and his son Carl brewed quality beer and, later, gave their breweries to two foundations, the Carlsberg Foundation and the New Carlsberg Foundation. Both of these foundations support Danish sciences and arts. The story of these two talented Danish entrepreneurs and patrons of the arts is an essential part of the history of Denmark. Neither Denmark nor Danish science would have been the same without beer or without large commercial foundations such as the Carlsberg Foundation. Nor would arts in Denmark have thrived as well without the New Carlsberg Foundation.

The Carlsberg Story was only fragmentarily illuminated in earlier works written by, among others, three previous chairmen of the Carlsberg Foundation.[1] The historian Kristof Glamann—member of the board of the Carlsberg Foundation from 1969–1993—took his account to the beginning of the 1990s but touched only briefly on the time after 1970. Before Glamann,[2] two earlier chairpersons of the foundation[3] had discussed their chairmanship in autobiographies. Every age needs its own history of the past. It has its charm that former chairmen write the history of the foundation or their own stories, but this also holds the risk that their own efforts will be placed at the center, while more controversial issues are underemphasized or not mentioned at all. Often, when it comes to business history and, particularly, when it comes to the people affiliated with the business, daylight hours are best counted with a sundial, as they say. Less flattering parts of the story remain in darkness or are dismissed or excused with brief remarks.

For this new story of Carlsberg and the foundation behind, a unique set of sources in the form of minutes from meetings at the Carlsberg Foundation, interviews, correspondence exchanges, etc., were made available to this author. Diligent minute-takers carefully reproduced often lengthy negotiations on leadership issues and much else, which is important to understand the history of Carlsberg. It has been a great pleasure in itself to be able almost to listen along when these people (who had responsibility for the foundation over the years) discussed the affairs of the foundation and its relation to the Carlsberg brewery. They were all scholars; and, if nothing else, it is characteristic of such people that they think about what they say and, as a rule, mean at least some of it. Therefore, this book is not a continuation of older works but tells the history from the beginning based on new material.

We start out with a description of the founder, J. C. Jacobsen, and his son Carl Jacobsen, their mindset, and the establishment of the Carlsberg Foundation in 1876, followed by an account of events in the relationship between foundation and firm that are relevant to understand how Carlsberg and the foundation behind it came into existence and are still in existence today.

The main subject of this book is how the Carlsberg Foundation has run its breweries, while the foundation's just-as-important work for Danish science and culture in connection with the distribution of research funds is

[1]Pedersen (1942), Glamann (1976 and 1993).

[2]Glamann (2002).

[3]Bjerager and Krogsgaard-Larsen (2011) and Matthiessen (2017).

dealt with only more sporadically. To the extent the book is read as an occasional critical commentary on the foundation's competence and work, it is only in relation to the management of the brewery and not about the great effort the foundation makes in supporting Danish science and culture. Today, the foundation distributes millions of Danish crowns to the natural sciences, the humanities, and the social sciences, and it is important to remember that when the foundation's efforts are to be judged.[4]

The history of the Carlsberg Foundation, breweries, beer, and science is no less interesting, considering the fact that, as of 2020, Carlsberg is (still) the world's third-largest brewery concern and a player on the world market, a market dominated more and more by a few very large breweries. Just twenty years ago, not many would have predicted that Carlsberg would be among them today. This book tells the story of how Carlsberg and its foundation, the Carlsberg Foundation, not only survived in a highly competitive beer market but even climbed to the top of the international heap—albeit at the lower end of that top echelon. In reality, the board of the Carlsberg Foundation is not in a position to know very much about either beer or business management, and the book recounts how the foundation nevertheless led the Carlsberg brewery to success over the years—especially since the turn of the millennium when Carlsberg grew truly large. It was not always a cheery story, but it seems at the moment to be chugging along happily.

Hopefully, the reader is now ready to undertake an extended pleasure trip during which, of course, it is permitted to stop and enjoy the brewery's products, which includes both beer and soft drinks. It is not for nothing '*that calls for a Carlsberg*' is one of the brewery's many slogans.

References

Bjerager, A.-L., Krogsgaard-Larsen, P. (2011). *Bryggerens lærling : Povl Krogsgaard-Larsens erindringer.* Gyldendal.

Glamann, K. (1976). *Carlsbergfondet.* Copenhagen: Rhodos.

Glamann, K. (1993). *Carlsbergfondet siden 1970* [Eng. trans. *The Carlsberg Foundation since 1970*, 1994]. Copenhagen: Carlsbergfondet.

Glamann, K. (2002). *En blandet landhandel.* Copenhagen: Gyldendal.

Matthiessen, P. C. (2017). *Følg med tiden. Ikke med strømmen.* Copenhagen: Gads Forlag.

Pedersen, J. (1942). *Carlsbergfondet* [Eng. trans. *The Carlsberg Foundation*, 1956]. Copenhagen: Munksgaard.

[4]You may read about this in other works, in the foundation's annual reports, and, recently, in the Carlsberg Foundation's illustrated annual review.

Contents

1

Introduction

1.1 You Can't Be a Real Country Unless You Have a Beer

Beer is a national drink. In two almost immortal sentences, the American musician Frank Zappa summed up the connection between a country and its beer:

> You can't be a real country unless you have a beer and an airline. It helps if you have some kind of a football team, or some nuclear weapons, but at the very least you need a beer.

When it comes to beer, Denmark is, indeed, a real country. The Carlsberg brewery occupies a special place among Danish businesses as one of the country's oldest and largest industrial concerns. As producer of what is modestly called "probably the best beer in the world," the brewery has had a very clear view of itself; and, in Denmark, the brewery and its products are still considered a national treasure that must and will remain in Danish hands. Terms of ownership today are far less clear-cut than they were at the time of the founder,[1] but Carlsberg's beer is and remains "our beer," and "our"

[1]Today, the Carlsberg Foundation owns around 30% of the capital with a voting influence of around 76%.

D. Tamm, *The Carlsberg Story*,
https://doi.org/10.1007/978-3-030-52670-2_1

quite unambiguously means that we are talking about a Danish product—one Danes gladly share with others but one that fundamentally belongs to and must remain in the country.

Nor is beer just any drink. It is a product with an ancient history of brewing reaching back to antiquity and before, a local anchoring, and its own traditions. Smaller and larger breweries the world over have been bought up in recent years like never before, but one part of the purchasing strategy is to allow local breweries to maintain and stand out with their own, often national, idiosyncrasies. It is not the point for the French beer consumer to think of Carlsberg when enjoying a Kronenbourg 1664, a brewery owned by Carlsberg since 2008. Nor are Norwegians to remember that their national brewery Ringnes went to Carlsberg in 2004, Italians who drink Moretti to think of Heineken, or the connoisseurs of the Belgian beer Hoegaarden to be reminded that the brewery was taken over by InBev and is today part of the international beer mastodon AB InBev. There are still national beer labels; but, as a rule, they are not so national after all when it comes to ownership. Just under half of the world's beer consumption is met today by breweries owned by one of the three large international beer concerns just mentioned. AB InBev is by far the biggest, followed far behind by Heineken. Carlsberg is still among the top three, and the powerful connection of Danes to Carlsberg today, therefore, is more of an exception than the rule.

Beer is beer, but not all beer is good beer. The co-existence of beer and humans is almost a fundamental condition that can be traced back thousands of years. Beer consists basically of water, barley, hops, and yeast. With that and a few other ingredients you can play around with, you can get a more or less good-tasting product. A Tibetan brewery director caused a stir at one point at the beginning of this millennium when Carlsberg was on the lookout for opportunities in western China and Tibet. He said, "Beer is all pretty much the same."[2] But even if he was too outspoken, he was a little bit right. Producing beer is not in itself anything special. Therefore, it requires an effort to get consumers to prefer a particular beer label. Beer belongs to the type of product today known as FMCG, "fast moving consumer goods", that is, consumer goods that have a very short shelf life and quick turnover. In the beer industry, however, people like to consider beer, with its long cultural history, as something different and more exclusive than razor blades, batteries, detergent, food and drink, toilet articles, headache pills, or whatever other FMCG convenience goods might be mentioned, intended to have as large a turnover as possible. For beer especially, there is the fact that it is a relatively

[2] *Financial Times* (23 July 2004).

heavy good that requires some effort to ship and the production of which requires a large and expensive apparatus. Therefore, it is better to be big than small if you are producing beer.

The history of Carlsberg has to do with "our beer" as something entirely special. Yet, beer is also just a trade good and, in modern business terminology, a good with an expiration date that must—and preferably in great quantities—be distributed to buyers for consumption and even exported without too much questioning of the sustainability of long distance carriage. "Supply" is the economic term for the quantity of a particular product available to consumers. This sounds technical, and so it is. Quantity in such a calculation can be a target more important than quality; but, in the end, success depends on providing both within the given economic framework. Therefore, there is a constant danger that beer will become a bulk commodity without any great prestige or, put in another way, that industrial-made beer will lose terrain, for example, to artfully-produced and expensive so-called craft beers. If one talks about beer as an FMCG, it has fundamentally more to do with business than culture. One challenge for the beer producer, therefore, is to unite the recognition that beer is a product for sale—preferably, to be sold quickly and in great quantities with a certain tact and sense that beer is a quality product with its own identity.

The beer market and the forces that control it are an exciting field in which there is constant movement. Carlsberg succeeded until now by not only surviving but growing and avoiding so-called "hostile" takeovers, when one or more businesses (often, competitors) aim to take over management of the company against the desire of a sitting board of directors by tempting the company's shareholders with a favorable share price—an enterprise in which Carlsberg itself gladly participated. How it happened that Carlsberg not only avoided this fate but even became an aggressive buyer is a long story. It begins at the dawn of Danish industrialism in the mid-19th century, and it has to do with how technology and science met to create an entirely new epoch for beer brewing. Much has happened—particularly, in the last twenty years, and it has gone fast. Virtually a revolution has taken place both with respect to the rules that apply to the foundation and to the reality in which they are used.

As a business, Carlsberg is and definitely conceives itself to be unique. This goes hand in hand with its special form of ownership and the way in which the brewery's history is exploited by the business as a part of its "branding". The founder's "spirit" and the use of profits to support basic scientific research is part of a comprehensive story that can be instrumental in keeping the business together and, hopefully, sell more beer. A modern term for the exploitation of a firm's history as a part of its product marketing is "heritage branding". It need not be a century-old history. It can also be a more ordinary and contemporary story of, for example, the firm's strong social consciousness or respect for climate and environment. The term of art *corporate social responsibility* (CSR) may also be used, and no company with any respect for itself today avoids presenting itself as an entity that places great weight on CSR. The most important thing is how to incorporate history positively into the narrative of who you are and how you got so far in order to sell something that others, in principle, can do just as well. Carlsberg has been particularly good at it, and precisely this side of the brewery's history is burgeoning right now.

The tale of Carlsberg and its founders is not only an important part of Danish industrial history and the story of how Denmark became rich by industrializing its agricultural products, it is simply a part of the history of Denmark. It is an extended, coherent story in which references to Carlsberg's founder, brewer J. C. Jacobsen, and his governing principles of life are constantly repeated whenever major decisions about the brewery and its future are to be made. It is a story that could even form the basis of a Danish TV series in twelve episodes, which garnered two million Danish viewers in 1996, even though opinions were divided as to whether it successfully presented the story dramatically enough over so many episodes.[3] The history of Carlsberg and the Carlsberg Foundation has to do with much more than beer and breweries. It has to do with support for science, art, and culture and what you can do for them with the sale of beer. However, it is not the story of the Carlsberg Foundation as patron and pillar supporting Danish research throughout the years that is told here. [4] Rather, we trace how the business behind the Foundation, the Carlsberg brewery, developed from a local and, later, a large regional brewery with a well-known international brand into one of the major players in the world's super-league of brewery concerns. This is a story that deserves to be told in its own right.

[3]On the brewery's involvement in the series, see Overländer Jensen (2013), pp. 133 ff.

[4]It is an exciting story in itself about, *inter alia*, the foundation as initiator of Niels Bohr's research in nuclear physics or about its support for spectacular archeological excavations in Denmark, the Middle East, and elsewhere, for scientific expeditions and publication of major works on Denmark's churches or of hard to access sources in the country's ancient history. Or it may be the history of the foundation's financing of major projects such as the Danish cultural institutes in Rome and Athens or individual scholars with their own exciting projects within the natural sciences, the humanities, and the social sciences.

1.2 Shareholders and Foundations

Since 1888, the Carlsberg breweries have been run by a foundation, the Carlsberg Foundation, which is closely linked to the Royal Danish Academy of Science and Art. Linking the ownership of the brewery to a foundation that supports science and art is a part of the Carlsberg brewery's international branding: "It all comes from beer". It has to do with the history of the brewery, Carlsberg's founder J. C. Jacobsen, his special mindset, and his peculiar relationship to money for an industrial entrepreneur. Jacobsen was a manufacturer who went for quality, and it was not for money's sake that he brewed his own beer in the then suburb of Copenhagen, Valby, starting in 1847. For him, money and the achievement of profits were not goals in themselves but means. He rejoiced at producing quality products—in this case, beer—and at doing something for others with whatever profit might come out of it. Jacobsen himself once wrote, perhaps coyly, to his son Carl, who was residing in England, of his pleasure that the son had received "some of the spirit of practical enterprise that distinguishes the population of this country to so high a degree. This pleases me all the more since I myself lack almost any aptitude in a commercial direction ...."[5] In this way, he and his firm differ from many of his contemporaries—particularly, from the shareholder companies that were beginning to see the light of day in 19th-century Denmark, whose primary purpose was to acquire financial dividends for their shareholders. One of them was the Tuborg brewery, which was founded in 1875 and became Carlsberg's largest, natural competitor on the Danish beer market until the two merged in 1970.

The Carlsberg brewery (or breweries[6]) developed over time into a something quite different from the one the Carlsberg Foundation took over in 1888, after J.C. Jacobsen willed his Carlsberg brewery to the Carlsberg Foundation. A charter for the Carlsberg Foundation was drafted and later amended several times, especially in the last twenty years, with a view to strengthen the brewery's opportunities to acquire capital in order to gain ground in the more and more competitive international beer market.

Brewer Jacobsen had run his brewery as a sole proprietor. In principle, he disliked shareholders and shareholder companies and the idea that the controlling aim was not quality but the shareholders' desire for profit. Nevertheless, as we shall hear, despite the brewer's reservations about this construction, Carlsberg wound up becoming a shareholder company, Carlsberg A/S, in 1970 with the Carlsberg Foundation owning a significant part,

[5] Letter to Carl, 5 Feb. 1869.

[6] For the period in which J.C. Jacobsen and his son Carl ran separate businesses.

though far from most of the share capital. On the other hand, the foundation has a decisive majority of votes. That is actually an important feature to understand the present ownership structure. Due to the distinction in Danish law on shareholder companies, it is possible to operate with shares that have different numbers of votes. You may be a minority shareholder as to capital but have a vast majority of votes, and this is how the Carlsberg Foundation today runs Carlsberg even though it owns only around 30% of the capital.

Ever since its establishment in 1876, the foundation's board of directors has been selected from among the members of the Danish Royal Academy. Since 1888 when J.C. Jacobsen donated the brewery to it, the Foundation has also had the responsibility of running the Carlsberg brewery. This means that, in the end, the brewery is run by people who definitely are not schooled to be businessmen—an entirely strange construction, which went together with Jacobsen's special trust in science and its devotees. How has it gone, and how is it going? Can it continue? Can you really expect professional and effective business management this way? Can this sort of foundation-owned company raise the necessary capital? Or: can you adapt an old charter for a foundation established in 1876 to the reality and economic needs of a new era? These are some of the fundamental questions raised in connection with a foundation-owned company such as Carlsberg, and the foundation's management has grappled with many of them over the course of time, as we shall return to repeatedly. This story is about how the brewery's owner, the Carlsberg Foundation, and the brewery itself since 1888 have supported each other over the years, about the way management has run things, and about how times changed, so that concerns involving the brewery were pushed more and more into the foreground.

Just as there would not be a foundation without beer, we can today state that there would hardly exist a Danish Carlsberg brewery with its headquarters in Denmark without the Carlsberg Foundation or even an independent Carlsberg, much less a Carlsberg of international dimensions with the ambitions the firm has today. Does the brewery exist for the foundation's sake to earn money for science, or does the foundation serve the brewery, so the business is at the center? What is the goal, and what is the means? These questions are posed at intervals, and not everyone answers the same way. The answer today is different. On the other hand, there is a consensus that foundation ownership is a successful ownership model for a large commercial enterprise. Therefore, Jacobsen chose the proper model if what he wanted was to secure the survival of his brewery,[7] and the history of Carlsberg and the Carlsberg Foundation does not contradict this claim.

Foundations are not for sale. Today, a number of the major Danish firms and many smaller ones are foundation-owned, but as a rule they did not start out as such. A foundation can and—as far as larger foundations are concerned—often will be a shareholder or majority shareholder, as it has been the case with the Carlsberg Foundation since 1970. A foundation is regulated by a charter peculiar to that foundation with provisions on the purpose of the foundation, which will often be a nonprofit goal or have to do with securing a firm or a family or both. Often, it will be determined that the foundation is to own a particular quantity of shares in the firm behind the foundation, which can create problems if new capital is to be acquired, as we will see later. Problems may also arise if the foundation charter contains provisions that limit the ability to adapt the charter to the needs of a new era or prevent certain forms of operation. Such problems became familiar to the Carlsberg Foundation, and in the following we will see how they were dealt with over time.

Foundations already existed in Denmark when J.C. Jacobsen established the Carlsberg Foundation in 1876. There were at that time no laws that particularly defined or regulated this form of disposition. Foundations like the Carlsberg Foundation with a controlling influence in a firm are called commercial foundations as opposed to non-commercial foundations; and, in Denmark, the two types of foundation have been regulated since 1984 by separate statutes and have different supervisory authorities. In the charter, there are also rules about the composition of the board of directors, which in today's Denmark is under the supervision of a public agency.[8] Today, commercial foundations are under the supervision of the Danish Business Authority (*Erhvervsstyrelsen*), which maintains contact with the foundation in the form of annual inspections and an operating review of the foundation's business. Previously, the Danish Ministry of Justice supervised the Carlsberg Foundation and allowed a number of quite radical adjustments of the foundation charter. Large foundations are important for a country's economy. Therefore, the Carlsberg Foundation has enjoyed a great deal of benevolence from its supervisory authorities, when there has been a question of accommodating the Charter to new conditions.

---

[7]"It's probably the best ownership form in the world", says an expert, Professor Steen Thomsen from the Copenhagen Business School, *Finans* (22 Dec. 2015).

[8]The Carlsberg Foundation once owned the whole of Carlsberg. That is not the case anymore. The firm itself—the brewery Carlsberg A/S—is today a corporation, but the foundation still exists and owns approximately 30.3% of the share capital. Due to the fact that shares may have different voting power, the Carlsberg Foundation still has controlling influence in the brewery.

There is a fundamental difference between a shareholder company and a foundation-owned firm, and J.C. Jacobsen was very conscious of this fact. He wanted his brewery to remain independent and not be run as a business together with others. He felt more comfortable if his brewery Carlsberg (or Old Carlsberg) in its entirety were given after his death to the foundation he had formed and to the Danish Royal Academy in 1876. Thereafter, the Academy has designated the board of directors for the foundation from among its members. It was quite a risk to place responsibility for a large business in the hands of a scholarly academy. Brewing and managing a big brewery is professional work. It is typically not a profession which you qualify for as a scholar or scientist. On the other hand, many businesses managed by people who appeared to be professional, talented businessmen have collapsed. J.C. Jacobsen's effort, therefore, might not have been so risky after all. At any rate, the brewery still exists, and the business is bigger than ever.

A lot has happened since J.C. Jacobsen established his foundation in 1876; and, effective as of 1 October 1888, the Carlsberg Foundation took over responsibility for Jacobsen's breweries, but the Danish Royal Academy still designates the five members of the board. Over the course of time and especially in recent years, developments in the beer market have gone in a different direction than Jacobsen could predict, and most of Jacobsen's principles have had to be modified with the dramatic developments in the international beer market in recent decades. Being owned by a foundation has its strengths and its weaknesses. Like a bulwark, the foundation has protected the brewery from buyouts and, thus, secured Carlsberg against takeover by more capital-rich businesses. On the other hand, the construction has also led to difficulties in connection with necessary capital injections, and precisely the lack of understanding of the need for capital by a very conservative foundation board was for a while in the decades after 1970 a dangerous hindrance for the expansion of the brewery.

In recent years, some existential choices were made about the future of Carlsberg. One chief question was whether and to what extent Carlsberg should expand internationally—which required capital and the willingness to take risks—or whether the brewery should remain a national or regional brewery and count on being able to survive primarily by selling in the Danish market with some exports to other countries in the region and elsewhere.

Carlsberg, as is well known by now, decided to expand and is today a worldwide business with a position as the smallest of the world's three largest breweries.[9]

The vast majority of Danish firms began as one-man businesses. Some were later transformed into shareholder companies in order to gain capital or ease a generation shift once they had reached a certain size.[10] It was only as late as 1917 that the first statute was enacted in Denmark, outlining more detailed rules for corporations.

Bequeathing a foundation, the Carlsberg Foundation, with a large brewery was in its time a unique and bold construction. Later, other large Danish foundations came into existence with a background in a commercial firm. It is actually something of a Danish specialty that a great number of the larger Danish firms are owned by commercial foundations. The presence of a large number of headquarters for major foundation-owned firms in Denmark has positive effects not to be ignored. It creates international prestige, brings jobs for many at a high level, and increases the need for intensive air traffic and airports, for specialized attorneys and accounting assistance, and much else that fosters growth even though the production takes place elsewhere. Therefore, it is of more than symbolic significance that the Carlsberg breweries have and retain their headquarters in Denmark.

References

Jensen, Jørgen Oberländer (2013). 35 år og en sjat på Carlsberg. Erindringer fra et hus med øller i. Odense: Historia Forlag.

Johansen, H.C., & Monrad Møller, A. (2005). *Fonde som fundament for dansk industri*. SDU Press

Lund, A.B., & Berg, E. (2016). *Dansk fondshistorie*. Copenhagen: Jurist- og Økonomforbundets Forlag.

Thomsen, S. (2017). *The danish industrial foundations*. Copenhagen: Jurist- og Økonomforbundets Forlag.

[9]Today (2017) after the two giants on the beer market, A(nheuser-)B(usch) InBev (20.8%) and SABMiller (9.7%), merged in 2016, these breweries account for approximately 30% of global production. In second place is Heineken with approximately 9%, and in third place is Carlsberg with approximately 6.1% followed closely by China Resources Enterprise Ltd. with 6%.

[10]On this, see the historical account in Johansen and Monrad Møller (2005), p. 13 ff., Brink Lund and Berg (2016), and Steen Thomsen (2017).

2

1847—Foundation and Founding Fathers

2.1 For Thinking Brewers

In 1847, J. C. Jacobsen founded the Carlsberg breweries. A year later, in 1848, the absolute monarchy was abolished in Denmark. A constitutional monarchy was introduced in 1849. The period from around 1800 until 1848 is often seen as a 'golden' age for Danish culture and arts. It was a time of renowned painters and poets but also a time for professors of natural sciences, represented first and foremost by H. C. Ørsted, who also took an interest in the practical use of chemistry for brewing beer.

"Thinking" brewers were the target group for a small 93-page book published in 1828 about the principles of brewing beer by a former brewer and distiller in Copenhagen, Christian Anton Brøndum, the man who gave his name to the popular Danish Brøndum aquavit.[1] Beer and aquavit complement and oppose each other. You can drink beer and aquavit together, but aquavit must be imbibed with moderation in order to avoid alcoholism. Therefore, beer is a better quencher and a healthier alternative to aquavit, which, by contrast, can slake one's sorrows more quickly and with less quantities of liquid. If schnapps is too cheap, it is easy to drink too much of it. For sobriety and public health, therefore, it is best for schnapps to be expensive and beer to be the cheaper to encourage drinking more beer than schnapps—all the more reason for an idealistic brewer to brew good beer. At that time, beer in Denmark was far from being a quality product. Beer was necessary

[1] C. Brøndum, *Grundsætninger for Ølbryggeriet* (1828).

D. Tamm, *The Carlsberg Story*,
https://doi.org/10.1007/978-3-030-52670-2_2

to drink as a substitute for polluted water, but brewing in itself was at a rather low stage, and the poor quality offered by brewers in Copenhagen or in other towns was often lamented by the consumers, who had no free choice in their provider of beer. At that point, beer brewing in Copenhagen was not held in high esteem. It was a protected trade, and many brewers could only survive thanks to the protectionist system, which ensured sales without regard to quality. To get good and tasty beer in Copenhagen, it was necessary to buy expensive imported beer from Germany, which was the closest market.

H. C. Ørsted wrote the introduction to Brøndum's manual of brewing and J. C. Jacobsen's father, Chresten Jacobsen, a brewer about whom we shall hear soon, received thanks for good advice. Fermentation processes and their significance for brewing were something that interested Ørsted. The introduction also revealed that Ørsted himself with interest in improving brewing by scientific means had contributed to the book with comments both of a more scientific nature and about brewing in other countries—especially England. Ørsted's concluding remarks that "thinking brewers" would be able to see from the book's "scientific truths" which improvements could be introduced to "our breweries" became a guideline for Brewer Jacobsen's future work. He was the epitome of the "thinking brewer" to whom the book referred, and it is this story we shall hear now.

As an introduction to his book, Brøndum describes in a few words what beer is: "Beer is a wine-like drink made by the fermentation of beer wort, which is prepared by allowing water to extract the soluble components of malt. Malt is made by taking a grain in such a condition that it begins to sprout and then interrupting the sprouting as soon as the flour-like components of the grain are transformed into sugar and have sufficient solubility to be extracted by water of a moderate heat; with which change a great many more follow". The problem, however, was that most brewers did not understand the way to influence this process. Of the general state of brewing in Denmark, therefore, he ascertains: "Most pursue this treatment without knowing the causes of the changes that take place beneath their eyes and, therefore, pursue it without, or without any certainty of, a good outcome, which they want since, to their benefit, they understood how to adapt their procedures to the variations in the type of grain, air temperature, and other circumstances." After this introductory, almost literary description of the quizzical brewers who, without insight into the process, see water turn into beer, Brøndum fixes the principle that also became J. C. Jacobsen's: "In order to attain the pertinent proficiencies, one must borrow some principles from science." As technical support, Brøndum pointed to the thermometer, which at that time was still a "foreign" word, and the hydrometer to judge the beer's strength; one had to know the water, type of grain, and yeast "since one does not want to work blind."

In a small autobiographical sketch from 1828,[2] Ørsted himself highlighted Brøndum's practical books as a model for the cooperation between science and commerce. "Everywhere, science and commerce must approach each other in absolute confidence in order to understand each other," wrote Ørsted here. He also said that it was part of "the perfection of science to have beneficial effects on civil society." This was something brewer Jacobsen could also endorse.

Jacobsen's father was one of the admirers of the great physicist and had challenged his son to pursue the natural sciences as well as he could without getting a degree from grammar school and without striving for an academic career. The young Jacobsen also became a member of the Society for Natural Sciences (*Selskab for Naturlære*) founded by Ørsted, and he attended his stimulating lectures on the importance of science at the just founded Polytechnic College (now, the Technical University of Denmark). Ørsted was the great attraction; the chemist Zeise had a reputation for being dry, but the mineralogist G. Forchhammer also had a lecture style that appealed to listeners. Much later, on 2 September 1865, J. C. Jacobsen wrote in a letter to his son Carl, who was away in apprenticeship abroad, about his own lack of real education: "the task for the brewers of today and the near future lies beyond my own abilities, for I was not so fortunate as to fulfill my desire to complete a course at the Polytechnic College and become a true chemist and physicist. Therefore, I am well on my way to being surpassed as a rational brewer—perhaps, it has happened already—of course, not in Denmark but in Europe".

The important recognition at that time was that the production of good beer is not a magic trick or dependent on chance but a result of successful malting and fermentation processes and storage. This was something one could study and learn to translate into practice. In the letter from 1865 to his son Carl, J. C. Jacobsen also wrote: "Whoever possesses the fundamental knowledge in chemistry and auxiliary sciences in connection with the necessary practical skill and insight, he will be Europe's leading brewer in the coming generation. This must be your goal. Otherwise, you will soon sink down into the rightly disdained class of empiricists to which I will be counted before long if you do not before then take me under the arm and keep me above water ...." This was something of a declaration of confidence to be considered binding.

[2]Printed in H. A. Kofod's *Conversations-Lexicon* (1828), pp. 515–541.

2.2 A Brewer for His Time

J. C. Jacobsen, later on simply known as the "Brewer",[3] was born in Copenhagen on 2 September 1811. J. C. stands for Jacob Christian. J. C. Jacobsen was the only child of brewer Christen Jacobsen and his wife, Caroline Frederikke Schelbek. Jacobsen senior was a true *self-made man.* He was the son of a small farmer, originating from Vendsyssel at the northern tip of the Jutland peninsula. In 1800 as a 27-year-old, he went to Copenhagen, became a brewer's apprentice, and ran a brewery for a number of years as leaseholder on what is now the street of Brolæggerstræde in the city's center. Later, he acquired the property and set about expanding both the house and the firm. It went well for Jacobsen, who was both talented and intelligent. So, J. C. Jacobsen grew up in a relatively well-to-do brewer's home with a father who was good at his craft and also had an understanding of the importance of science for brewing beer. Chresten Jacobsen had kept up with the lectures of H. C. Ørsted and others—particularly on chemistry, and he also encouraged his 17-year-old son to attend these lectures. J. C. Jacobsen had had to shelve any thought of studying himself, however. He was needed in the brewery business, and from the beginning of the 1830s as his father's health declined, he had to take over larger and larger portions of the operation of the family business. Upon his father's death in 1835, the 24-year-old son took over responsibility for the brewery on Brolæggerstræde.

Four years before the brewer's birth—in 1807—as a small piece in a great game for European domination, Copenhagen was attacked and set afire by English troops who stole what was left of the Danish fleet;[4] that is the way Danes saw it, and Denmark was thereby forced into an alliance with Napoleon. Two years after his birth—in 1813—a reorganization of the Danish monetary system, known as the "great state bankruptcy", was implemented. In 1814, the centuries-old union between Denmark and Norway was dissolved by the Treaty of Kiel. The king at the time was Frederik VI. Much could be said about him and his style of governing and quite a bit negative, but not about the way the king wielded absolute power. The absolute monarch was resistant to critique, and it could be downright dangerous to express political opinions even though there might be good reason to criticize Danish unpreparedness against the English attack, monetary policy, and the dispositions that led to the loss of Norway.

[3]Glamann (1990).

[4]The Danish navy, apart from a few ships, was deliberately put in dry dock but was still seen as a threat by the English in the event Denmark became an ally of Napoleon, which was unlikely to happen before the British action 1807.

The otherwise unfortunate king was actually popular even though he had caused foreign policy disasters and stubbornly held onto absolute power. In his youth, the king helped implement important reforms; and, despite being a sourpuss, the king was an upright person and had some fine human qualities that, *inter alia*, were demonstrated by his support of the great artists of the time. One of those who benefitted from his largesse was the actress Johanne Louise Heiberg, who rose from the bottom of society and, in time, was admired by the king and became a friend of J. C. Jacobsen. In a letter on 22 April 1887 shortly before Jacobsen's death, she compared her relations to Jacobsen with her relationship to the old king: "Things with you are, for me, like with Frederik the 6th in his time. He lived so long I had a feeling that I had a father whom I could trust in time of need, to whom I could turn if it was ever needed. Such a friend I have had in you, a friend who has made me happy and proud …." It was at once an ambiguous and an apt comparison, whatever one might think of the somewhat awkward king. Whether this letter, written just a week before Jacobsen's death in Rome on 30 April 1887, reached him alive or whether he appreciated the comparison if it did is unknown.

Not everyone looked upon the king positively, and there were good grounds for that, too. A so-called free press ordinance from 1799 that tightly regulated freedom of speech had been an effective tool for shutting the mouths of critics, and it was definitely enforced, as proved by the banishment in 1800 of two of Denmark's most critical and intelligent writers, the authors P. A. Heiberg and Conrad Malthe Bruun. They both moved to Paris, where Malthe Bruun thrived better than Heiberg. This was a warning to the likeminded to think again before setting pen critically to paper. However, otherwise you could live quite well in the king's Copenhagen as long as you minded your own business and did not say anything unconsidered about the government. J. C. Jacobsen was born under the absolute monarchy, and his own way of running a business had pronounced patriarchal features, but he was among those who could gradually see that this form of political regime had outlived itself. Jacobsen also took his turn in politics and in the local, so-called citizens' militia in which he achieved the rank of captain. He was proud of this, and in his mature years, he enjoyed—perhaps a bit coyly in relation to his real efforts—to be called Captain J. C. Jacobsen, as Mrs. Heiberg would address him. Jacobsen was a child of his time, and the times were pivotal. His father had not had the same opportunities as he had, and his own son Carl came to live as the son of a wealthy man in a very different era in which the great breakthrough for industrial beer brewing would occur and the challenges and competition were different. J. C. Jacobsen's time was one of upheaval after the French Revolution and the Napoleonic Wars in which science, industrialization, and new technology came together. J. C. Jacobsen understood before many others that the requirements for beer brewing had changed. He also understood the necessity to keep up, as those who believed they could rest on their laurels might easily be left behind by the next generation.

Decisive for what ended up becoming one of the greatest success stories of Danish commercial life was the fact that, beyond understanding the connection between chemistry and brewing beer, Jacobsen recognized the poor quality of Danish beer in comparison with German beer, which was imported to Denmark, and he had the will and the skill to do something about it. He noted the methods of storing beer used in Germany, the so-called Bavarian method of brewing Bavarian beer, and he began to experiment with this new type of beer in Denmark.

Later, in 1859, J. C. Jacobsen himself recorded how, after a trip in 1844 to master brewer Georg Sedlmayer's brewery "Zum Spaten" in Munich, he "in the year 1845 had … established beneath Copenhagen's walls the first Bavarian storage cellar, … whereupon the following winter I began to brew Bavarian lager at my brewery in Copenhagen. The production, however, was limited in the first year to about 300 barrels but rose already the following year to about 1800 barrels of beer".[5]

In October-November 1845, Jacobsen had been on yet another trip to Munich and brought home in his hat case a batch of so-called bottom-fermenting strains of yeast, which was an important ingredient in the Bavarian method, and this process became the foundation for his future brewing. Jacobsen's Bavarian beer *made in Denmark* was an immediate success. Sales opportunities outstripped production speed, as it often happened also later in Jacobsen's history. In his account from 1859, he wrote how he, when production "proved insufficient to supply both the capital and the provinces from which orders began to be received, had … in 1847 erected a complete Bavarian brewery, Carlsberg, near Valby, reckoning on a production of 5000 barrels a year …." This is where the history of the Carlsberg brewery begins.

J. C. Jacobsen was—as already stressed—a manufacturer, someone who wanted to found and further production, and he was not and did not want to be seen as a businessman—at least, not in a traditional sense. Countless stories circulate about how he rejected the opportunity for an immediate profit by raising prices or expanding production beyond what he himself considered sustainable. His products were successful by virtue of their quality,

[5]J. C. Jacobsen's account of his work until then dates from 1859.

and Jacobsen became a very well-to-do man who could not only care for himself and his family but was also capable of contributing to society as a generous patron. J. C. did not care for the word "patron" even though he was very close to being the epitome of one. He would rather talk about being "public spirited".[6] It was not just generosity, he displayed as a solidly established wealthy man in his later years. Rather, patronage was a part of his lifestyle, which meant that he provided all possible support with the means he had. Sometimes when his business required it, there might be an interruption of patronage, but it began again as soon as the coffers allowed it. When in 1868 his son Carl asked, during a stay in England, whether he might mention to his friends there that his father was a millionaire, his father replied that he would leave that to his son but that, if he did, he should inform them that the fortune was tied to the breweries and that his father personally was in debt. Money for him was a means, not an end in itself. For Jacobsen, it was all about beer and its quality and about whether profit from this might do society some good.

J. C. Jacobsen's political sympathies originally lay with the members of the so-called National Liberal Party, which wanted a closer connection between Denmark and Schleswig and a loose union (if any at all) with the Duchy of Holstein, which was also part of the vulnerable Danish "*Gesamtstaat*" that, thus, included a strong and increasingly aggressive German-speaking minority. In the years 1854–1863, he was a member of the second chamber of the Danish Parliament. In 1863, he was appointed by the king to be a member of the so-called Council of the Realm (*Rigsråd*), which was established for the joint affairs of the Danish realm and the Duchies of Schleswig and Holstein. Politically, he was at that time a dyed-in-the-wool "Eider-Dane", who advocated for Denmark incorporating territory "to the Eider River". Therefore, he voted for the fateful constitution of 1863, the so-called November constitution, which on paper and against international agreements tied Denmark and Schleswig together—ultimately, leading to war with Prussia and Austria and the devastating defeat of 1864. Jacobsen later felt a personal responsibility for having supported what afterwards had to be recognized as an irresponsible policy that proved harmful to the country. His cultural patronage became a kind of recompense for what he felt was a debt to the nation.

Jacobsen's nationalist temperament and desire to strengthen Danish national consciousness in the years after 1864 were given strong expression in his eagerness to rebuild the Royal Frederiksborg Castle in northern Zealand,

[6] Glamann (1990), p. 195 ff.

which had been ravaged by a fire in 1859. Rebuilding and refurbishing the castle, so that one could learn from and be proud of one's national history, became a cause dear to his heart. In 1878, the Frederiksborg Museum became a part of the foundation he had established in 1876. We shall return to this.

Business historian Camillus Nyrop wrote a biography of Jacobsen on the centenary of his birth in 1911,[7] followed a year later by a biography by philologist Johannes Østrup.[8] The successful brewer and the responsible citizen but not the father is at the center here. After the writing and studies of Sigmund Freud, it has been difficult to avoid a more psychologized analysis in which the relationship between father and son has been given an important place. Kristof Glamann's books about the Brewer and his son Carl have allowed a psychologizing father complex to dominate his presentation of Carl,[9] and the father-son relationship was also a primary theme in the TV series *Bryggeren* (The Brewer), which was shown for the first time on Danish television in 1996. It would hardly have pleased the Brewer, who might also have furrowed his brow at one thing or another that later took place with his breweries.

Carl, J. C. Jacobsen's only son, came to play an important role in the history of the Carlsberg breweries. Unlike his father, he had a thorough education as a brewer with long trips abroad and the opportunity to learn about international breweries. At the same time, from birth, great demands had been placed on the only child Carl; his father would go charging in even if it had to do with something as personal as his love life. Carl, unlike his father, was raised as the son of a rich and demanding man. His education as a brewer was a real one, one in which you were thrown into the deep end and learned to swim. And so he did, forging a large network of contacts. He later proved to be quite talented at both brewing beer and making money. Many letters preserved from father to son in those years deal with more personal issues as well as technical issues of brewing. J. C. Jacobsen did not keep journals, and he later destroyed the correspondence from his son.[10] The letters from him that are preserved, however, throw a powerful light on the relationship between father and son—particularly, on the father's obsession with his son's education.

Especially important for the story is how the relationship between father and son became complicated when Carl's own beer since the beginning of the

---

[7]Nyrop (1911).

[8]Østrup (1912).

[9]See, for example, Glamann (1995), p. 302: "In Carl Jacobsen's letters and records, there are a number of 'key situations' in which it is tempting to allow his behavior was dictated by the subconscious and a father complex.".

[10]Glamann (1990), p. 113.

1870s became a success. In the father's view, it was not always of the quality he thought it should be. Therefore, Jacobsen was skeptical when it came to the question of the son's ability to weigh earning opportunities and quality against each other or to prioritize expenses and, thus, whether he was the right person to take over the "Brewer's" businesses. This skepticism, which proved unfounded in the long term, was an important part of his decision to convey his breweries to the Carlsberg Foundation and not to his son after his death.

In 1867, Jacobsen's brewery was ravaged by fire, but it was quickly rebuilt. In a letter dated 30 September 1867 to Carl, who was on his Grand Tour of Europe, the Brewer described drily but precisely the new facilities after the fire. It is reading as dry as Julius Caesar's description in *The Gallic War* of how one builds a bridge across the Rhine. However, in the same way as this passage in *The Gallic War* reflects parts of Caesar's personality, the letter says a great deal about Jacobsen's engagement in and understanding of the importance of every detail. Carl was certainly an interested reader because, at that point, he was educating himself quite thoroughly to become a brewer. The letter runs like this:

> … the exterior of the buildings are quite as before, with the exception that the stairwell between the kilns and the brewery wing is elevated a few feet above the roof ridge like a sort of tower with a platform and bricked parapet and the little connecting building between the malt house and the grain store, where the steeping tanks are located, is likewise raised to the level of the stairwell.

J. C. Jacobsen described how, "… iron water containers, holding 120 barrels each, have been erected, while the 2 larger water containers holding 440 barrels, as before, are placed nearby under the roof beams", and Carl also learned that, in the cellar, there was a bricked cistern "holding 500 barrels into which the water was pumped from the well in the garden" and that precautions had been taken with "more fire hydrants". All the details are there—also about the interior of the buildings in which much was changed, and "the heating chambers have been moved to the north end where the workers' room was before and in the earlier place of the heating chambers are now placed the 3 steam boilers. In the brewery, the mash and straining vats are in their old place …. The floor of the engine room is made of marble slates and the walls are covered with delft tiles …." Jacobsen was not so happy about "the almost white galvanized roof tiles that shone very strongly in the sun". On the other hand, Jacobsen thought that "the two tower sections mentioned [look] good, and there is a beautiful view up there and easy access to it …."

This was the brewery that twenty years later was not to become Carl's but was given to the Carlsberg Foundation.

Jacobsen placed great weight on discipline and creating supportable living conditions for his workers in return for the dedication of the workers to his Carlsberg, which became a model business. At Carlsberg, a patriarchal structure prevailed that presumed complete loyalty to the firm in recompense for pay, pension, and security in the form of healthcare and permanent employment. Once you were employed, you stayed employed as a rule, and a very large number of employees remained then and later at Carlsberg all their lives, so that 25-, 40-, and even 50-year anniversaries were the order of the day. Workers were cared for, but requirements were also made in the form of devotion to duty and precision. There were fixed rules for worktime and general behavior, and anyone who did not follow these provisions could be levied a fine, which did not go to the Brewer or the firm but to charity at the "Valby Asylum, whose treasurer issues a receipt".[11] Such rules furthered discipline, and they created a fixed daily framework around the worker's life, so that they did not waste time but could put all their energy into the business. They were, as Foucault has reminded us, reminiscent of corresponding regulations for schools, barracks, hospitals, or prisons, all of which presumed disciplining and, by governing the spirit and the will of those who were subject to the rules, induced them to contribute their best for the enterprise. At that time, there were no rules of maximum work hours. Only Carl Jacobsen introduced later to his brewery a fixed 10-hour work day from 6 a.m. to 6 p.m. (with a break), and he wrote (but much later in 1896) that he hoped that "the eight-hour work day would be introduced everywhere abroad, so it will also necessarily benefit brewery workers".[12]

Work at a brewery takes place around the clock. The product must be monitored, and the process can easily be disturbed by carelessness, so it is important that the right working spirit is present. Of the actual work conditions at Carlsberg, the Brewer himself later wrote rather self-consciously but also surprisingly candidly in a letter to his chief competitor, the founder of the Tuborg brewery Philip Heymann. He stressed that the risk of dissatisfaction was poor at Carlsberg: "because all my people know that I myself am a 'worker' with my life and soul and consider all my people as my 'co-workers' for whose reasonable desires I always have an open ear and gladly welcome them of their own accord. Therefore, it will hardly occur to any of them to come to me with demands that they well know that I would refuse from my

[11] Regulations for people at the breweries 'Old Carlsberg' from 1887, art. 17.

[12] See Nyrop (1886), p. 102.

whole way of thinking and acting ...." The letter had to do with the work and pay conditions for the coopers, who produced the beer barrels.

Of this, Jacobsen could also relate that, "at times, such as on dark winter days in which I avoid as far as possible having work done on the floor by candlelight, the work hours are very short and, even though the day is long enough, I let them off early when they've been doing stressful work .... At other times ... when it is urgent, work needs to be done until late in the evening. Work is also done as a rule on Sundays ... My apprentice coopers, therefore, get a monthly wage of DKK 95, and they also get after their term of employment an annual award of DKK 150–200 as well as free doctor's care, medicine, and hospital care. Likewise, the other workers are after 10 years of service enrolled into the pension fund". Rights corresponded in the Brewer's universe to duties: "On the other hand, all without exception are obligated to carry out all the work required without respect to the hour or whether it is day or evening or night. However, when my people know that I do not demand more work from them than is necessary and that I would like to give them all the rest and free time that can be united with the requirements of the brewery, I never see anything other than zeal and satisfaction with their positions".[13]

2.3 Augustus

In addition to his work as a brewer, Jacobsen was an active socialite, and it is a part of his history and that of his brewery that his home in Valby became a gathering point for a large portion of Copenhagen's intellectual and political elite. Jacobsen was at ease with the most prominent authors, philosophers, composers, artists and scientists of the time. In the same letter to Carl in which he described the fire, he wrote about "the evening at Jerichau's[14] in their new residence—formerly, Thorvaldsen's at Charlottenborg. We met here, in addition to R. Nielsen (philosopher), Gade (composer), H. C. Andersen (the world-famous author), Marstrand (painter), Worsaae (archaeologist) and others, a French artist, elocutionist, Madame Ernst, who gave a reading of a number of poems and dramatic pieces in French ...." He writes that, by hearing her declamation, he had the desire to learn more French. Jacobsen had moved up in the "*beau monde*". A somewhat more prosaic description of the aforesaid lady we find from the later famous Danish critic

---

[13]Letter to Haymann 16 March 1884.

[14]The sculptor J. A. Jerichau, who created the later Ørsted monument. The other names mentioned are those of important philosophers, artists and scientists of the time.

Georg Brandes, who mentions "a Mme Ernst" as a mediocrity, a "*declamatrice assez mediocre*", who "has been here for some time and delighted the posh world".[15] The young Brandes did not belong among those with whom the Brewer rubbed shoulders in society; but, like Brandes, Jacobsen had a great weakness for France and French culture, and he also appreciated French beer. In a letter dated 22 July 1865 on a trip to France, he talked about sights and visits to breweries, adding that "I am ashamed at being unable to speak French properly, and I cut a poor figure", but he knew sufficient business French to talk about brewing: " … of breweries I can speak French well".

Jacobsen liked to stage his large parties. In a letter dated 26 January 1869 to Carl, who was studying beer brewing in Scotland at the time, we hear how the following Friday he was to "have my usual party for members of Parliament …. On this occasion, the port wine and sherry you sent me will do the honors. As usual, there will be music from the gallery of which I have required a good deal of Mozart, whose *Magic Flute* I'm looking forward to hearing tomorrow. Politics now has so little interest and pleasure that I prefer to give my parties a predominantly aesthetic stamp, which seems to coincide with the taste of my guests …." This was one of his last parties for politicians. He was approaching the age of sixty. Jacobsen had achieved much but still had not established the Carlsberg Foundation. Nor was he spared a future and bitter family conflict. To use his own religious language, he still had to go through Good Friday to reach Easter Sunday.

Of his interest in Rome, Jacobsen wrote in 1887, on his way to the eternal city that: "Even since my youth, ancient Rome has occupied my thoughts a great deal, and the development and destiny of the Roman people has had major influence on the entire civilized world and also is in itself so instructive that my interest in the history of Rome has even grown".[16] J. C. Jacobsen knew his Roman history and, of course, was entirely familiar with Augustus, the first Roman emperor, who—as it is well-known—called himself modestly 'first among equals', *princeps*, even though he implemented with a firm hand radical changes in Roman society and certainly knew how to stage himself. Augustus was a despot and did not belong among the house gods in the Brewer's home, but we may assume that Jacobsen was still quite impressed by his achievements and appreciated his efforts to consolidate government after the fall of the Roman Republic.

Out of politics, Jacobsen had more time to cultivate other sides of his personality and even to think about the Emperor Augustus. In a letter from

---

[15]Letter of 5 December 1867 to his mother Eva Bendix in *Breve til forældrene* ([1859–1871] 1978/2016).

[16]Letter to Mrs. Heiberg 20 Feb. 1887.

April 1869, he wrote directly to his son Carl that it "is generally in the company of women that one develops the spirit best". And by that he was not only thinking of his wife. By the end of the 1860s, new and challenging female acquaintanceships also entered Jacobsen's social circle, which gave him the opportunity to play the attentive gallant and get a bit of variation from the daily interactions with his wife Laura. In a letter to Carl dated 6 December 1867 in which he again touches on his wide-ranging sociability, which the son should imitate to a high degree, he mentions that he "was with Krieger last week, where I as usual met Mrs. Heiberg, whom I had the honor of escorting to dinner. It was a highly interesting evening". Krieger was the leading National Liberal politician at the time, and his relationship with the legendary Danish actress of the day, Johanne Louise Heiberg, had developed into a close friendship. To Carl, then in Scotland, Jacobsen (as he signed his letters to his son) wrote a year later: "I had not dreamed that I would ever enjoy the enviable—and by many desired in vain—distinction of being invited by Mrs. Heiberg to a private dinner and spending 4 h with her quite alone". He was, he wrote, "not so foolish as to imagine that my company and my entertainment have had any special attraction for her". To the contrary, he realized that "she has only wanted to show me this attention" in order to achieve financial help for another "and … perhaps gain access to some other assistance on occasion, but I feel rightly flattered that she has shown me attention in this way. It is at any rate an aid to enlighten me as to the level of cultural sophistication with which I may stand in the eyes of others, and I can only rejoice that my mostly autodidactic efforts have given me such a character of such an examiner".[17] Jacobsen viewed himself as self-taught, and someone who contributed to his intellectual development in this way and presumably to a significantly higher degree than his wife was precisely Mrs. Heiberg. A couple of later letters to her show an accelerating talent for polite interaction with the fair sex such as a 'bird greeting' on 22 November 1871 in which he asked her "to receive the accompanying small birds and to grant them some place in your room". Jacobsen believed he could "vouch that they will not give you any difficulty but may in all modesty chirp a token of the warm wishes that are sent to you by all friends of art and passion and, particularly, by your respectful and devoted J. C. Jacobsen".

Or, on Christmas Eve 1872, in the accompanying letter to a quite generous Christmas present in the form of an ancient bust of Augustus, he introduced it as "the great actor Augustus", who "desires to serve his fellow artist Johanne Luise Heiberg". The Brewer wrote inquiringly: "As I hereby have the honor

[17]Letter to Carl dated 8 December 1868.

of introducing him, I ask you to grant him a kind reception with which you will associate and please your respectful J. C. Jacobsen". With the mention of Augustus as a fellow actor, the Brewer might refer to his famous death-bed words that the comedy was over and now it was time to applaud: *Comedia finita est, applaudite!* Whoever reads the letter today could get the impression that the successful brewer might just identify with the Roman actor-emperor. There are many stages upon which to be an actor, and it is not entirely without humor to imply that the management of the Carlsberg breweries is one of them.

Mrs. Heiberg, the famous actress, and Jacobsen, the successful brewer, had in common that they both had struggled their way into the country's highest circles through their talent. Mrs. Heiberg had come all the way from the bottom of society,[18] while J. C. Jacobsen had support from home, which made him, like the actress, strive to be the best in his field, and, perhaps, also gave him a perspective on life, once seen from below, now seen a bit from above.

Also after having bowed out of active politics, Jacobsen moved in a more and more politically conservative direction. He regretted his earlier National Liberal stance and his participation in the events that led to the 1864 war and the national disasters that resulted therefrom. In time, he became a warm devotee of the conservative 'landowner government' of J. B. S. Estrup from 1875 which opposed any claim that the King was not free to appoint his own government without being bound by a majority of the First Chamber of Parliament. Jacobsen had been an opponent of A. S. Ørsted's dictatorial way of ruling over the Parliament,[19] but now he had changed his mind and desired a firm hand to control divisive forces. The Franco-Prussian War of 1870–71 had briefly awakened a hope that the Danish-speaking northern part of Schleswig, lost in 1864, might return under Danish rule with a French victory, but history went otherwise. France was beaten in a blitzkrieg, Napoleon III had to abdicate, and the country became a republic. These were all events that J. C. Jacobsen could only look upon gloomily. In a letter, dated 23 March 1886—a year before his death—he wrote to the then popular Danish poet, Holger Drachmann, whom he secretly gave economic support,

[18]Johanne Louise Heiberg (born Pätges, 1812–1890) stemmed from a poor family of emigrants and grew up in Copenhagen in very poor social conditions. Due to patrons, however, she entered the ballet school of the Royal Theatre 1820, became actress and since her early debut in 1827 was the leading Danish actress with a high position in Danish society of her time not lest due to her intelligence and wits. She married the Danish poet (and Director of the Royal Theatre) J. L. Heiberg and even wrote a much appreciated biography of herself and her times.

[19]The Danish lawyer Anders Sandøe Ørsted, brother of H. C. Ørsted, assumed the position of prime minister 1854–55 but became unpopular for what was seen as disrespect for the new constitution in his attempts to find a solution to the complicated constitutional problems of the Kingdom of Denmark in relation to the Duchies of Schleswig and Holstein.

of the importance of "a strong, hereditary monarchy", adding that "it … is France's misfortune, under which it still groans, that, in 1793, it cut its historical cord by chopping off the king's head …, now France lacks the historical fundament for a strong monarchy …."

An employee of J. C. Jacobsen said that, in his later years, he "takes respite in nothing, there is uninterrupted building and gamboling. He knows neither Sunday nor holidays".[20] Always to be doing something was an important part of his survival strategy. In the following history of the Carlsberg Foundation and the brewery, we shall rediscover many of the elements we have seen developed in the founder himself: entrepreneurship, technical dexterity, a sense for detail and product quality, political interest, a deep understanding of the importance of science, and a conviviality that was not necessarily linked to beer. At the same time, all this was confined within a distinctive patriarchal spirit and, thus, in a mental universe in which the Roman Augustus, the king and his prime minister Estrup, and courting Mrs. Heiberg could find room.

2.4 Tuborg A/S

"Hof or Tuborg?" has traditionally been the choice offered at Danish pubs to inquire whether the patron would prefer to drink a Carlsberg or a Tuborg. 'Hof' was—and still is—the popular moniker in Denmark for a Carlsberg pilsner. 'Hof' actually in Danish means "court" in the sense of a royal court, but 'Hof' was not considered a specifically aristocratic beer. On the contrary. The 'Hof' had to fight with the image of being a rather ordinary product. In reality, the difference between the two went far deeper than nuance of taste or the design of the label. Carlsberg was founded as a sole proprietorship for the purpose of producing good quality beer. For the Brewer, earning money was a subsidiary concern, while Tuborg was founded as a corporation to create profits for shareholders through the production and export of beer, which—thanks in no small part to J. C. Jacobsen's groundbreaking efforts in Denmark—had become a bulk commodity that could be sold and even exported for gain. Two very different worldviews are at the base of these two brewery concepts. The entrepreneur, the manufacturer, or the industrialist faces the merchant and capital. A great deal of the history told here has to do with this difference between the breweries, which became less pronounced over the years. Tuborg also put weight on having a quality product, and Carlsberg also employed—and to that degree—merchants to sell goods. There are,

[20]Glamann (1990), p. 18.

after all, more or less idealistic approaches to life, and there is a deep truth in the economist Adam Smith's often quoted statement that it is not from the benevolence of the butcher, the brewer, or the baker that we expect our dinner but from their regard to their own interest.[21] One part of the story, therefore, is about how Carlsberg and Tuborg as two companies, each with their own form of management and "spirit", nevertheless came to resemble each other and, ultimately, merge under the same management. Paradoxically, it has even proved that the Tuborg label, especially in East Asia today, continues to sell well—and better than Carlsberg—as a result of an entirely different mechanism, the modern marketing techniques by which Tuborg was launched as a beer in tune with a younger lifestyle as opposed to the classic Carlsberg pilsner. This is an entirely different story that has to do with modern marketing and not about quality.

The brewery Tuborg A/S (founded in 1873) began its life as the competitor of the Brewer and his Carlsberg. Since 1891, it was the dominant partner of the United Breweries Group (*De Forenede Bryggerier* (DFB)). Subsequently, Carlsberg and DFB, as it is correctly called, but often just called Tuborg, entered into an agreement in 1903 on cohabitation and profit-sharing without moving in together until the two finally united in 1970 at an event reminiscent of a great beer wedding. As mentioned, the beer world in many ways is a man's world and a tough one often dominated by football sponsorships and big bellies, but the relations between breweries are described, often aptly, with sexual undertones as between consenting partners who get together, break up, or just engage in a one-night stand. Seen by such a measure, the relationship between Carlsberg and Tuborg early entered into such routine cohabitation and regulated paths, so that quarrels were often part of the day's agenda. At the same time, they still saw financial benefits from staying together and sharing an economy.

1864 was and remains a decisive year in Danish history. The loss of the two duchies, Schleswig and Holstein, in the brief war of 1864 with Prussia and Austria was considered a national catastrophe. Two-fifths of the territory and the inhabitants of the Realm were gone, as was the idea of a nation with both a Danish- and a German-speaking population living together. Since that time, Denmark has been a geographically small, Danish-speaking nation-state. Just as important, perhaps, was the fact that the defeat became an occasion for finding new paths and, thus, a turning point in the history of Denmark by spurring many new initiatives that made Denmark into a different and much more extroverted country. These many activities showed that the country was

[21] *The Wealth of Nations* (1776): "It is not from the benevolence of the butcher, the brewer, or the baker that we shall expect our dinner, but from their regard to self interest.".

far from beaten, that people were minded to get over the loss by developing new industry and energy. If the country were to survive, it was necessary to develop a business community and much else as a firm foundation for a new dynamic. Denmark was an agricultural country, but if growth was to be created and real money earned, then industrialization was required that could translate agricultural production into refined products that could be sold in greater quantities in order to create capital with which to improve work. Beer is just such a product. The raw materials came from agriculture, but the production was industrial and the results could even be exported. The wheels started turning, and it was actually only after 1864 that the history of Danish industry seriously began. J. C. Jacobsen was one of those who charged out and picked up the gauntlet laid down by 1864. He became a role model, and Carlsberg's success provoked in others the desire to brew beer in larger quantities and earn money from their breweries.

It was in these years that the groundwork was laid for the structure of the Danish beer industry: there would be two large breweries, Carlsberg and Tuborg, and a whole series of small local breweries of various sizes and ability to survive. From the old days, there were many larger and especially smaller breweries in Copenhagen and "the provinces"—as the rest of Denmark was called in beer distribution language. Carlsberg's largest and only real competitor was *A/S Tuborgs fabrikker* (Tuborg Factories, Inc.), which was founded in 1873 with wholesaler Philip W. Heymann as promoter. The relationship between Carlsberg and Tuborg became an important part of Danish brewing history, which had great significance for the promotion of the Carlsberg Foundation. The new Tuborg business was located in Hellerup by the sea north of Copenhagen near the newly-established Tuborg Harbor. There was a point in this in that they were considering exporting to South America, among other places. With him in this enterprise, Heymann had the great Danish industrialist of the time, C. F. Tietgen, wholesaler Rudolph Puggard, and a prominent Supreme Court attorney G. E. Brock. The men behind Tuborg wanted to construct both a brewery and a glassworks that could produce bottles, so they could sell beer tapped directly into bottles and not, like Carlsberg and others, still distribute beer in barrels that were to be tapped later by the receiver. The main shareholder was the great Danish industrialist C. F. Tietgen, who subscribed to DKK 800,000 of 1 million in capital. This was a corporation and not a sole proprietorship, which was the salient characteristic of Carlsberg. It was precisely this form of company about which the Brewer harbored great skepticism. Responsibility was spread among a number of "capitalists", who wanted to profit from their shares, who did not want to incur losses or take risks, and who did not necessarily have any eye for the importance of the development of high-quality beer. That was not Tuborg's problem either then or later. Carlsberg was good at profiling itself as particularly quality-conscious and independent of profit, but in actual practice there was no great difference between either the product or the ethics of the two firms. Tuborg employed a talented Norwegian brewer, Hans Bekkevold from Kristiansand, to be responsible for production, and it was not long before Tuborg's beer was known as a quality product.

J. C. Jacobsen did not fear competition as long as his competitors maintained quality. He feared competition based on lower standards for the product. From the early phase of Tuborg's business (from 1875)[22] comes a letter from Jacobsen to the Tuborg investor Tietgen: "Since I do not know who the operations manager at Tuborg is, I permit myself to address you with a report of a matter that may have influence on the mutual relations between the Tuborg and Carlsberg Breweries." Jacobsen raises directly the question of whether Tuborg was trying to lure good employees away from Carlsberg in order to exploit their know-how: "One of my son's cellar men, who after a few years' service has a wage of DKK 920 a year and to that point seemed very satisfied and eager has now terminated his services because he has been hired by Tuborg with a monthly salary of DKK 100. On this occasion, I would like to know whether this salary is usual for diligent workers at Tuborg ... or whether the operations manager has promised the worker in question ... an unusually high wage in order to lure a worker trained by my son from him. I am convinced that you would not appreciate the aforementioned method .... Should my suspicion be confirmed, Tuborg must be prepared for me to take my own measures thereafter."

In its way, the letter was the first of many that, over the years, were to be exchanged between the leaders of these two breweries on often apparently trivial matters. It also became a guideline for the very direct style that came to dominate mutual communication between the two breweries, whose histories became closely intertwined.

Tuborg's production of beer began with a lager, the later so-called "Red Tuborg". The South American market they were banking on proved not to be accessible for Danish entrepreneurs due to high tariff rates. Moreover, the production of bottles proved to be uneconomical. Therefore, Tuborg had to undergo a major readjustment in the 1880s. One of the people who helped Tuborg without concern for the latent competitive implications was Brewer Jacobsen. In a letter to Heymann dated 27 April 1882, he wrote that it "would please me much if I could give you useful advice with respect to the

[22]Letter of 9 Aug. 1875.

illness in Tuborg's beer, and I would like to inspect the localities in order, if possible, to find out where the fault lies…." Tuborg also repaid this generosity later by placing at the brewery a bust of Jacobsen in the best conceivable company for Jacobsen. In a letter of 16 November 1884 to Heyman, Jacobsen wrote: "It is truly all too great an honor you show me in erecting my bust beside Pasteur and Ørsted, but since you desire to have a bust of me, I must thank you for such evidence of your good will …."

Competitors may assume the outward air of behaving like gentlemen in their mutual relations, and the courtesy the old Brewer showed to the new brewery created a good atmosphere and a sympathy that explains how the two breweries could later enter into the collaboration that, ultimately, led to a merger. The course of events was not always easy, and we shall return to this story several times. Jacobsen favored patriarchally-run sole proprietorships of a manageable size; but, even though he was against a construction such as the Tuborg breweries, one could easily be polite and show an interest in each other's products, even learn from each other. The above-cited letter to Heymann about working conditions also ends with an amiable but determined recommendation to create equal conditions, which were to become so characteristic of the relationship between the two breweries.

Tuborg's beer was not sold in barrels but directly in bottles tapped at the brewery. Thus, sales became easier without beer bottlers or other intermediaries. Only later did Carlsberg move from lager to pilsner, which was a fresher and easier type of beer than lager and gradually became the preferred beer type. It also took a longer time for Carlsberg to begin bottling beer directly, which proved to have a future. Heymann was good at marketing and came up with the characteristic "Tuborg" logo, and Tuborg's pilsner, "Green Tuborg," really took off in the 1890s. In 1895, they even launched a "Gold Tuborg". Heymann was a quick study. As mentioned, he paid J. C. Jacobsen a visit to comment on production, and after 1883 he was quick to use Emil Christian Hansen's pure yeast to which, thanks to the Carlsberg laboratory's generous principles, there was free access.

2.5 The Ørsted Monument

The day of unveiling in September 1876 of a monument to honor the great Danish scientist H. C. Ørsted in the presence of the king was the day J. C. Jacobsen chose to establish his foundation, the Carlsberg Foundation. It was not announced in advance, but the date 25 September marked the great significance that H. C. Ørsted had had for Jacobsen, for his work, and for his decisions to establish a foundation to promote science and to convey the foundation to the Danish Royal Academy of Sciences and Art. This date was also inscribed in the monument.

The history of the Carlsberg Foundation, therefore, begins on 25 September 1876 on a part of Copenhagen's old ramparts in what a few years later received the name Ørsted Park. Here, beneath Copenhagen's old bastions, J. C. Jacobsen had earlier constructed his first storage cellar. It was also here that the monument, dedicated to physicist H. C. Ørsted, was erected depicting him high above the old ramparts with great stature and an enthusiastic gaze, giving a lecture to passers-by on electromagnetism with a magnetic needle in his hand and a galvanic apparatus in front of him. The statue itself was designed by one of the great Danish artists of the time, the sculptor J. A. Jerichau.

The 25th of September 1876, however, was to be Ørsted's day and not the Brewer's. Therefore, the announcement of the establishment of the foundation took place later once Ørsted had received his due. For posterity, 25 September became the Carlsberg Foundation's day, and it was later marked by an inscription at Carlsberg in which Jacobsen declares "how much I owe H. C. Ørsted's teachings and animating influence" and that he, therefore, is "linked to the establishment of the Carlsberg Foundation to this day".

It was only under the new constitutional regime after 1848 that a practice began of honoring not only kings with a statue but also ordinary citizens. Fund-raising for the monument began in 1861, ten years after the scientist's death. Ørsted's monument tells a story of Danish science at the highest level and about one of those people who learned something from it. At the same time, for the initiated, it tells about the establishment of the Carlsberg Foundation. The story of the Ørsted monument, therefore, is not only a random account of the erection of the first monument to a late Danish scientist. Ørsted was in his time and thereafter the personification of the science that was especially relevant to Jacobsen's product. He contemplated him every day. In Jacobsen's study, the Captain's room as it was called, "hung Marstrand's great portrait of H. C. Ørsted."[23] Ørsted had been indefatigable in his exploration and understanding of nature, as was Jacobsen himself, who had spared no exertion when it came to promoting and maintaining beer as a Danish quality product by replacing the mishmash of barley and water with which generations had to put up and which only poorly served the name of beer once it was known how beer could be brewed.

[23]Carl Jacobsen in *Mit Hjem* (1911), p. 41.

J. C. Jacobsen had heard about Ørsted since he was a little boy. His father Chresten Jacobsen, an autodidact brewer and a great fan of Ørsted, had conveyed this admiration to his son, who now in 1876 was a famous, well-to-do master brewer, someone who stood out as an example of how far you could go when you understood the role of the natural sciences in practical life. He had therefore supported and kept close track of how things were going with the monument. In 1869, in a letter to his son Carl, he described a visit to the artist's atelier, where he had seen "a new sketch with small changes to the protagonist, Ørsted himself"; and a year later when the figure was finished, he said that Jerichau "has been very fortunate both with respect to likeness and expression ...."[24] The artist reluctantly had to accept the fact that the commission behind the project (consisting, *inter alia*, of the writer Hans Christian Andersen) wanted a statue of the physicist in normal, everyday clothing and not dressed or represented as a Greek god as was often the case to honor the person.[25]

In his time, Hans Christian Ørsted achieved a fame in Danish society that may only be compared to that held by the Danish astronomer Tycho Brahe over the centuries or as the physicist Niels Bohr achieved in the 20th century combining a great and winning personality with being a scientist of genius. Bohr knew this as well. He also had in his study a picture of Ørsted, a reproduction of a wall painting in the university hall of Ørsted speaking in the 1840s at a meeting in Roskilde of Nordic natural scientists. Ørsted was a central figure in the Copenhagen of the early 1800s. As mentioned, he was the founder of the Polytechnic College (now, the Technical University of Denmark) and an eager distributor of the message of how important a role the natural sciences played for development and progress. He was not only known for his research, but his natural philosophy, which was based on the idea of the unity of spirit and nature, also provided a generally accessible understanding of existence with which many people could identify. He was quite simply at one and the same time a highly gifted, a highly beloved, and a highly inspirational figure in Danish society, generally known, liked, and admired.

In 1876, the 65-year-old J. C. Jacobsen was one of Denmark's leading entrepreneurs. As a brewer and industrialist, he had fought his way into the front ranks and now stood not only as a leading figure of Danish industry but simply as one of the country's most prominent citizens. The establishment of the Carlsberg Foundation was a way of demonstrating that someone who has the abilities and achieves results and serves something can at the same time

[24] Letters to Carl 14 Jan. 1869 and 5 March 1870.

[25] Christensen (2009), p. 26.

show public spirit by giving to others and, in this case, to the promotion of science. The important realization behind Jacobsen's industrial success was that quality beer should be produced scientifically. First science, then beer. In this context, science was, first and foremost, chemistry.

Ørsted was one of J. C. Jacobsen's role models not only as the epitome of a scientist but also as a man of honor and a citizen who acted to benefit society. Jacobsen spoke of his "house gods", and Ørsted might have been the greatest of them all for the Brewer, holding a place beside (or, rather, above) the sculptor Bertel Thorvaldsen and the contemporary businessman and politician L. N. Hvidt (who is less known today). As chairman of the Copenhagen city council—of which Jacobsen had been a member from 1843 to 1857, Hvidt had shown civil courage in March 1848 as the man who led the procession of citizens from seat of the Council at the New Square of Copenhagen to the Royal Palace of Christiansborg to ask the king for a new constitution. This was something Jacobsen liked: A union of political engagement and action with an appropriate flair and sense for business and quality.

Jacobsen's three Danish house gods, Ørsted, Thorvaldsen, and L. N. Hvidt, had as their counterparts three of his ancient heroes who reflected other sides of his personality. Of course, they were three of antiquity's greatest men—at least, as history has delivered them to us (one of them might not have existed, but Jacobsen and his era knew nothing of that debate). Homer was and remained the creator of the great epics of the *Iliad* and the *Odyssey*, and reliefs with motifs from them decorated the large Pompeii room in Jacobsen's home. Poetry on one side and Greek democracy (which, of course, might not have been so democratic after all) on the other in the form of Pericles. He was the second ancient house god, who in his famous funeral oration had praised his fatherland Athens and the city-state's ideals of freedom and equality, as expressed in its constitution: "Its name is democracy (*demokratia*) because the government is not gathered in the hands of the few but the many". The Roman general Scipio Africanus had during the Second Punic War between Rome and Carthage defended his fatherland. He had beaten Hannibal in 202 B.C.E. and thereby ended the war. Upon his return to Rome, he withdrew to his own pursuits—yet another example of public prominence on the fatherland's behalf but without any desire to benefit one's own career. He was the third of Jacobsen's ancient heroes or house gods.

Shortly after the erection of the monument to H. C. Ørsted in Ørsted Park, a bust of L. N. Hvidt was erected at the foot of architect Vilhelm Dahlerup. Much later in 1954, Einar Utzon-Frank's monument to Thorvaldsen was erected in the park. Thorvaldsen is depicted as resting on a couple of wooden boxes beneath his work "Hope" from 1839, while a winged genius hovers above his head. In this way, Ørsted Park came to mirror precisely the values that J. C. Jacobsen stood for: insight into nature, creativity, civic-mindedness, a sense of political and personal responsibility, diligence, and talent. Later, Carl Jacobsen adorned the park with statues, donated by a foundation created by him with name of Albertina—in honor of 'Alberto' Thorvaldsen. Copies of ancient artworks from Roman museums blend together with modern French art such as Chapu's *Jeanne d'Arc*. The generous Carl actually wanted to surpass his father as a patron. He knew Henri Chapu, who had told him about his artists' group in Rome, which called itself *semper ardens*, always burning. These words had captured Carl, who placed them above the gate to his own brewery buildings; here, they were much later spotted by a bright Carlsberg employee as a good idea for a name both for a series of specially-brewed Carlsberg beer and the Carlsberg Foundation newly created research grants.[26]

Much later, in 1911, a statue was added of H. C. Ørsted's brother, the jurist A. S. Ørsted, a famous lawyer but also a politician who, after 1849, had followed a controversial political line in order to secure the so-called "whole state (*Gesamtstaat*) policy", which aimed at preserving the monarchy intact, keeping the Kingdom of Denmark together with the duchies of Schleswig-Holstein. Thus, the park became a park named by both of the Ørsted brothers, even if the lawyer brother never became quite as famous for his legal work as H. C. Ørsted for the discovery of electromagnetism.

As a physicist, H. C. Ørsted was known far outside the borders of his country, as Jacobsen's beer later would be. Together with Galilei, Leibnitz, and Linnaeus, he was one of just four modern European scientists who, in the 19th century, found their way into Oxford University Museum's Hall of Fame. When the collection was set up, Ørsted was missing, and it was Brewer Jacobsen, who in 1885 acquired and saw to it that a clay model of Jerichau's Ørsted monument in Ørsted Park was sent to Oxford as model for a statue by the Scottish sculptor Alexander Monro.

Today, Ørsted has given his name to the great energy company, previously known as DONG. It would presumably have amused the old brewer that his scientific idol came to live on in Danish and international consciousness in this way. Had J. C. Jacobsen known the slogan '*This calls for a Carlsberg*', he might have thought it was an appropriate moment here.

---

[26]Hatch and Schulz (2017).

2.6 The Royal Danish Academy of Sciences and Letters and the Carlsberg Foundation

J. C. Jacobsen had decided to establish the Carlsberg Foundation as a gift to Danish science, personified for him in the institution that bore the name *Det Kongelige Danske Videnskabernes Selskab* (The Royal Danish Academy of Sciences and Letters). This institution at that time numbered 50 members, all prominent academics, who were supposed to represent the best in Danish sciences and humanities. They saw it this way themselves, and so did J. C. Jacobsen. It was decisive for the gift that the Academy accepted on 29 September 1876 to be responsible for selecting the Foundation's board of five directors from among its members.

The Royal Academy was created in 1742. It publishes scholarly works, and meetings are held regularly twice a month in season in which the members present the results of their research to each other in an exclusive, closed circle in the form of so-called "reports". Members of an academy of this character are selected by the Academy itself. At one time, there had been four small departments called classes, but, in Jacobsen's time and still today, the members of the Danish Royal Academy are divided into two classes. The number of members (which today is more than 200) was limited to 50, divided into the mathematic-scientific class (at that time, 30 members) and a humanistic class (at that time, 20 members) including social sciences.

The Academy's protector is and was in 1876 the king (or, as the case may be, the queen). As members, only highly qualified academics are accepted—not people with a prominent position in society or attractive for their possession of a lot of money to be spent on science but without academic qualifications, as is the case in certain foreign academies. Jacobsen himself would not have been accepted into the Academy, and he had no such ambition, as he did not consider himself a scientist. He saw the Danish Royal Academy "as our only institution that is so fortunate as to stand independent of all alien, unscientific considerations and influences", and this was crucial for his decision.

In 1876, the president of the Academy since 1867 was Johan Nicolai Madvig, a famous classicist. In this capacity, he received a separate letter about the establishment of the Carlsberg Foundation in which Jacobsen stressed his enormous debt to physicist H. C. Ørsted, who for a long period of time was the Academy's general secretary. These two became major figures in the early history of the Carlsberg Foundation. Jacobsen and Madvig had in reality a great deal in common even though they represented different worlds. They were both iconic figures in Danish society at that time. Madvig was one of the country's great men by virtue of his personality and as a humanist. Just as the Brewer was the greatest in Denmark in his field and probably the country's most prestigious businessman—with the financial genius C. F. Tietgen as his only competitor—Madvig was probably the most prestigious humanist of the time. He was a distinguished, internationally-known classical philologist who for long periods had been rector of Copenhagen University. Madvig was born in 1804 and, thus, was 72 years old when the Carlsberg Foundation was established and seven years older than Jacobsen. Both came from rather modest circumstances, and they had reached the pinnacle in their fields.

In the Denmark of the 19th century, there was social mobility for whoever had the will and the ability, but access to the highest levels of education was limited, and persons from a poor background were dependent on luck to be spotted by a teacher or a relative and gain appropriate support along the way. J. C. Jacobsen was the son of a gifted and ambitious first-generation brewer. Madvig's father was a town clerk in a small town on the distant island of Bornholm. There was not much money in the home, and Madvig owed his education to good teachers and private support. Thus, he could attend grammar school, completed a secondary education, and entered the university, where in 1825 he attained a degree in classical philology, Latin and Greek. He had specialized in the Roman politician and orator Cicero, who did not belong among the Roman patricians but achieved the highest position of power even though his entire life he was considered a "*homo novus*", a new man. Madvig became famous throughout Europe as publisher of his texts. In a critical moment in his life, however, Madvig began to doubt the purpose of a classical education, a crisis that led him to the recognition that education is not a goal in itself, it is a means to develop oneself as a useful citizen; and, in this, he also resembled Jacobsen. As a scholar, he had a meteoric career, becoming a professor of Latin in Copenhagen at the age of 25 in 1829. Unlike Jacobsen, Madvig remained a political liberal. He was part of the assembly that drafted the Danish Constitution of 1849, a member of Parliament, and a member of the government as Minister for Church and Education 1848–1851. In 1867, he became the president of the Danish Royal Academy and, once the Academy accepted the foundation as a gift to Danish science, the first chairman of the Carlsberg Foundation.[27]

Classical philology is not just about ancient Greece and Rome. The classics from antiquity with their abundant number of observations about human beings and human society are read again and again with new eyes in every era. They do not go out of date, and familiarity with the ancients and ancient

[27]Pedersen (1955), p. 262 ff.

languages, therefore, provides a tool for engagement in and criticism of what happens in one's own time. Much of the Roman legacy has to do with politics and history and is written in such a way and with such keen observation that every generation learns something from ancient Rome that enhances its understanding of political life. The founders of the American constitution in 1787 read their classics, and the same was true of many of those who were influential in Danish politics at the end of the 19th century, including the members of the Danish Royal Academy, who at that time had all received a uniform education based largely on a cultivation of the classic languages. It is a part of the 19th century's educational history that humanists, scientists, and brewers such as Jacobsen had the same horizon of classical education. Rome and Roman history was also a passion for Jacobsen. Another member of the Danish Royal Academy who particularly infused Jacobsen's confidence in the Academy and its members was the natural scientist Japetus Steenstrup (1813–1897), who was related to J. C. Jacobsen's wife Laura. Steenstrup, a strong and controversial personality, was regarded as one of the country's most prominent natural scientists. In a couple of treatises in the 1840s, he demonstrated the great significance of peat bogs for research and an understanding of climate change. He also touched on zoological topics and thus created quite a name for himself at a young age. Already in 1842, only 29 years old, he became a member of the Royal Academy. In 1845, he became professor of zoology at Copenhagen University. His field of interest was broad but did not include classical languages, which were Madvig's specialty. To the contrary, he had given up taking exams at the university since it required a test in the field of classics. But he made a success anyway and is today, perhaps, most well-known for his research of so-called "køkkenmøddinger", kitchen middens, whereby he helped elaborate our knowledge of Denmark's antiquity and Stone Age culture.

Like Madvig, Steenstrup was a central and leading figure in Danish science in the 19th century, and Jacobsen had great confidence in him. Others were more skeptical of him and found many examples of superficiality or outright misinterpretations in Steenstrup's writings. Steenstrup had power and was a good ally who helped with the formation of the Foundation Charter from 1876 and Jacobsen's will from 1882. Steenstrup sat on the Foundation's first executive board until his death in 1897, together with Madvig as chairman and the historian Edvard Holm, along with P. L. Panum, who was a well-known physiologist, and the chemist C. T. Barfoed, also close to Jacobsen and who had advised him on the design of the Charter of the Foundation.

Madvig was already informed beforehand by Jacobsen about the plans for the Foundation and had also already learned that Jacobsen intended to leave his business to the Foundation at his death. The prospect of the Carlsberg Foundation's executive board running an entire brewery gave Madvig reason for concern.[28] None of the members of the Academy were businessmen or supposed to know about running a brewery or any other bigger business. This lack of business experience on the Foundation board is one of the themes that will be running throughout this book. The scientist's approach to life, as a rule, is theoretical; and, even though scientists are often good at asking questions, they usually lack—for good reason—experience and understanding of the decision-making process and its consequences in running a business. Science creates new knowledge, which is something different from the management of a company and the production of goods that consumers enjoy.

Madvig was a scholar, and he was understandably worried that scientists such as himself might one day be responsible for a business of Carlsberg's dimensions. One could learn much from Cicero and the ancient Romans but not how to brew beer or how to run a major modern industrial enterprise. Madvig expressed his concerns in a letter to J. C. Jacobsen on 1 October 1881 in which he proposed that the brewery, instead, go to an independent brewer. This irritated Jacobsen,[29] and seen in hindsight, we must acknowledge that Jacobsen's decision was correct. Without the breweries, the Foundation would have remained a minor fund without any opportunity to have the societal impact it ultimately had. And we may even go further and say that, without the Foundation, there would hardly be a Danish Carlsberg brewery today.

The Danish Royal Academy played and still plays an important but not altogether clearly defined role in connection with the establishment and operation of the Carlsberg Foundation. The idea for its founding was J. C. Jacobsen's own, but his letter on the establishment of the foundation was styled to the Royal Academy. The Brewer stressed here that the Carlsberg Foundation must be secured by "a permanent board with scientific insight and competence" and that the "idea" must necessarily fall to the Academy as the only institution "independent of all external, unscientific considerations and impulses". The Academy's job thereafter was to designate five members from among its members as the board of the Foundation.

[28]Madvig (1955), p. 269; Glamann (1990), p. 215, 242 ff.

[29]See letter from J. C. Jacobsen of 13 October 1881 to Steenstrup.

Particulars of the relationship between the Foundation and the Academy are not described in the charter documents, nor does the current charter for the Foundation describe the relationship in more detail other than a rule that the Carlsberg Foundation's board has a right to remuneration as fixed by the Royal Academy. The Foundation and the Academy today are located in the same building. The Academy has an unlimited free right to use the uppermost floors, while the Foundation's administration is housed on the ground floor. The Danish Royal Academy has an important function, as we have seen, in connection with approving amendments to the Foundation's Charter: "Amendments to the charter of the Carlsberg Foundation may occur through a proposal unanimously presented by the board approved by the Danish Royal Academy". The Foundation also contributes a significant subsidy to the Academy's operation. The daily business of the Foundation is independent of the Academy, whose influence is exercised in the designation of the board's members. Since the establishment of the Foundation, it has been customary to choose three members from the sciences class of the Academy and two from the humanities class. Each Academy class nominates its own candidates, who are thereafter elected by the overall Academy.

Very little in reality has changed in the relationship between foundation and academy since the meeting on 29 September 1876 in which the Royal Academy discussed and accepted J. C. Jacobsen's offer to designate the executive board for the newly-established Carlsberg Foundation. On this occasion, the president, J. N. Madvig, expressed his fear that the designation of some of the Academy's members for this task could lead to an "equilibrium disturbance" in the Academy. Upon the establishment of the Foundation in 1876, J. C. Jacobsen had set the remuneration for foundation work at DKK 1200 and DKK 1800 for the chairperson. In 1902 when the Foundation had taken over his breweries, Carl Jacobsen had encouraged the Foundation to accept a considerable increase. The Foundation at that time did not go along but found it appropriate for the remuneration for this significant work to be set at about 67% of a professor's salary.

The management of the Foundation was and has been independent without interference from the Academy, and the Academy in principle has no responsibility for the Foundation's economy and dispositions. Neither is there any fixed procedure in the Academy nor any expressly formulated criteria for a designation of candidates for the Foundation board. Terms for election used to be for ten years without restrictions as to reelection. Today, there is an age limit of 70 and a limit of serving on the board up to three periods of five years, which are still long periods compared with other foundations.

On the Foundation's first executive board were members whom Brewer Jacobsen knew personally. As they gradually fell away, others were chosen and, frequently, with a profile that was reminiscent of their predecessor's. In this way, overlapping series of chemists and physiologists may be identified in addition to physicists, mathematicians, zoologists, botanists, and geologists. On the humanist side, languages and history have dominated. After J. N. Madvig followed a series of classical philologists, a representative of comparative linguistics, Semitic and Oriental languages, and later modern languages such as German and English. Historians were very strong for a long time until the end of the 1980s when the line was broken by the selection of a series of economists.

For Jacobsen, the primary purpose of the brewery business was to produce the best quality product possible, and the connection to the Royal Academy was to ensure that the people who governed the foundation would secure this goal after his death. The Brewer and his beer were to be and remain the best. Jacobsen would probably not have cared for the "probably" that later slipped its way into the Carlsberg advertisement for "Probably the Best Beer in the World" and might perhaps even have doubted whether it was actually correct English.[30]

The legal basis for the establishment of the Carlsberg Foundation is a charter and deed of gift dated 25 September 1876 supplemented by more detailed bylaws dated 18 October 1876 and a number of other later documents. The charter received royal confirmation on 18 October 1876. This sort of confirmation does not in itself imply any particular legal significance, but it helped stress the importance of the gift and, for Carlsberg's sake, showed Jacobsen's respect for the royal house as a stabilizing factor in society.

In the charter, the new Foundation was named the "Carlsberg Foundation". Its purpose was described as dual, and the first purpose mentioned—designated A—was and still is the continuation and expansion of the work at the Carlsberg Laboratory, which was established by the Brewer the year before with a view toward research in topics important to beer production. We shall return to this. The second purpose—designated B—is support for basic research within the primary disciplines at that time: natural sciences, mathematics, and humanities such as philosophy, history, and linguistics. For many, this purpose was and is the epitome of what the Carlsberg Foundation stands for.

[30]Probably the "the world's best beer" would come closer to English standard.

In 1878, a new part C was added to the charter, which provided support to the Museum of National History at Frederiksborg Castle. How this could happen was explained by business historian Camillus Nyrop in a book about Jacobsen from 1901. He mentioned how the "Carlsberg Foundation was established in 1876 'for the benefit of science' but also 'for the honor of the fatherland'. He stressed in this context that 'devotion to the fatherland deepened in Jacobsen bit by bit' with the result that, not only for the Frederiksborg Museum but also for the Foundation's part B, the central thing has ... become its relationship to what is peculiarly Danish." The promotion of Danish science was essential and has always been so in the work of the Foundation—but not in a retrospective way but with a view to the future of science: "The primary emphasis, however, is not respect for the dead. This part is to work with Denmark's living scientists, and it has also demonstrated that it is up to the task."[31] The Carlsberg Foundation was established—and still works—as a distinctive Danish national foundation financed by income from what is still considered a national Danish brewery. Hardly anyone had at that time the ambition or imagination to think that could be different, and even today the Brewer's will is carried out on this point. As ways to support science, the bylaws mention the distribution of travel stipends, financial support for young scholars, or paying salaries to older scholars doing basic fundamental research. To promote these goals, the Brewer granted the foundation capital in the amount of DKK 1 million—a large sum at that time—with security in the brewery's properties in Valby. The capital was to yield 5% interest annually after the death of the Brewer and his wife and, until then, 2% a year as semi-annual contributions. As early as 1879, however, Jacobsen increased it to the stated 5% annually. According to the charter, the Foundation was to be governed by an executive board consisting of five members selected by and from the members of the Danish Royal Academy. The term of office according to the Brewer's wish at that time was 10 years with an opportunity for several re-elections without respect to age.

A charter is like a constitution, which lays out the general rules that determine how a foundation is to work. It reflects the wishes of the founder at the time of its establishment. However, time goes by, and certain articles may later prove to be outdated or even detrimental to the life and work of the foundation. One theme in the following is the amendments to the Carlsberg Foundation's original charter, especially about ownership, which were necessary to adapt the rules to the conditions of the time and, particularly, the

[31]Nyrop (1911), p. 131.

desire in certain cases to go in a different direction and run the business in another way than the Brewer had wanted or foreseen.

To amend or change a charter is a bureaucratic procedure that demands the intervention of supervising public authorities. For most of the time, it has been the Danish Ministry of Justice, which on several occasions has authorized changes to the original charter. Today, the charter is set out in a newly revised version from 2012, but until then the charter and its many addenda[32] might seem quite confusing. Old material was cleaned out, and the charter became better systematized.[33] Charter, bylaws, and appendices were gathered into a whole, and provisions about the Carlsberg Laboratory became a part of the charter. The former division into paragraphs was replaced by the more anonymous but functional division into numbered points and sub-points. One important, material change in 2012 was that the terms of office for the board members were reduced to only five years instead of ten and a (still high) maximum of 15 years for members of the Foundation's executive board. There are no specific rules about the chairman even though, as we shall hear, this position became a full-time job long ago and far more demanding than an ordinary membership on the Foundation board. Nor were more detailed rules laid down, concerning the relationship between the Royal Academy and the Carlsberg Foundation.

2.7 Pasteur, His Beer Studies, and Jacobsen

J. C. Jacobsen's great foreign hero was the French scientist Louis Pasteur, whose yeast studies had paved the way for new insights into methods of beer production. Pasteur was born in 1822 and educated in physics and chemistry at France's elite university, the *École Normale Supérieure* in Paris. His fundamental effort, which made him world-famous as the "father of microbiology" and a legend and icon for science even during his lifetime, is linked to the development of vaccinations against diseases (primarily, rabies), studies of fermentation processes, and the form of heat treatment that was named after himself, pasteurization. Jacobsen knew and recognized the value

[32]From 1888, 1916, 1931, 1970, 1972, 1977, 1991, 1997, 2000 and 2007 (and again 2013).

[33]The work was prepared by the Foundation's attorney, Jørgen Grønborg, and the Carlsberg Foundation's responsible manager, lawyer Gunver Kyhn, together with questor J. O. Veile, and the Foundation's CFO Anders Garrigues.

of Pasteur's works and studied, among other things, his book on wine, *Sur le Vin* (1866).[34]

Pasteur's study of beer production, *Études sur la Bière*, published the same year the Carlsberg Foundation was established, in 1876, is one of the classics of beer brewing. Both brewers, J. C and his son Carl Jacobsen, granted the work an authority on a similar level as the Bible. In the two representative portraits of J. C. Jacobsen and of his son Carl, made by the (at that time) leading Danish painter Jerichau, the book with Pasteur's name in bold type can be seen lying in front of them on the table. It was a book that—in Carl Jacobsen's words—shows "the path brewers must follow".[35] A few years before in the Franco-Prussian War of 1870–71, France had suffered an ignominious defeat to Prussia that, just as in Denmark after its 1864 defeat, gave occasion for reflection about what went wrong and what new activities could recover some of what was lost. The French, since the Napoleonic Wars justly proud of their *Grande Armée*, had clearly shown themselves to be inferior to the Germans on the battlefield. They even had to admit that, in a war over the quality of beer, the Germans would probably also run off with the victory. His work on the book, therefore, says Pasteur in the preface, began immediately after the war in order to help the French beer industry achieve a level comparable to that of the German art of brewing.

Pasteur had worked in laboratories and in practice with some of France's most prominent brewers. He was above all—like Jacobsen's 'house god' H. C. Ørsted—a person who understood what it meant to exploit research results to the benefit of industry. The book was expressly written with the aim of increasing the level of French beer brewing, and Pasteur proved that the fermentation processes in connection with beer brewing were different from wine production. They were more complicated and could give rise to spontaneous fermentation processes that were difficult to control. The yeast used in connection with the brewing of beer contained impurities in the form of microscopic organisms such as fungi, etc. Therefore, it was a matter of minimizing such organisms during the brewing process. This could happen by heat treatment, by preventing access by air-borne bacteria, and by observing utmost care with respect to the cleanliness of the vats used, etc. Pasteur's work on beer is richly documented, it is illustrated with descriptions of experiments and trials, and it is supplied with fine illustrations and tables that showed the developments in connection with fermentation processes.

Jacobsen's 'official' biographer, Camillus Nyrop, evokes in a book published on the 100th anniversary of J. C. Jacobsen's birth an image of a

[34]Letter to Carl 19 Feb. 1868.

[35]Carl Jacobsen in Nyrop (1886), p. 92.

quasi-magician to illustrate Pasteur's influence and significance for Jacobsen. He tells us that, "when Pasteur appeared and proved that the (until then) incomprehensible fermentation process was due to the life functions of yeast fungus and that beer yeast must and could be protected from numerous, harmful microbes in the air, present in great numbers in the summer months, Jacobsen was so enthralled by the genius behind Pasteur's work and so full of admiration at the results achieved that he wanted to erect his bust in the Carlsberg Laboratory."

Jacobsen contacted Pasteur asking him to allow a bust of him to be executed by Paul Dubois. Pasteur accepted and showed Jacobsen his gratitude by dedicating a book to him in 1879, *Examen critique d'un écrit posthume de Claude Bernard sur la fermentation.* He thanks Jacobsen for the establishment of the Carlsberg Laboratory and as a famous man in the world of European brewery.[36] Visitors still today are greeted at the Carlsberg Laboratory by this bust.

Pasteur definitely was not without academic or personal flaws, and some of his basic assumptions proved not to hold up, including the fermentation of yeast cells. Much later, there was also sport in showing that the great scientist was not entirely above board on all points. J. C. Jacobsen would probably not have liked this debate, which took place both in his day and later about Pasteur's apparently somewhat self-asserting personality and around some of his results. Pasteur operated from different ethical core values than those with which we are familiar in science today. He kept results secret, manipulated experiments, had a hard time acknowledging the efforts of others. Many of his experiments would today have provoked a storm of protests from animal welfare proponents. Fortunately for the old Brewer, Pasteur's private notebooks with his own sometimes revealing notes from his laboratory remained sealed, and not until long after his death in 1895 did the public become familiar with portions of their contents. This set off a debate on Pasteur's often arrogant personality, his self-promotion, and his method of determining research results, just as it has been pointed out that he relied to a high degree on discoveries of his predecessors.[37] At the same time, the recognition of his talent was maintained to create order within fields in which uncertainty earlier reigned as well as his unique proficiency when it came to exploiting his research results and creating a connection between science and practical life. Not least on this last point, he enjoyed the Brewer's admiration. To do Pasteur justice, we must not forget, either, how much benefit the world has

---

[36]Nyrop (1911), p. 56.

[37]In particular, the American researcher Geison (1996), *The Private Science of Louis Pasteur* initiated a debate about Pasteur's talent for promoting himself and his scientific methods.

had from his vaccine, his discoveries of pathogenic bacteria, and his method of pasteurization to combat them.

For J. C. Jacobsen, Pasteur was a role model to be referenced on beer brewing and science in general but also when it came to politics. As in beer brewing, so should it be in politics: there should be clean lines. Pasteur and chemistry could show the way, as Jacobsen wrote in a letter in 1886: "The air in the whole of Europe and, thus, here with us, will, therefore, probably remain filled with poisonous contagion. Therefore, it is a matter of striving to cleanse the intellectual atmosphere of all the toxic organisms or making them harmless just as we have learned to do from Pasteur in the physical world ...."[38]

2.8 The Carlsberg Laboratory

Pasteur and his experimental research was one of the most important sources of inspiration for J. C. Jacobsen. Pasteur had achieved his results through scientific experiments; and, in Jacobsen's opinion, it was on this basis that beer brewing should rest. An important part of 'the Carlsberg family' is still today the research institution, Carlsberg Laboratory, which as part of a "family" that sticks together and jointly supports the brewery and its products, has contributed much to the fame of Carlsberg. J. C. Jacobsen in 1875, the year before the establishment of the Carlsberg Foundation, had founded this 'Lab' with an eye toward experimental research and as a replacement for a smaller brewing lab. In the word 'laboratory' is included the Latin word *laborare*, which actually means to stagger under a heavy burden but also simply to work. The word was new to the Danish language, but in the second half of the 19th century, the laboratory became popular as a place, where scientific and medical experiments with the help of modern technical equipment could be carried out. The word 'laboratory' thus connects the idea of empiricism and professionalism, scientific method and honesty, and the researcher's inexhaustible search for the right connections. There already existed such laboratories in Copenhagen, and in 1875 a new one was added when Jacobsen established his Carlsberg Laboratory in connection with the brewery. It was a scientific institute, and it was essential for Jacobsen that the laboratory did not become a sort of brewery school. On the other hand, students were welcome at the brewery itself.

[38]Letter of 23 March 1886, comp. above. p.

The Charter of the Foundation from 1876 clearly reflected the Brewer's thoughts about the purpose of the Carlsberg Laboratory and his desire to ensure a durable link between the research of the laboratory and the exigencies of the beer industry. At the laboratory, they were to study malting, brewing, and fermentation processes, which formed the basis for the production of high-quality beer. One result of Jacobsen's generosity and fundamental vision was that scientific results should be freely accessible; therefore, it was his determination that there would be openness about research, so that no important practical or theoretical result of the laboratory's work should be kept secret. Jacobsen had himself learned the basis for modern beer brewing from Sedlmayer in Munich and brought home the necessary yeast from there. In this way, he had helped raise the level of Danish beer brewing. Now, in his view, Denmark could contribute to improving the state of beer brewing internationally, and it had an obligation to do so. Beer quality was decisive for the Brewer. The history of the Carlsberg Laboratory is a story in itself and an important part of the history of Danish science.[39] The maintenance of his research unit as an institution that could help increase the quality of beer production was also an essential reason for establishing the Foundation to secure the perpetuity of this work. Supervising the research at the laboratory that was an essential part of J. C. Jacobsen's lifework became an important part of the Foundation's efforts, which primarily rested with the natural science-oriented members of the Foundation.

Over the years, research at the laboratory went in many different and sometimes even erratic directions. It is a good question how this could happen under the supervision of the Carlsberg Foundation and whether the board of the Laboratory has consistently lived up to expectations. The Brewer had established a fixed framework around the research, stressing that it should be relevant to beer brewing. At the head of the laboratory was a board of directors consisting of three natural science members of the Foundation in addition to one or two other members selected by the Royal Academy, in practice often people with leading positions in the brewery.

The everyday management of the laboratory was placed in the hands of two research directors at professor level. It was stressed in the Charter of the Carlsberg Foundation that they should keep abreast of foreign research and disseminate the laboratory's work abroad, so other people could see "the honorable part Danes are playing in the development of science". The laboratory's history has primarily been told as the story of a series of more or

---

[39]On this, see Holter and Møller (1976); Larsen (2001 and undated).

less distinct personalities who generally, by virtue of their scientific excellence, influenced the work of the laboratory and understood how to construct research groups and attract foreign guest researchers. It also became a story of the relationship between the brewery's desires for targeted brewing research and a laboratory with individual researchers with their own ideas about how best to contribute to science. In the laboratory's initial years, the work and method of the outstanding chemist J. Kjeldahl to find nitrogen in organic materials was one of the results that helped cement the laboratory's reputation. A monument recording his efforts is found in front of the laboratory. Of even greater importance for Carlsberg was Professor Emil Christian Hansen's path-breaking work with yeast and yeast reactions. In front of the laboratory today is a more than well-deserved monument to this extraordinary man originally a botanist, who, due to his yeast research, achieved a step beyond Pasteur, when it came to bacteria studies and the understanding of yeast cells as living organisms. Pasteur's method was still not certain, and there were still surprises waiting for the brewers of the time. In 1883, however, Hansen succeeded in isolating single cells of the yeast fungus and purifying the kind of yeast that was later known as *Saccharomyces carlsbergensis.* This so-called "pure" yeast became an international success and a turning point in the history of beer brewing. Carlsberg Laboratory pursuant to its basic values of openness did not take out a patent on Hansen's apparatus. Jacobsen's idealistic approach—about which he was not alone at the time—meant that such results were made available without remuneration to anyone interested, and of course such interest was especially found among the brewers of the time and even those who would later be competitors.

One was the Dutch brewer Heineken. The Dutch brewers were even inspired by the discovery to establish a corresponding laboratory in connection with their brewery. The Brewer's generosity in connection with pure yeast later became a part of Carlsberg's branding as a brewery with a good story to tell. Heineken, at that time a moderately-sized national brewery, had surpassed Carlsberg in size on the international beer market. In 2010, there was correspondence between Carlsberg and Heineken on former relations including how in the mid-1880s Carlsberg had sent *sacccharomyces carlsbergensis* to Heineken's brewmaster Wilhelm Feltmann, whom the founder of the Heineken brewery, Gerard Adriaan Heineken, had in his day brought from Germany. Feltmann knew or had turned to Carl Jacobsen (who had originally spotted Emil Christian Hansen and had access to the laboratory), asking for a shipment of the new yeast that made it possible for Heineken to develop so-called type A yeast.

Hansen became a European celebrity for his yeast studies. Personally, he was known as a difficult and introverted character, very touchy, and he often felt undervalued. On the other hand, his observational abilities and assessments of others—and this included the Brewer—were sharp and self-assured.[40] With all his excellent traits and great respect for science, J. C. Jacobsen also had the not infrequent character flaw that he was subject to moods, generally wanted to decide everything, and was sometimes not good at praising others for their achievements. This created an occasionally adversarial relationship with Emil Christian Hansen, who might occasionally feel that his yeast research, which was vital for the brewery, was not appreciated, much less rewarded, as it deserved. Hansen had overcome great personal difficulties to reach the position he had achieved. He believed that others had often too easily come to theirs or got more out of it than he, and he was right about that. Hansen knew, if anyone did, the brewer's personal weaknesses; but, in his summary of the brewer's actions, he turned to magnanimity, stating that "Jacobsen [was] as with all great figures; if we consider them from the proper distance, we see only the great in them. And what they have contributed evokes such a vibrant admiration in us that we do not even notice the flaws".[41]

A stellar moment in the history of the laboratory was Louis Pasteur's visit during a conference in Copenhagen in 1884, where he also met Emil Christian Hansen. Pasteur truly appreciated Hansen as a researcher, and the feeling was mutual, while Jacobsen, like the noble family in Hans Christian Andersen's story about "The Gardener and the Family", had a more difficult time recognizing that his own Hansen was actually just as good as Gallic Pasteur and, perhaps, even more groundbreaking in his field.

The laboratory quickly acquired a good reputation after a flying start with Hansen's studies of yeast and Kjeldahl's simultaneous determination of nitrogen in organic substances.[42] In addition, there was S. P. L. Sørensen, who in the years 1901 to 1938 was head of the chemistry department. He studied the functionality of proteins and enzymes and became known as the person who established the pH scale for acids and bases for which he was several times, however without success, nominated for the Nobel Prize. These were all discoveries that also had great significance for the brewery.

The importance of the laboratory was stressed when, in 1897, it was housed in a brand-new, impressive—for its day—red-brick building on its own grounds across from the brewery. The spacious lobby was adorned

[40] Glamann (2004).

[41] Emil Christian Hansen's eulogy to Jacobsen 1901.

[42] On this and the following, see Larsen.

by busts of Pasteur and the German Liebig, thus linking what was going on in Copenhagen to international research. In the years thereafter, excellent research was done at the laboratory but not always with any special affiliation with the brewery. One of the problems in connection with the laboratory's work in the years after the triad, Kjeldahl, Hansen, and Sørensen, was whether there was sufficient connection between the laboratory and the brewery. Another hot question was how to establish a fruitful exchange between the chemistry and the physiology departments, each of which had a tendency to work in their own direction. A considerable part of the laboratory's work certainly was excellent science but not relevant at all to the brewing of beer. An important—and classical—question at that time and later, therefore, was whether it was better to be generous and go down the path of contributing to free research or whether the laboratory research should be kept within certain limits and stick to research that was of interest to the brewery.

In particular, such questions were raised in relation to the biologist Johannes Schmidt and the relevance to the brewery of his research that took place during his term as research director from 1910 to 1933. Schmidt participated in marine expeditions and was often far away in connection with his important marine biology studies. It could be asked what natural connection these *per se* important and truly interesting, internationally-recognized studies had for a laboratory affiliated with the Carlsberg breweries. However, Schmidt was a nephew of the famous laboratory director Johan Kjeldahl and had even lived in his home for a time at the laboratory; he was married to the daughter of legendary Carlsberg CEO S. A. van der Aa Kühle, and he was the protégé of the laboratory's board chairman Eugen Warming. He was even more than ordinarily talented at what he did. A later chairman of the Carlsberg Foundation, the pharmacist Povl Krogsgaard-Larsen said in 2011 of Johannes Schmidt, called "eely Schmidt" after his preferred object of research, that he was far more interested in the migration of eels than in beer and yeast.[43]

People could have—and had—diverging opinions as to the relevance of the laboratory's research for the brewery, and they were also aired and wrestled with in the years to come.[44] Fundamentally, what happened was that researchers at the laboratory, regardless of the charter's phrasing about relevance to the brewery, received or took for themselves significant freedoms with respect to the formulation of their research tasks, and the Carlsberg Foundation's members of the laboratory's board actually accepted this. In

[43]CF 27 Jan. 2011.

[44]On the Carlsberg Laboratory, see Holter and Møller (1976); Larsen (2001, 2016).

a memoir written much later, Povl Krogsgaard-Larsen, chairman of the Carlsberg Foundation (2003–2012) and for a period also the board of the laboratory, described such deviation from the charter directly as "treason against the Brewer".[45]

In 1929, Carlsberg had established its own more targeted research laboratory, and S. P. L. Sørensen, among others, was related to this laboratory to provide advice on a number of questions about beer quality. However, the extent to which one could give the lab's researchers a free hand and let them decide for themselves whether their research fell within the purposes of the lab was and remained a major open question closely connected to the Brewer's understanding of the cooperation between science and enterprise. The excellent research results that were achieved at the laboratory in the years to come in a variety of fields all helped to give the laboratory a very good international scientific reputation and created research environments at the laboratory that attracted younger as well as more experienced international researchers. It was research that was carried out under the leadership of such great researchers as S. P. L. Sørensen and the versatile Johannes Schmidt[46] or by the multi-talented chemist K. Linderstrøm-Lang or the fungus researcher Øyvind Winge. Heinz Holter, who had his own department for cytochemistry, and Martin Ottosen with ground-breaking enzyme research should also be mentioned. The most brewery-relevant research in those years came from the geneticist Øivind Winge, who was supervisor at the laboratory in 1933–1956. In the spirit of J. C. Jacobsen, his research focused on the refinement of hops and barley, both of which were of great significance for the brewery, and there were developments involving the crossing of yeast strains and special types of barley, so -called Carlsberg I and II barley, at the laboratory's experimental farm.

However, earlier and over the slightly longer term, the laboratory's affiliation with and the research's relevance for the brewery continued to be problematic. In 1955, when Carlsberg had a serious problem with too much foaming, the laboratory was only helpful to a rather limited extent in finding the cause, and the problem was not even mentioned in the minutes of the laboratory board or in accounts from the laboratory.[47] Characteristic of the frustrations one might have in the Foundation board with respect to the breadth of the research in relation to what was said in the charter is a remark by Aksel Tovborg Jensen, who was one of the Foundation members on the laboratory's board (1956–72). In connection with the laboratory's

---

[45]Krogsgaard (2011), p. 235.

[46]See Winge and Tåning (1947), *Naturforskeren Johannes Schmidt. Hans liv og ekspeditioner.*

[47]Larsen (n.d., p. 128).

100th anniversary, he wrote of two of its leading researchers, Linderstrøm-Lang and Holter, that, in the Foundation's eyes, they "solved more problems about animal and human organisms than problems relating to barley, yeast, and hops".[48]

2.9 Frederiksborg Castle

The three-winged Renaissance castle in Hillerød some 40 km north of Copenhagen in the midst of an old royal hunting district, Frederiksborg, was a creation of the Danish King Christian IV in Dutch Renaissance style and a national symbol. It was still used as a royal residence but burned down in 1859, and the castle had been in ruins since, as a reminder of this national catastrophe. For the Brewer, restoration of the castle was to be seen as a national duty, which he undertook himself with the idea of establishing a national historical museum in the former royal apartments. Establishing such a museum with public access at the restored Frederiksborg Castle was a cause dear to J. C. Jacobsen, which he was willing to finance even at the cost of delays for new facilities at the breweries. His primary idea in this connection was that the castle should be outfitted as a national historical museum by which he meant that important historical events should be illustrated and the country's great men should be honored by portraits or historical pictures. The idea was to tell the history of Denmark through historical images in order to strengthen patriotism and Danish national consciousness and knowledge of history by presenting major historical events in a direct and immediately accessible way.

Jacobsen participated enthusiastically in the refurbishing of the museum. It was expensive to decorate. The walls were standing, but the restoration of the castle's interior was something of a project that would have cowed less indomitable souls than Jacobsen. He eagerly corresponded with the head architect Ferdinand Meldahl, and here we can read about how support for the castle restoration had to be weighed against considerations for brewery operations and about how Jacobsen found inspiration in the restoration of a similar Swedish historical museum that he liked to visit at Gripsholm Castle.[49]

---

[48]Quoted from Larsen (2016), p. 243; comp. Holter and Møller (1976), p. 273.

[49]Letter to Meldahl 3 April 1877. Comp. Glamann (1990), p. 299, on J. C. Jacobsen's last birthday 2 September 1886, when he visited Gripsholm alone.

Jacobsen wanted his Carlsberg Foundation to support the operation of the museum.[50] The National Historical Museum at Frederiksborg, therefore, became its own letter as a specific department C of the Carlsberg Foundation since 1878. The new collection at the castle was to contain historical paintings that highlighted important events in the history of the fatherland, and Jacobsen's sense for detail came in handy here. At a certain moment in 1882, the museum board suffered political reservations about a monumental picture referring to a well-known incident of Danish history depicting a group of men leaving the scene of the killing of the medieval Danish King Erik Klipping, which took place near the village of Finderup in Jutland in 1286. The board was reluctant to accept the picture by a then famous Danish painter Otto Bache as they feared such an act could be seen as a Danish museum expressing sympathy for regicide. The Danish monarchy at that time held this theme close to its heart since the Danish Princess Dagmar's father-in-law, the Russian Czar Alexander II, was killed the year before on the open streets of St. Petersburg. And with reservations about the depiction of a regicide, how do you deal with a depiction of the perpetrators? Jacobsen had commissioned for the museum what became an almost iconic Danish image by Otto Bache with the title: *Marsk Stig and the Conspirators Ride from Finderup after the Murder of Eric Klipping St. Cecilia Night 1286*. In a letter to the architect Meldahl, Jacobsen wrote sharply that he himself was willing to buy the picture if, out of touchiness on the theme of regicide, the Frederiksborg board did not want a picture of the presumed killers hanging there."[51]

Over time, the portraits of contemporary persons were supposed to be added to the collection of historical portraits at Frederiksborg Castle. One of the first to enter was of the Brewer himself, but that was definitely not upon his own initiative. The initiative apparently came from the royal court. It was, however, at the instigation of the architect Meldahl and Edvard Holm from the Carlsberg Foundation, who knew that the Brewer would not allow his bust to be placed in the new museum if it was not by an order from the highest circles.

---

[50]The primary work on the castle and museum is Bligaard (2008), especially volume II.

[51]Letter of 20 May 1882.

2.10 Laboremus Pro Patria

Laboremus pro patria, let us work for the fatherland, was Carl Jacobsen's motto—a bit more lively than his father's "work and moderation" but still earnest. The two, father and son, were different in attitude, as it often happens when one is a founder and the other has more given to him but must live up to great demands. Still, they were both brilliant brewers, and both believed that wealth and prestige brought responsibility, that from wealth flows an obligation to do something for the society in which they worked and whose growing thirst for beer gave them the economic possibility to do so.

The story of the relationship between father and son, J. C. Jacobsen and Carl Jacobsen, which veered between admiration and hatred but ended up in reconciliation, belongs to Danish history and has been told a number of times. As a family history, as a prototype of an ancient, almost mythical, struggle between father and son, and as a chapter in something that resembles a *Bildungsroman*, it is deeply fascinating, but it can overshadow the real story, which has to do with two talented businessmen and their efforts to spend their income for the benefit of their country and its science and art. Traditionally, J. C. Jacobsen is described as a "rock" and his son Carl as a less rigid and somewhat softer type. There is, however, much to indicate that old Jacobsen also had feelings and his own "crazy" sides and not only in relation to courting charming actresses and the reconstruction of ruined castles. Yet, Carl was a most professional brewer and entirely on board with the program that beer must be sold and a brewer may also be a merchant (who does not always have clean hands). Just like his father, he sacrificed his family's interest to preserve the family enterprise. Both the opposition and the symbiosis between father and son, the old brewer's ideas and Carl's somewhat different—but not radically different—way of viewing life, and their ultimate reconciliation are important ingredients for understanding the story of the Foundation's existence and its later history.

Carl was the person who, as a five-year-old in 1847, gave the name to the newly-established Carlsberg Brewery, and he followed in his father's footsteps as a brewer as his own father had done. Ambitions for the son had been great since his childhood, and they left their mark. Now there is a difference in growing up as J. C. (who had the possibility of surpassing his father) and as Carl (who had to struggle not to be weighed down by his father's stature). Carl did not have an easy childhood; and, like others in this situation, he struggled with having a great man as a father who wanted to decide everything. From an early point, the correspondence from father to son is rich and revealing. At the same time, especially during Carl's apprentice years as a brewer abroad from 1865 to 1870, it is unusually candid from the father's side. With respect to concern for his son's education and his whole character development, the correspondence comes close to the "mirror for princes" from which Renaissance kings learned the art of statecraft. Carl was to be the brewer of the future and, preferably, the best of them all when his time came. The letters are important for history, and many of them are cited here. Nor is being born with a silver spoon in one's mouth generally to be despised. It provides opportunities, and Carl exploited them. They must be lived up to, and he did in his own way. After what could be called a "pissing match", father and son wound up more or less on equal footing.

A letter from father to son on 2 March 1855, a proper birthday greeting to a 13-year-old, may explain more than many words about a demanding father who wanted to be generous but expected the person who receives a large present to deserve the gift: "My dear Carl! Since you have been a very good and diligent boy this past year, the enclosed watch should have been your property today. But now I cannot give it you because you have not earned it. However, I hope you will strive to deserve it. Therefore, I will lend it to you to look at and be guided by in your room, but you may not wear it before you have moved up to the place in class you previously had. Your loving father, Jacobsen."

The letter strangely anticipates what happened 21 years later when the Brewer gave another, much larger gift—namely, his breweries—to others, because he did not trust that the son had lived up to his father's strict requirements for beer quality. It is, however, also a part of the Carlsberg story that Carl actually learned from these experiences and later proved to be just as talented a brewer as his father as well as a patron of stature. Still, Carl was a different kind of person, and his background was also different. If he did not remember it himself, others could remind him that he belonged among those privileged by birth and had been given not only good advice by his father but also "a highly-regarded name and who, by giving you a business and operating capital, laid the groundwork for your welfare and wealth".[52] Voila!

After a thorough practical and theoretical education and as soon as he could stand on his own feet, Carl began to go his own way with his own brewery. This is something a father could be proud of, and so this father was—deep down. However, with a father like J. C. Jacobsen, the son's own development could not avoid creating conflicts, which for a period seemed

[52]See Glamann (1992), p. 242 ff.

insurmountable. Nevertheless, they ultimately resolved their issues. Carl's mind was different. Even though he was a talented brewer, he was even more captivated by his interest in art and culture and in such a way that it affected the balance between business and patronage. They merged. Both the Glyptotek as a universal art collection and Carl's New Carlsberg Foundation have become indispensable parts of Danish culture for which Carl deserves just as much gratitude as his father for his foundation and his national historical museum.

From the end of the 1860s, when Carl was on his long Grand Tour to Germany, France, and England, we have weekly, sometimes daily, letters from father to son. One of them, dated 2 June 1865, sets out J. C. Jacobsen's ideas about Carl's education and personal development: "My primary goal with the education I have tried to give and acquire for you has been (1) to lay a solid foundation for your comprehensive, intellectual development as a human being, (2) to provide you with sufficient cultivation to ensure you a distinguished position in society and allow you to harvest the benefits of personal development through convivial interaction with educated and knowledgeable people, and (3) to make you capable as a brewer of developing a business that can be satisfactory for you as a man and a citizen and give your life rich content for the benefit and honor of your fatherland …." In hindsight, we must acknowledge that Carl lived up to expectations and that these three goals were more than achieved but, perhaps, not really until after his father's death. On Carl's 25th birthday, this admission was even given by the father: "You know that it is my custom to allow my feelings to be expressed in deeds."

Jacobsen stressed his ability and wish to manage his brewery himself; and, like other business founders after him, he grew concerned that it all might become too much to keep track of. Therefore, when it came down to it, he did not want his son Carl involved in his business when he returned home from abroad. The solution was to have Carl found his own brewery and begin to brew in accordance with methods he had learned during his long study tour abroad. In 1871, Carl leased land from his father on his brewery's premises in Valby, the so-called Annex Brewery, to brew English beer types, which he had studied during his stay in England and Scotland. Shortly after that, Carl also began to produce the more sought-after lager, and he eventually was given by his father the brewery's customer portfolio outside of Copenhagen. With the establishment of the Carlsberg Foundation in 1876, Carl was well on his way to establishing his own brewery business.

In 1879, J. C. Jacobsen decided to completely break off business collaboration with Carl. He terminated his son's lease and suggested the son build his own brewery—this despite attempts by his wife and friends, lawyers, and the executive board of the Carlsberg Foundation to mediate. Carl's new brewery was opened on adjacent land in 1881. Jacobsen demanded of Carl that he not use the name Carlsberg, but he got no legal support in this since Carl had already announced "New Carlsberg" as the name of the company. Therefore, it ended with J. C. Jacobsen's two breweries acquiring the name "Old Carlsberg" and them being spoken of in the plural as breweries, while Carl could call his new brewery "New Carlsberg". The relationship between father and son developed thereafter in a catastrophic direction that could not help but corrode both parties—perhaps, the old man the most. It did not help the atmosphere that, after terminating his son's lease of the Annex Brewery, the father had been excluded from the dedication of Carl's new brewery in 1881 or that, shortly thereafter, he bestowed his breweries upon others.

The relation reached the point that gifts were returned, doors and gates to homes barred, and grandchildren kept from their grandparents. Even road names became an apple of discord for what third parties had to consider as two slightly insane people. The causes of the strife were many. The old father, who felt estranged from his son, believed the son had been assisted too much and had come to his success too easily. He thought Carl had thereby been afflicted with a sort of megalomania, which made their relationship difficult. Nor was the Brewer convinced of Carl's ability and will to keep up the quality of the beer, and he also looked skeptically upon his son's expensive art purchases, which consumed means that, in his opinion, could better be used to develop the business. All this might very well be correct, but it is hard to get around the fact that J. C. Jacobsen was hard on and not entirely fair to Carl, who was a talented brewer and, later, showed excellent leadership abilities. Old times and new clashed, which led to a break between the families for several years until, at the last moment, two years before J. C. Jacobsen's death, they reconciled.

2.11 Jacobsen's Legacy

The establishment of the Carlsberg Foundation came in the form of a donation to the Danish Royal Academy in 1876. At first, the Foundation was a money donation, but it later became commercial when J. C. Jacobsen left it the breweries in his will after his death. Thus, there are two phases in this foundation story and two founding documents, a charter from 1876 and a will from 1882, which came into effect as of 1 October 1888 with respect to the takeover of the breweries.[53] In 1881, the Carlsberg Foundation received an additional DKK one million from the Brewer, so that the capital, together with DKK 200,000 contributed in 1878 to Frederiksborg Museum, totaled DKK 2.2 million.

A will is a document in which a person determines what is to happen to his fortune after his death. J. C. Jacobsen had quite a bit of wealth but the most important asset, of course, were his breweries, and his will of 20 February 1882 reflects, first and foremost, his concern about how things would go for the breweries after his death. A key word in the will—and, generally for understanding him as a person—is "perfection". Jacobsen was a perfectionist. The word appears in article 8 of the will, where we find the so-called "golden words" of beer brewing, which are still an important part of the brewery's heritage, still written with the old orthography.

"In the Operation of the Carlsberg Breweries, the constant Purpose without respect to immediate Advantage must be to develop Manufacture to the greatest possible Perfection, so that these Breweries and their Products may always stand as a Model and by their Example have the effect of keeping Beer Brewing in this Country at a high and honorable Level."[54]

The perfection mentioned here was best secured in the long term, the Brewer believed, by making the Carlsberg Foundation heir to the brewery and the land appurtenant thereto. The ideas that the Brewer had aired and already discussed with his son Carl in connection with the establishment of the Foundation were now being realized. The Brewer at that point had terminated Carl's lease at Carlsberg and merged the so-called Annex Brewery with his own, so that it accompanied his own breweries and became the property of the Carlsberg Foundation. Now it was about the business itself, the breweries. The establishment of the Foundation and, later, the donation of the brewery to the Foundation meant that his son Carl would not inherit his father's business. However, Carl consented to the will. He received as heir a considerable amount of money but renounced for himself and his descendants any additional inheritance from his father. At the time of the donation, the relationship between father and son was tense but had not yet broken, which it did shortly afterwards.

[53]At a Foundation board meeting on 23 May 1986, the chairman at the time, Kristof Glamann, mentioned the possibility of celebrating the centenary of the takeover with publications, CFP, meeting 23 May 1986.

[54]"Ved Carlsberg Bryggeriernes Drift skal det stadige Formaal uden Hensyn til øjeblikkelig Fordeel være, at udvikle Fabrikationen til den størst mulige Fuldkommenhed, saaledes at disse Bryggerier og deres Produkter altid kan staa som et Mønster og ved deres Eksempel virke til, at Ølbryggeriet her i Landet holdes paa et højt og hæderligt Standpunkt".

Jacobsen was well aware that the Royal Academy did not possess either the necessary technical skills for brewing or the business know-how. A provision in the will, therefore, demanded that the breweries were to be run for the Foundation's benefit by an independent and professional manager as long as the production had a certain volume. Thus, Jacobsen's gift to science was a brewery with professional leadership included and a requirement that such a manager remain employed as long as the brewery maintained a certain output.

The Brewer's closest staff member at that point and for the rest of his life was S. A. van der Aa Kühle, whom he had employed in 1879.[55] Kühle was born in 1849 and, both upon employment in 1879 and even in 1882, was still a young but already experienced brewer, who had to be expected to last a few years yet. He was educated as an officer, which was a big plus for Jacobsen. Kühle had married into the Wiibroe brewery family in Elsinore, where he learned about brewing. Upon his employment at Carlsberg, he was running a minor brewery, Rabeshave, in the Copenhagen district of Christianshavn. The choice of Kühle proved to be a very good choice.

Another article (art. 4) of the will contained a provision that the operation of the breweries must not be merged with the operations of any other brewery: "The two breweries[56] erected on the property should always be run jointly, and their operation must never be merged with the operations of any other brewery…." What this implied and what it means exactly to run something "jointly", however, could be debated, and it was in the coming years until 1970 when the consolidation with Tuborg or The United Breweries (*De Forenede Bryggerier*, DFB), became a reality.

After Jacobsen's death in 1887, an addendum of 1 October 1888 was prepared for the 1876 charter in relation to his will in connection with the conveyance of the breweries to the Foundation. In article 4 of the addendum, it was determined that the brewery was to belong to the Carlsberg Foundation, and it was once again stressed that it must not be run together with other breweries.

At the same time, the "golden words" that beer brewing here in Denmark must be held "to a high and honorable level" were repeated in the charter addendum of 1888. The "golden words" are still referred to when talk falls to what Carlsberg is so good at. They remained not just words but became for the business an expression of the level of quality that was always to be strived for. They also became, as we shall hear, the mantra to which they later referred

---

[55]On Kühle, see Schmidt (1956). See also file 27/54 in archive box A 95-1954.

[56]The 'old' Carlsberg and the socalled Annex brewery are sometimes mentioned as two sometimes as one brewery.

and which legally paved the way to adapt Jacobsen's brewery to developments in the beer market. Even if the changes were great, the "golden words" remained fixed. They are still a part of the newly-revised charter of 2012. The consideration of maintaining the quality of "beer brewing here in this country" was a very good argument, when people later wanted to change the original charter to give the brewery the possibility of expanding beyond its original narrow framework.

2.12 An Easter Morning

Not until after several years of strife were father and son reunited and reconciled. J. C. Jacobsen's letter to Carl from the day after Easter Sunday 1885 is, in its way, gripping evidence of the personal suffering caused by intransigence on both sides during this long conflict: "Dear Carl, thank you for the Easter greeting you sent me by Theodora as evidence that you felt it would please me to see the innocent children and that you will allow me that pleasure in my old age. I see in this greeting a continuation of the long history of suffering that may also for me be replaced by a resurrection to a new and better life here on earth, and I can now with hope and consolation join in: 'Good Friday was a bitter day, but beautiful was Easter morning!' Your devoted J. C. Jacobsen."

Father and son could finally speak together again. Carl's daughter Theodora had been sent out on a reconciliation quest, and it turned out to be at the very last moment. Two years later, the Brewer set off on what would be his final journey—to Rome in the chilly spring of 1887. In a letter to Mrs. Heiberg dated 20 February 1887—shortly before his departure—Jacobsen summarized his work in a few lines: "Since I have now roughly concluded my work of many years with the erection and organization of my brewery and also have an operations manager to whom I may leave the management thereof with security when the Lord recalls me, I feel a need to consider the progress of the whole work at a distance and thereby, as I hope, gain certainty that everything can go as it should when I am gone".

It was chilly in Rome that spring. The Jacobsen family and entourage were quartered in one of the city's newest and most elegant hotels, *Hotel Quirinale*, which is still located on the then newly-constructed Via Nationale, not far from the Terminus railway station. Rome was different from the time Jacobsen first visited there. Back in 1862, he traveled with Carl to what was still the Rome of the Popes. Since 1870, the city had become the capital of a united Italy. Jacobsen wrote to Carl (who was then in Greece) about his stay in Rome on 18 March 1887 that "this dark and cold weather" has "put a powerful damper on our outings and given us all head colds … Therefore, after a 14-day stay in Rome, there are a multitude of things that must be seen and studied that none of us have viewed … I have always on my travels engaged in intensive activity, which has not allowed me to miss my accustomed activity at home, but I have been prepared for the fact that, at my far advanced age and on a journey with my family, I could not indulge in such activities as before; yet, I had not prepared myself for such diluted activities as in these last days, and I therefore have not been able to keep from thinking of swapping a stay in cold, rainy Rome with the region of Naples in this inclement March month until Easter, but I have not yet seen how the weather in Naples is at the moment, and it is against my principles to change plans without pressing need, and I will therefore probably stay where I am until after Easter".

On 25 March 1887, an attentive "Grandpapa" could tell his grandchild Theodora that he was "perfectly healthy and can still be on the go, so that I can tell you many things about Rome when I return", and he sent "little Theodora" an anemone, which "I plucked today in the grass at Pamphylia—Doria garden".

Grandpapa was not perfectly healthy. He was deathly ill; and, in the coming weeks, his condition worsened. The final greeting from Carl to his father was a telegram on 21 April 1887 on its way from Greece to his father's deathbed in Rome. Carl arrived before his father died, but it was just as important that he was able to say in the telegram some of what can be difficult to say between father and son and that, with a nice turn, he mentions the role of the father as a citizen before his biological paternity. It is not a letter to a loving father but to a father as a professional role model: "For me, you are the best citizen and a dear father. You are the role model whom I always seek to emulate, and you should know that, just as I myself desire to follow in your footsteps as a brewer, citizen, and man, so I hope that your spirit may also live in the next stage through my children. If God wishes to give me his blessing, then they and I would not have lived in vain. I long only to come to Rome to be with you".

On 30 April 1887, J. C. Jacobsen died in Rome. Almost by a miracle, Carl arrived the same morning from Greece and could be present at his deathbed in the last moment. His notes about the Brewer's last hours are testimony to the reconciliation between father and son. We can read there how Carl arrived at six o'clock in the morning by train and was received by Louis Pasteur's son,[57] who said: 'Il est bien, bien mal, vous allez le voir'. Carl records how

[57]A son, Jean-Baptist (1850–1908), of Louis Pasteur, who worked at the French embassy in Rome, see Glamann (1995), p. 23.

'my poor father' lay in bed with panting breath and a dull gaze. He did not seem to notice that they had arrived and were standing beside him. When he did notice us, Carl writes, he asked how it was that we were there, but there was no joy of reunion in seeing in him. He was in a visible delirium, spoke a gibberish of languages without much connection between thoughts. His speech was labored, indistinct, often incomprehensible, constantly interrupted by a staring that also seemed to break the connection. It struck Carl that he had never seen him like this: "I tried several times to find a clear moment. Do you not know me Father? Yes, of course, I know you, Carl, or the like, but after a few coherent words, he began to speak about French verbs, etc. … I bought some roses and gave them to him to hold to his nose. He only said they do not smell and did not seem to care for them. When the others said to him that these are roses that Carl is giving you, he said thank you and looked kindly at me. He fumbled for them and placed his hand on them … at 12 o'clock, he rose in his bed and recognized the doctor, Neotani. I prayed Our Father for him, but he did not seem to notice it. A bit later, Durante came, but he did not recognize him. After 1 o'clock, he just lay with closed eyes, gasping. When the clock was approaching 2, it became weaker. Ottilia and I went into him. Were alone with him. I held his right hand in mine, while he took his last breath. Just before the moment of death, his head lowered toward his left side, where Ottilia stood, and his eyes fell on her with an expression as if he recognized her. That was the last impression he received in life. I bowed over him in order, perhaps, to get a look, but he drew his last, weak breath. I said then, "Look at me, Father", but he did not look at me. I said, I'm squeezing your hand, squeeze mine again (but he did not)".

And what about afterwards? Of course, J. C. Jacobsen had thoughts about that. The Brewer was religious but in his own independent way. In an 1867 letter to Carl, J. C. described his religious views and stressed the individual faith of the Protestant: "Among Protestants, the self-determination of the individual in the domain of faith is a right—and a duty—and the individual's faith, therefore, has a more or less individual character. For me, almost all dogmas seem unimportant, either irrational or alien from the true nature of Christianity".

He also touched on the question of life after death:

"But now the doctrine of immortality! Can one prove its truth philosophically?

No!

Can one conceive immortality?

No, just as little as we here on earth, as finite creatures, could conceive infinity in time or space.

Am I to believe in what I cannot conceive, much less prove its correctness?" The Brewer's answer here was an "unconditional: Yes!" He believed in the immortality of man: "For without immortality, the whole of human existence seems to me utterly unreasonable. Without immortality, there is no eternal justice, for the evil man is suddenly ripped away without getting his punishment and the good man as well without his reward: It seems clear to me that all of human life necessarily presumes a continuation after death...." On the other hand, he did not believe that it made sense to ponder more "over the form of this continued life". Eternity lay beyond the capacity of the human horizon to grasp. Pictures of "this state of existence" are the play of imagination and not thought: "For life down here, they are without meaning".[58]

J. C. Jacobsen nevertheless lived on as a role model, and Carlsberg afterwards referred time and again to his "spirit" when decisions were to be made. Several later chairpersons for his Foundation have recounted their internal dialogue with the Brewer. Considerations of what he might have thought and done in hypothetical situations that he could not have foreseen but happened later also belong to the history of his breweries told here.

2.13 1 October 1888

Whoever originated the idea that, in addition to leading the scientific laboratory, distributing funds for research, and maintaining a museum, the Carlsberg Foundation should also take over responsibility for a major brewery is uncertain. If they had been able to ask the Brewer J. C. Jacobsen himself, he would presumably have responded that, even when the Foundation itself was established in 1876, he had ideas in that direction, that he had mentioned them to his son Carl at that time, and that Carl had approved the idea. It was all about securing the future of the breweries. A letter dated 17 September 1876 from Carl Jacobsen to Japetus Steenstrup confirms that, prior to the establishment of the Foundation, Carl had been briefed on the Foundation and his father's intention to convey the brewery later to the Foundation and that he might have been part of the idea, in principle, to convey his father's breweries to the Foundation. On the other hand, Carl wrote to his father

[58] Glamann (1991), pp. 36–38.

already in November 1876[59] that he had been the one to broach the idea when he heard about the Foundation for the first time but that it had gone no farther than the thought. That he had expected it to be something to be discussed in more depth and that his father should have waited to tell others until they had discussed it more appear in a letter of 6 November 1876 from Carl to his father after a dinner party the day before: "Dear Father, the report you made last night to the party of your decision about Carlsberg was just as unexpected to me as it was significant. So far as I remember, I myself was the one of us two who first proposed the idea of this in a conversation in the spring. It follows from this that I cannot disapprove of the step, and I hope that, in its time, it will really be to our country's benefit. I also assume that you will give me the right to believe that, more than most, I understand and appreciate your high-minded actions. But even more the way in which you reported to me—your son—this significant testament has made me sad—indeed, offended me greatly. A fleeting and loose expression half a year ago about a possibility about which you did not even enter into a discussion since it 'was not at hand' (as opposed to the 'foundation' whereof you gave an exact account) is all the information with which you have deigned to satisfy me".

For Carl, the report of his father's decision was "just as surprising as for anyone else. I do not write this to chastise you but so that you might possibly think to understand that this action of yours—which testifies so powerfully about your civic-mindedness—will for me be accompanied with the memory of a disregard that has rarely been shown to a son by a father, however little your mind otherwise could be open to trust on a daily basis. You have gained in my thoughts of you as a historic personality but not in the same degree as a father. Your dearly devoted Carl."

Later in 1896, Carl wrote again about the establishment of the Carlsberg Foundation. His version now was that he was briefed by his father in May 1876 and "received this idea with warmth and added that he thought his father could give the foundation the brewery as well to which Jacobsen replied that he had not thought of this but, as known, he implemented this idea later …."[60] Much indicates that it was correct when, in a letter to the Foundation board dated on the closing day of 1 October 1888, Carl took paternity of the gift. He wrote: "When my father one evening in the month of May 1876 reported to me his intention to establish the 'Carlsberg Foundation', I did not only receive this idea with undivided applause, but I also recommended to his consideration that he convey the old brewery itself. When he did not

[59]Glamann (1995), p. 175.

[60]Carl Jacobsen in Nyrop (1886), p. 64.

mention that he himself had had such an idea and when he later reminded me of *my* suggestion that evening, I must assume that the initial idea for his later disposition derives from that evening's conversation ...." In the letter to the Foundation board, Carl expressed the desire that "this harmony between father and son, which described the establishment of the Carlsberg Foundation and which was also expressed in the last part of their life together, must also describe the relationship that is now developing between you and me ...."

In the time between the establishment of the Foundation in 1876 and its takeover of the brewery in 1888, there had been the fierce family conflict, which was resolved only at the last moment before the old Brewer's death in 1887. Harmony was restored, and on 1 October 1888 Carl wrote to the Foundation's executive board: "Now the future lies open to any possibility; but in this I wish the Carlsberg Foundation welcome in my former home, I want to repeat my desire that the two fraternal establishments may always be worthy brothers".

Whether it was the father or the son, or the two jointly, who had the idea of giving the old Carlsberg brewery to the Foundation must remain open. It is a nice thought that the idea came from Carl and was executed by the father in order later to be repeated by Carl as to his brewery. At least, Carl proved to be just as generous when in 1901–25 years after the establishment of the Carlsberg Foundation—he followed his father and, with effect from 20 January 1902, gave this brewery, the New Carlsberg, which he himself had founded and run to become a modern business, to the Foundation. What makes the Carlsberg Foundation into something special was the gift to the Foundation in the form of the breweries, which made it probably one of the world's first if not *the* first commercial foundation.[61]

The closest in time and content to the Carlsberg Foundation is the foundation that the physicist and businessman Ernst Abbe established in 1889, which he named after his companion of many years Carl Zeiss. Abbe originally wanted to give his comprehensive business, which dealt with optics, precision technology, and glass cutting, etc., to the University of Jena. However, it was not legally possible and, therefore, ended with the establishment in 1889 of an independent foundation, the Carl-Zeiss Stiftung to which Abbe already in 1891 conveyed his shares of the large enterprise. In 1919, his co-owner Otto Schott transferred his shares to the foundation. The story is a little reminiscent of the conveyance—first, by Jacobsen and, later, by his son Carl—of their breweries to the Carlsberg Foundation. The purpose

[61]See Johansen and Møller (2005), loc. cit.

of the Carl-Zeiss Stiftung was also to ensure the operations and social obligations of the business to employees, to promote its precision technology industry and charitable arrangements in the city of Jena, and to promote research and education in the natural sciences and mathematics. So, there are parallels. Like the Carlsberg Foundation, this foundation also ran the businesses without intermediate companies, but it had a construction that brought it into closer contact with state authorities than the—in principle—independent Carlsberg Foundation. The executive board of the foundation was designated by the Ministry of Education of the (at that time) German state of Saxe-Weimar-Eisenach and was separate from the business itself.[62]

2.14 Carl Jacobsen and New Carlsberg

After his father's death, Carl no longer had a dominant father figure to take into consideration or stand in the shadow of. His father's brewery was donated to the Carlsberg Foundation, so Carl could concentrate on the operations of his own New Carlsberg and develop it as a modern, well-functioning business. The operations of old Carlsberg were managed by J. C. Jacobsen's man, S. A. van der Aa Kühle. Like the Brewer himself, he was vitally interested in the scientific foundation of beer brewing and helped to get Emil Christian Hansen's results with pure yeast put into practice. As mentioned, the Brewer had designated him as his successor and sole director with an obligation to follow the instructions set out in his will, including maintaining the high quality of the beer. Kühle and Carl Jacobsen had developed a trusting relationship, which also explains Kühle's special role when, fourteen years later after his father's death, Carl repeated his father's gesture of giving his brewery to the Carlsberg Foundation. Carl's foundation, the New Carlsberg Foundation, provided generous support for Danish art; and, like the Carlsberg Foundation with respect to science, this foundation is today an invaluable partner on the Danish cultural scene.

In an almost literary flash, Carl Jacobsen's lawyer, Michael Lunn, recalled in a report to the Carlsberg Foundation what happened when, many years later in November 1914,[63] he analyzed the relationship between the Carlsberg Foundation and the New Carlsberg Foundation, which Carl Jacobsen had established in 1901:

---

[62]Carl-Zeiss Stiftung has since undergone a number of changes and, in recent decades, an adaptation to the conditions of the global market has occurred which resulted, inter alia, in a separation of the business operations and the preservation of the foundation's non-profit purposes.

[63]CF 1914-15, 295/961, box A 21.

> One day at the end of August or, maybe, right at the beginning of September 1901, the now deceased brewer Carl Jacobsen came to me in my office, pulled his watch out of his pocket, and said: 'It is 2 o'clock. This is a historic moment. Right now, Kühle is with the board of the Carlsberg Foundation as the bearer of my declaration to give the Foundation my brewery New Carlsberg to be consolidated with Old Carlsberg and for the establishment of a New Carlsberg Foundation as a new, special department of the Carlsberg Foundation, and at the same time I am coming to you with a request for your assistance in arranging this conveyance.

On 25 September 1901, the 25th anniversary of the Carlsberg Foundation, Carl Jacobsen thus made public his plans to give the Carlsberg Foundation his brewery and the establishment of the New Carlsberg Foundation. The New Carlsberg Foundation was Carl Jacobsen's gift to the Carlsberg Foundation and, thus, indirectly to Danish society. The Foundation's income derived from Carl Jacobsen's own brewery, but the business of the two foundations became closely connected when Carl also gave his brewery to the Carlsberg Foundation in such a way that a part of the income of the Carlsberg Foundation from the brewery operations was to go to the New Carlsberg Foundation.

Carl Jacobsen's gift was generous, but it needed a more thorough investigation into what an acceptance would mean for the existing foundation. At first sight, it might look promising to be given a brand-new brewery, but it did not require much imagination to realize the complication of managing more breweries and, at the same time, understanding the intentions of the donor. Moreover, the art lover Carl Jacobsen had tied himself up tightly economically, and one had to be clear about all that before an otherwise attractive gift could be accepted.

Carl Jacobsen's interest in art was legendary, but he was not a fan of moderation like his father. His need to acquire ancient objects and modern French art was insatiable. It was an expensive hobby, and some of his dispositions seem irresponsible in relation to the brewery's need for capital. It was a problem at the time, but posterity has reason to be deeply grateful to him for his inexhaustibility when it came to acquiring beautiful objects. Without him, Copenhagen would not have one of the world's most distinguished private universal museums.

Like his father, Carl was not just interested in his own business. He wanted to be a true citizen. The conveyance of the brewery was "a magnificent gift from him to the Foundation", wrote Michael Lunn, and the purpose of the gift may have been primarily to erase the last vestige of disagreement that may have existed between him and his father. His mother Laura, who saw the establishment of the New Carlsberg Foundation before her death as a 92-year-old in 1911, spoke directly of the gift as "a peace offering".[64] J. C. Jacobsen's 1882 will was from a time when father and son stood far apart from each other, and Carl tried to influence the Carlsberg Foundation not to accept the brewery as a present or, at least, not the so-called Annex Brewery, which was built for him. However, he ended up approving the disposition.[65] Now, the son appeared as a donor and a patron at the same level as his father. As a third element, there was a certain assurance for Carl Jacobsen's children, who, like himself, were deprived of most of their inheritance by the dispositions of their fathers.

The Carlsberg Foundation accepted Carl Jacobsen's gift after thorough negotiations between Kühle and Michael Lunn. Thus, the Carlsberg breweries were merged into a materially and distinctly larger unit than before. The final arrangement was somewhat different than Carl Jacobsen had imagined. He wanted to have funds for his art purchases, but this side of the gift had low priority in relation to a necessary consolidation of the two foundations. They ended up with a split of 55% to the Carlsberg Foundation as opposed to 45% to the New Carlsberg Foundation or, later, 5:4 based on an evaluation of the worth of the businesses at the date of conveyance. In that way, the Carlsberg Foundation became the big brother, but respect for the New Carlsberg Foundation was something to be taken into consideration in running the business in the future.

Kühle shared J. C. Jacobsen's view of life and also his way of running the breweries—however, not unconditionally, and he took it upon himself to represent Jacobsen's values in a way that adapted them to the requirements of the times. He was also the person who, after the Brewer's death and in an understanding with historian Edvard Holm as chairman of the Carlsberg Foundation, had contacted Carl to encourage him to leave his brewery to the Carlsberg Foundation. In Kühle's view, there was no reason for Old and New Carlsberg to compete against each other. To the contrary. Carl Jacobsen's New Carlsberg was a more modern brewery than his father's, and it produced and was managed in accordance with more contemporary principles that could be a nice shot in the arm for the two old breweries.

In 1881, Carl's brewery had outperformed his father's in production. In 1888, Old Carlsberg was once again the largest, but the two breweries both produced lager and were competitors in a declining market. Kühle understood how important in the long term it was for the two businesses not to compete but to work together, and he had spoken to Carl Jacobsen about this.

[64]Pedersen (1955), p. 269; Glamann (1990), p. 312; Glamann (1995), p. 47.

[65]Pedersen (1955), pp. 267 ff.

In the first years after Carl's conveyance of New Carlsberg to the Foundation, however, the two breweries were separate, each with their own management. The fence between Old and New Carlsberg was still there, and Carl Jacobsen did not trespass on old Jacobsen's territory. At Old Carlsberg, they had Kühle; and, at New Carlsberg, the boss was Carl Jacobsen, who was assisted by his director Poul C. Poulsen, who was for Carl what Kühle had been for his father. Poulsen as future CEO guaranteed the continuity in management up until the beginning of the 1930s.

An official authorization to run Old and New Carlsberg as a unit was never given. After Carl Jacobsen's death in 1914, the interpretation of the board was that the old Brewer's will did not directly stand in the way of a joint operation of the two breweries, which were so closely tied. Since the Danish Ministry of Justice did not step in even though the conditions were well-known, it was assumed (at least, after 1916) that this form of operation was tacitly approved.

2.15 The Agreement of 1903

The operation of the brewery was, for the interim, in good and professional hands. Until the last, Jacobsen trusted his man, Kühle, who came to play an important role in the transition phase following the Brewer's death. Jacobsen's testament required the business-untutored Carlsberg Foundation to keep Kühle as the experienced director of the brewery at least until 1891. It was a very good idea that proved its sustainability. Up until his death in 1906, Kühle enjoyed the Carlsberg Foundation's full confidence. He was the manager of all business operations and thereby made the Foundation's job easier. He was also good at handling the not always easy to handle Carl Jacobsen, so operations management went very well in those years.[66]

In 1891, a Danish beer tax was levied for the first time, which helped repress the great progress that beer production had had in the 1870s and 1880s. On the other hand, spirits were not submitted to taxation; and the sale of spirits, therefore, surged. This did not suit Carl Jacobsen. He now acted as spokesman for the Danish beer industry, which began to feel hard-pressed. As part of his lobbying work against the law, Carl Jacobsen called attention in an inquiry to Parliament to the fact that the law "would have a deleterious effect

[66]Kühle was paid pursuant to merit DKK 54,000 annually in addition to free board, horse and wagon, etc. By comparison, a day wage for a worker was about DKK 3, and a brewery worker received around DKK 1200 a year with certain supplements, while the chairman of the Carlsberg Foundation received remuneration in the amount of DKK 1800 a year. This gap is even bigger today with the present (2020) CEO of Carlsberg receiving annually more than 50 mio. Danish crowns and the annual salary of brewery worker being around 360.000 DKK.

on one of the country's most unblemished industries" and that "the law in its present form cannot be counted on to bring any significant income into the state treasury". At the same time, in an 1890 lecture that was distributed in printed form, Kühle warned against the law's high tax rate, which "is almost taking the form of a persecution against Danish bottom fermentation breweries." His starting point was that it was often "stated and repeated with emphasis that Denmark was the world's most 'drunken' land." He pointed to the danger that, as a consequence of the tax, more cheap spirits would be consumed when beer prices rose. In an inquiry directed to the Parliament, he stressed the risk of increasing alcohol abuse and criticized the size of the levy and the "fateful consequences" it could have for Danish breweries. But the state needed money in the treasury; and, since income taxes at that point were unknown, industrially-produced beer, which was now traded in great quantities, was the obvious new target for taxes.

Another threat, seen from the breweries' perspective, was a powerful temperance movement. If it achieved the same political foothold as in the other Nordic countries, they might risk a prohibition or a limitation on the sale of beer with higher alcohol content. If one tried to look at the matter idealistically, one of the pleasures of brewing good beer—beyond earning money—was precisely helping to change the drinking habits of the population from strong schnapps to healthier beer. Therefore, the beer tax and cheap schnapps, on one hand, and the temperance movement, on the other, were the primary antagonists.

In 1897, the beer tax was raised, resulting in additional stagnation of sales. Moreover, pilsner began to outpace lager as Carlsberg's main product. Tuborg produced the now more popular pilsner beer and gradually became a serious competitor in the slightly more pressed market. As the worst-case scenario, a beer war between the Danish breweries loomed in which they would underbid each other, which might cause quality requirements for the beer to slacken in order to win market share. If it was about quality and not just about earning money, calm in the market was decisive. Kühle had a very clear vision of this. In 1895, an initial agreement was entered into for ten years between Old Carlsberg, New Carlsberg, and a consolidation of minor breweries established in 1891, *De Forenede Bryggerier* (abbreviated in the following as DFB or sometimes just Tuborg) in order to regulate competitive conditions. In 1894, Tuborg was a part of DFB and, by virtue of its size, trend-setting to such a degree that we often equate DFB and Tuborg. In 1895, they entered into an agreement on the distribution terms between Carlsberg and DFB. The agreement calmed the market, but it was now about to expire. Pursuant to the agreement, Carlsberg had desisted from producing tax-free beer; and, among other things, a new agreement was necessary to maintain this sort of division of labor. The question was whether the agreement was to be continued, changed, or whether they should embark on a brewery war of all against all in order to see who could survive.

Persuading Carl Jacobsen to give his brewery as a gift to the Carlsberg Foundation, a disposition that in the longer term led to a consolidation of the Carlsberg breweries, was an important piece in the plans that the strategically-thinking Kühle had for future brewing policy. With the gift, competition was eliminated between Old and New Carlsberg, and something that resembled a sufficiently large and profitable unit was established. Now they had to move on and find a solution to how to treat the real competitor: the union of other breweries called *De Forenede Bryggerier* or DFB. Negotiations began as soon as the agreement between the Carlsberg Foundation and Carl Jacobsen was settled on 20 January 1902. Kühle was the primary force behind the new agreement or accord between the breweries, which was entered into in 1903 and which for the next 67 years was to regulate the relationship between the two parties, the Carlsberg breweries, Old Carlsberg and New Carlsberg, and the corporation DFB.

The agreement occasioned great advantages for the parties, but it could also become—and became—on the inner lines a source of irritation, since it presupposed negotiations and agreement between the breweries on many internal matters. The contract defined "common interests, which this agreement concerns" as "all matters touching on the sale of beer and other products such as ice cream, carbonated and mineral water, and the division of profits between the contracting parties as well as the operations of the brewery and all other business ...." On the DFB or Tuborg side, Philip Heymann, manager of Tuborg, was succeeded by his son-in-law Benny Dessau, who ran Tuborg for the next half century and who, together with Kühle, was the primary architect behind the agreement.

Competition is normally considered to be something positive that fosters a certain market. Competition ensures customers a broader selection of products and helps keep prices at an appropriate level. No one wants to pay more than necessary for the same product. For the same reason, there are today competition authorities to watch over competitive conditions that are threatened if some businesses acquire a dominant influence on the market. Seen from the producer's side, it looks different. Competition from their point of view is not necessarily an advantage but could, on the contrary, lead to relaxed quality requirements in order to lower prices—with a deterioration of product quality as a consequence. So, why compete instead of cooperate and save money on unnecessary advertising, discounts, and other schemes to lure customers from each other instead of using the money that sales bring to create a good product? It was from this point of view that the 1903 agreement that tied the two competitors, Carlsberg and Tuborg as the chief competitor within DFB, closely together in the next decades was entered into. Whether such an agreement could have been implemented at a later time when cartels were brought under the spotlight must remain unanswered here, but the plan was for the agreement to hold for most of a century until the year 2000. The agreement, in fact, was so attractive that it survived until 1970. Kühle's idea was that the breweries were not to be competitors that tried to outbid each other in offers to purveyors or distributors or others parties. Rather, they should be connected in such a way that what was considered harmful competition and unnecessary cost was avoided. Instead, they were to emphasize quality. Thus, in principle, the agreement had nothing to do with maintaining a high price or acting as a harmful cartel in relation to customers. Rather, the basis for the agreement was to avoid a form of devastating competition that had an effect on quality.

Kühle was the man behind the leading principle of the agreement: that competition should not be free but had to be regulated. Pursuant to a specific calculation method, the net income of the breweries was pooled; then, profits were shared and losses balanced. In this way, one party would not have an interest in knocking the other off the playing field since, in that case, they would just pay more into the common treasury. On the other hand, the agreement was not meant as a social benefit either but presumed that the two parties would have more or less equal earnings in the long run, so that one party did not contribute its income to the other for longer periods. This last consequence of the agreement proved to be particularly problematic. Already in the 1930s, people at Carlsberg felt that were in the lead and were critical and spoke about getting out of the deal. However, it was not until the 1960s that the mechanism began to show its weaknesses so decisively that the agreement could no longer stand. Only then did Danish breweries begin to rethink their position in the international struggle for buyouts and survival in the brewing industry.

In accordance with the provisions of the 1903 agreement, the breweries each continued as entirely independent businesses, while profits were evened out between them. Thus, the one that earned most had to yield profits with deductions for investments to the other party. According to the agreement, Tuborg was responsible for lager beer and soda water; and, in accordance with the 1895 agreement, Carlsberg continued to disclaim the right to produce light ale.

In reality, Kühle had already prepared for an arrangement in which the Carlsberg breweries in the long run would be transformed into a shareholder company. The agreement contained a provision in its article 19 that gave the Carlsberg Foundation the possibility of entering into *De Forenede Bryggerier* as a shareholder with one or both breweries and, in this connection, acquire up to half of the share capital, which would then be doubled. The agreement ran for a period of 100 years, but it foresaw a possible merging of Carlsberg and DFB before the year 2000. It did not take that long. Carl Jacobsen was not entirely happy personally about the new agreement and the presumed closer relations to Tuborg but allowed himself to be persuaded of its advantages. At the end of December 1902, the concluding negotiations took place. The agreement was dated 6 May 1903.

"When the breweries were consolidated, it was a precondition that the special interests and, thus, mutual competition were to cease, that an intimate cooperation should take place to the greatest possible advantage for the common pool". Thus did Carl Jacobsen write in a letter dated 22 December 1908.[67] In many ways, this sentence provides an accurate snapshot of the relationship between the two breweries at this point. Not everything was idyllic. The agreement between the breweries was based on equipoise. Preferably, the parties were to earn somewhat at the same level. Otherwise, one party would have to give to the other, and this was not tenable over the long term. As long as there was a certain equipoise, things worked; but, once it proved that one of the parties could not keep up, it did not work anymore. Carl Jacobsen's words pointed toward an ideal state, which—to put it mildly—did not always correspond to reality. If one reads the comprehensive correspondence between the executive boards of the Carlsberg Foundation and Tuborg/DFB in the years after 1903, it is striking that both parties were making a whole-hearted effort to live up to the intentions behind the agreement. At the same time, it is also clear that, if the inequality became too great, the "common pool" would not work and the other party would be worried. In the early years, things went mostly downhill for Carlsberg. For a long period, conditions improved again and, for short period, they again went down until Carlsberg ended up as the invincible party in the mutual relationship. As mentioned, together with a number of other extrinsic circumstances, this led to the consolidation of the two breweries in 1970, which was in reality Carlsberg's takeover of a competitor. If anyone had any doubt, the end result, as director Kühle put it, showed that Carlsberg had "the right end of the stick" with the agreement.[68]

[67]Quoted in appendix 6, letter of 23 June 1949 in case 54/49.

[68]Kühle's own account, quoted in Glamann (1976), p. 67.

A so-called joint executive board between the parties was appointed, and a specific council to look out for the breweries' so-called "common interests", but otherwise each brewery looked after its own business. The joint executive board held meetings several times a year and discussed issues of common interest and compliance with the agreement under the surveillance of the council, which had the final say. The joint executive board had two members—as a rule, the administrative directors of the two breweries. Decisions were made unanimously. The council consisted of seven members from each side. Carlsberg chose to be represented by the overall board of the Carlsberg Foundation plus two additional persons with a professional background. The agreement did not detail what matters were to be considered as 'common interests', but it proved to encompass everything from new facilities, advertising issues, employee relations, and pensions to property purchases, production, closing down departments, accounting, and prices. Thus, many matters were considered to be common and in a time in which the breweries did not need to fear being bought out or outside competition, much time could be spent on discussing whether a particular matter belonged to the common area or not.

2.16 Holm's Foundation

J. N. Madvig had been chairman of the Foundation in its first decade until his death in 1886.[69] In his time, there was no reason to worry about the business operations of the brewery. The brewing and the management were in professional hands at the brewery. At a Foundation board meeting on 10 January 1887, Japetus Steenstrup, who was close to J. C. Jacobsen, "seriously" declined to be designated as Madvig's successor. Instead, C. T. Barfoed was appointed. It was during his brief management term that the Foundation took over the brewery itself in 1888. At that point, Barfoed was already ill, and the historian Edvard Holm looked after the duties of the chairman from the fall of 1888 until he took over completely as chairman in March 1889. He was one of the most significant Danish historians of his time; and, with him as chairman of the Foundation, a rhythm was found in relation to the brewery under new management and in relation to the competitor, DFB. Everything worked out more or less. The 56-year-old Edvard Holm, like his two predecessors, was a veteran of the first executive board of the Carlsberg Foundation appointed in 1876, and he became the longest surviving

[69] Madvig was succeeded as a board member by another classical philologist, J. L. Ussing.

member by far of the original executive board. Since 1867, Holm had been a professor in modern history and belonged to the generation before the breakthrough of the modern critical method in historical research introduced by Kristian Erslev in the 1890s. As they were for Jacobsen, the events of 1864 had been of great significance for Holm as well. He re-orientated his research from antiquity to the history of 18th-century Denmark, which he considered a precondition for understanding what was happening in his time. In the following years, he worked on what would become the primary work on the history of Denmark and Norway in this period, a magnificent performance in many volumes that was published in the years 1891–1912.

It was during Holm's twenty-year chairmanship that the Foundation was bequeathed with Carl Jacobsen's New Carlsberg brewery, that the New Carlsberg Foundation was established, that the agreement of 1903 on the relationship between Carlsberg and Tuborg was entered into, and that, in cooperation with Carl Jacobsen, a new way of management of the breweries was established. With Kühle as CEO of J. C. Jacobsen's breweries, the relationship between Foundation and breweries was unproblematic. With Kühle as CEO of J. C. Jacobsen's breweries, the relationship between Foundation and breweries was unproblematic, and the Foundation board did not need to go into business details.

As chairman (from 1889), Holm still had to do the work—unaccustomed for an academic—of burrowing into the entire accountancy of an already powerful industrial enterprise. Unaccustomed for him as well were discussions of beer prices and loans to beer distributors and restauranteurs. Moreover, applications to the Foundation increased from a beginning in which they were more than capable of granting them all to a situation in which choices had to be made.

At the time of the establishment of the Carlsberg Foundation, the Danish Royal Academy did not have its own premises but met in a room in the so-called Prince's Palais, which today houses the Danish National Museum in Copenhagen. This itinerant life is the way it has been since the foundation of the Academy. Holm had the bright idea of erecting a stately building for the Carlsberg Foundation and the Royal Academy in the center of Copenhagen as the seat for the Foundation. He also saw to it that the foremost Danish portrait artist of the time, P. S. Krøyer, was hired to paint the formidable picture of a meeting of the Academy, portraying all members at that time. Since Carlsberg came into the picture, the Academy had a lift. Beer had become a part of the Academy's sphere of interest and is served at the more informal get-togethers after the meetings. As the building stands today and with the function it has of housing both the administration of the Foundation and the Academy, the seat of the Carlsberg Foundation is in itself an expression of the symbiosis between the Foundation and the Academy.

By entering into the agreement of 1903, it was thought that the operations between J. C. Jacobsen's and Carl Jacobsen's breweries should be simplified, so that the overall earnings could be improved and Carlsberg would not be lagging behind Tuborg. Equipoise was a fundamental condition for the agreement to function. At that time, it was Carlsberg that could not keep up with Tuborg's pace. The death of S. A. Kühle in 1906 left the breweries that once belonged to J. C. Jacobsen, the "old" Carlsberg, with a management vacuum. A new CEO had to be found who could bridge the still existing gap between "old" and "new" Carlsberg. The result of the Foundation's considerations became the resolute but not exactly easy decision to assign Carl Jacobsen as director of New Carlsberg the task of unifying with this position the general management of Old Carlsberg until he turned 70, five years later in 1912.

However, it was not simple to maneuver in relation to Carl Jacobsen.[70] As an earlier owner, he should have been comfortable as manager, but things are not always so easy, especially not for a man with Carl Jacobsen's self-importance and temperament. He had, as historian and later Chairman of the Foundation Kristian Erslev expressed it, an "autocratic nature" and found collaboration with others "an oppressive yoke". Carl could be hot-tempered and impulsive; but thanks to the merits he brought to Carlsberg, he definitely deserves having one of the brewery's most popular beers today named after him, Carl's Special—followed by Carl's Lager, Carl's Christmas, and Carl's Easter, all of which let us remember this remarkable person.

Tuborg, at that time, was managed by a most competent and highly recognized CEO, who had a professional, business-oriented executive board behind him, and it remained a concern for the Carlsberg Foundation board whether they as "the professors" could keep up. In the years right after the 1903 agreement, Carlsberg was still hampered by a complicated production apparatus divided into many units. Seen from this perspective, therefore, the collaboration was not unproblematic, and the other party, *De Forenede Bryggerier* (DFB) with Tuborg as main negotiator, wanted a different basis for allocation to which Holm on behalf of the Carlsberg Foundation concurred in 1909. Consequently, the Carlsberg Foundation refunded the other party, DFB, the amount of DKK 150,000 a year for the next six years. Only in the year 1913/14 did Carlsberg achieve a better operating profit than Tuborg. The refund agreement of 1909 was, in reality, a break with the principle of

[70]Glamann (1995), p. 198.

equality, and it was not forgotten later at Carlsberg that Tuborg had squeezed them when they were on top. The DKK 900,000 that Carlsberg had to pay was raised repeatedly, when inequities arose between the breweries and finally even made it easier for Carlsberg to 'eat' Tuborg in 1970.

Holm withdrew in 1909 due to age, but he was also bitter when he left the management of the Foundation. His colleagues did not approve his acceptance of the 1909 agreement to refund DFB, and thus there was a bad atmosphere in the Foundation board. Another brilliant historian and a representative of modern historiography, Kristian Erslev was selected to the available spot on the Foundation's executive board and, from the beginning, became a leading figure in the Foundation.

Holm's immediate successor as chairman of the Foundation, chemist S. M. Jørgensen, was at that point 72 years old. He had been a member of the Foundation's executive board since 1885. He was a talented chemist and expert in cobalt ammonia complexes. In many ways, he represented something that was a weakness in the construction of the Carlsberg Foundation, namely, that academic ability was one thing, business sense and leadership ability something else. At least, that is the way his successor as chairman (from 1913), Kristian Erslev, saw it, and he wanted to do something about it.[71]

References

Bjerager, A.-L., & Krogsgaard-Larsen, P. (2011). *Bryggerens lærling: Povl Krogsgaard-Larsens erindringer*, Gyldendal.

Bligaard, M. (2008). *Frederiksborgs genrejsning. Historicisme i teori og praksis* (Vols. I–II). Copenhagen: Forleget Vandkunsten.

Christensen, D. C. (2009). *Naturens tankelæser. En biografi om Hans Christian Ørsted* (Vols. I–II). Copenhagen: Museum Tusculanum.

Geison, G. L. (1996). *The private science of Louis Pasteur*. New Jersey: Princeton.

Glamann, K. (1976). *Carlsbergfondet*. Copenhagen: Rhodos.

Glamann, K. (1990). *Bryggeren I.C. Jacobsen på Carlsberg*. Copenhagen: Gyldendal.

Glamann, K. (1991). Breve fra J.C. Jacobsen til sønnen Carl 2. marts 1855-22. December 1867. Copenhagen.

Glamann, K. (1992): Apparently error for: Kristof Glamann: *Carlsbergfondet siden 1970*. Rhodos (1993)

Glamann, K. (1995). *Øl og marmor. Carl Jacobsen på Ny Carlsberg* [Eng. trans. *Beer and Marble: Carl Jacobsen of New Carlsberg*, 1996]. Copenhagen: Gyldendal.

Glamann, K. (2004). *Nordens Pasteur: fortællingen om Emil Chr. Hansen*. Copenhagen: Gyldendal.

[71] Erslev (1926).

Hatch, M. J., & Schultz, M. (2017). Toward a theory of using history authentically: Historizing the Carlsberg Group. *Administrative Science Quarterly, 4*(62), 657–697.

Holter, H., & Møller, K. M. (1976). *The Carlsberg Laboratory 1876–1976*. Copenhagen: The Carlsberg Foundation.

Jacobsen, C. (1911). *"På Carlsberg" in Mit hjem 1* (pp. 40–42). Copenhagen.

Johansen, H.C., & Monrad Møller, A. (2005). *Fonde som fundament for dansk industri*. SDU Press.

Larsen, P. O. (2001). *Steerage-way. The Carlsberg Laboratorium 1976–2001*. Copenhagen: The Carlsberg Foundation.

Madvig, J. N. (1955). *Johan Nicolai Madvig. Et mindeskrift*. Copenhagen: Det Kongelige Videnskabernes Selskab.

Nyrop, C. (1886). *Ny Carlsberg. Et Jubilæumsskrift*. Copenhagen: Carlsbergfondet.

Nyrop, C. (1911). *J. C. Jacobsen 1811–1911. Et Mindeskrift. Med en Redegjørelse for Carlsbergfondets almindelig videnskabelige Afdelings Virksomhed 1876–1910*. Copenhagen: Carlsbergfondet.

Østrup, J. (1912). J. C. Jacobsen. Copenhagen: Det Schønbergske Forlag.

Pedersen, J. (1955). "Videnskabernes Selskab og Carlsbergfondet". In J. N. Madvig (Ed.), *Et Mindeskrift* (pp. 252–271). Copenhagen: Det Kongelige Videnskaernes Selskab.

Schmidt, I. (1956). *Blade af Carlsbergs hist. Kapt. S. A. v. d. Aa Kühle og hans liv på Carlsberg*. Copenhagen: Bianco Lunos Bogtrykkeri.

Winge, Ø., & Tåning, Å. V. (Eds.). (1947). *Naturforskeren Johannes Schmidt. Hans Liv og Ekspeditioner. Skildret af Venner og Medabejdere*. Copenhagen: Gyldendal.

3

1914—Carlsberg "Hof" or "Green" Tuborg?

3.1 Erslev—The Visionary

In 1914, Carl Jacobsen died and with him that epoch in the history of Carlsberg in which the founder's family was still influential in the business management. It was the year of the outbreak of the First World War. Denmark was neutral during the war, and many Danes could profit economically from trading with both parties in the war. For Carlsberg, it was a time for the brewery to consolidate itself after the decease of both its founders, and it became the time for the board of the Foundation to reflect on the future. Both J. C. and Carl were aware that the executive board of the Foundation was not to be composed of brewers or persons skilled in selling beer. Kristian Erslev, who succeeded S. M. Jørgensen as chairman of the Carlsberg Foundation in 1913, was one of Denmark's best-known and most influential historians. He also clearly realized that the members of the Foundation board lacked business skills; and, therefore, there was a need to consider the form in which the breweries were to be managed in the future and act in relation to their business-run counterpart, Tuborg.

As a professor in history at Copenhagen University, Erslev had introduced and developed new critical methods in history. In the decade after 1900, he published his collection of historical sources for the history of Denmark, his basic account of historical criticism, and his overviews of the history of the Middle Ages—a golden age of Danish history—and the 16th century based on this new view of history with another critical interpretation of the sources. Erslev was his generation's great scientific historian. A younger

D. Tamm, *The Carlsberg Story*,
https://doi.org/10.1007/978-3-030-52670-2_3

colleague spoke of his “cold-blooded judgment”, his “ability to put things together” in addition to attentive “vigilance” and inexhaustible “tenacity”.[1] In a memorial to him from 1931, his successor as chairman, the classicist A. B. Drachmann, speaks of “one of the most peculiar and most significant personalities our society has ever contained in its midst” and that the first thing “that caught the eye of anyone who had anything to do with Erslev in business matters was his proficiency, especially in the area of accountancy… Erslev mastered it all ….”[2]

In 1909, at the request of Tuborg and *De Forenede Bryggerier* (DFB), a special committee was appointed under a joint council, consisting of a representative of the Carlsberg Foundation, the chairman of the board of DFB, who was a Supreme Court attorney, and a third member. Erslev joined this committee, which was also a liaison between foundation and brewery. As a council member, Erslev had such influence that, in 1913 as a 61-year-old, he became the obvious candidate for the Foundation chairmanship with his authority, his legendary diligence, his talent for organization, and ability to mediate. He also proved to have precisely the insight into his own abilities and the abilities of others needed to understand the management problem the Carlsberg Foundation had, even though he did not himself need assistance. He had learned about accounting as a child by helping his father, who was a bookseller, and he was not only a historian at the highest level but also someone who could organize work and, therefore, had the desire and the guts to take on administrative tasks and to intervene in business operations. He could discern the weaknesses in the management structure of the Carlsberg Foundation and work to find solutions. As a visionary, he could see what the future would be for Carlsberg, even though he did not himself have the opportunity to implement the reforms he considered necessary.

In 1916, he left the university to become head of the Danish National Archives. He considered it a less demanding post than his professorship. There was also a lot to take care of there, and Erslev got it done in the years 1916–1924. Erslev himself wrote modestly in 1919 how the work of being liaison between the Carlsberg Foundation executive board and the brewery “still occupied his time and thoughts so intently that it was the main reason that, in 1916, I sought to leave the university for the calmer position of leader of the national archive”.

Erslev was good at cooperating with the brewery’s management, so that foundation and brewery could work together. The aforementioned younger colleague described his efforts this way: “He organized from the ground up

[1]Aksel E. Christensen art. on Erslev in *Dansk Biografisk Leksikon,* 3rd ed.
[2]Drachmann (1930–31), pp. 85–90.

the Foundation's very out-of-date apparatus of administration and accounting and carried out the great amendment of the Charter of 1916, which, as it was said, placed the Foundation's economy on certain ground.... The result was a powerful growth in the Foundation's means".[3]

Erslev had the indisputable advantage in his job as Chairman of the Carlsberg Foundation that he actually knew and understood brewery operations and, thus, realized the uncertainties that existed particularly in relation to Tuborg, which was in the lead in those years. His many reflections and concerns about the Foundation may at times seem almost prophetic to a reader today with respect to later developments and difficulties that the managers of the Carlsberg Foundation necessarily encountered when it came to *big business*. His basic concern was the lack of business skill in the Foundation. He, therefore, proposed a structure in which Tuborg and Carlsberg joined forces within a shareholder company structure. However, this idea was vehemently opposed by the Jacobsen family, represented by Carl Jacobsen's two sons Helge and Vagn. They started a press campaign against this idea, alleging as chief arguments that both the founder, J. C. Jacobsen, and their father Carl were against any cooperation with Tuborg and would never have accepted their breweries becoming shareholder companies. Erslev and the Foundation could not win this battle with their arguments based on economics and reason against family sentiments and had to give up this idea. In addition, the idea of turning Carlsberg alone into a shareholder company was abandoned. This decision was helped by the deliberation that Danish Social Democrats at that time were aggressive, and there was a real fear that big industrial companies could be targets for nationalization, which might be less likely to happen in the case of a foundation-run business. Actually, a proposal to that effect circulated among workers.

Instead and as an important innovation, Erslev fathered in 1922 a so-called brewery council (*bryggerirådet*) in which only one or two representatives of the Foundation, together with three recognized professional businessmen, functioned as an intermediary between the board of the Carlsberg Foundation and the Carlsberg brewery management. This proved to be a wise decision that, in the years to come, relieved the board of the Foundation of much worry about the beer business and attracted highly accomplished businessmen to fill in the positions of the council.

---

[3]Aksel E. Christensen, loc. cit.

3.2 Complicated Cohabitation Between Wars

The First World War with its many restrictions was a difficult time for the breweries, and much of Erslev's concern for the business survival of a weakened Carlsberg depended on the circumstances in those years. Yet, with the agreement of 1903, things could not go too far off the rails for either of the parties. To the contrary, the agreement provided a sort of safety net, and both parties benefitted from it. Each party took care of itself, and the atmosphere gradually became better since, after 1916, there was no longer a need to talk about a continuation of the skewed agreement of 1909 or the actual merger of the two parties. Since the end of World War I, Carlsberg's turnover and earnings had soared. Carlsberg's new pilsner, the "Hof", was successful, and Carlsberg had the biggest market share of the two in the years to come. Things were beginning to go the right way. After Carlsberg put a number of efficiency measures into effect, sales had gone so well by 22 April 1922 that Carlsberg's CEO since 1914, Poul C. Poulsen, could hold a lecture at the Danish Industrial Association about Carlsberg's importance to the country's economy.[4] It was a lecture title that testified to a healthy portion of self-confidence, and Poulsen did not hold back, either. With pride, he began with an overview of the history of beer brewing, which ended in the observation that beer, which was originally brewed around the Mediterranean and the Middle East, had in recent years reached such "perfection and goodness" in the North that it could now be exported to the South. Carlsberg's facilities were the largest in the world, and Poulsen reported how the brewery's volume had risen from its original 3,600 hl. (hectoliters) a year in 1847 to 750,813 hl. in 1921, corresponding to approx. 214 million bottles. In 1902, when the New Carlsberg Breweries became a part of the overall business, the production was 392,000 hl., so they had almost doubled their manufacture. Not so bad, he believed.

The history of Carlsberg in the following years has to do, in large part, with the relationship between Carlsberg and DFB—and, first and foremost, Tuborg, the leading brewery in the DFB group and the only one in size that could challenge Carlsberg. It could go up or down, as things do in these sorts of relationships. The balance between the two and the necessity of negotiating about many minor details, however, became an increasing problem. In the end, it mostly went up for Carlsberg and mostly went down for Tuborg. At the same time, the total national market share for Carlsberg and DFB rose to about three quarters. As the party that earned the most, Carlsberg

[4]Manuscript in CF.

had to put a large part of its profit into the common pool, to the detriment of science. This changed in the mid-1950s when, for a time, Tuborg Green overtook a large share of the market for Carlsberg's Hof—and it was Carlsberg that had to be supported. But this was only for a brief period until Carlsberg was once again the largest. This unequal earning relationship gradually became so pronounced that it was the beginning of the end for the 1903 collaborative agreement. Regardless of Erslev's concerns about business savvy, it turned out that the management construction they had established was viable and that Carlsberg could survive as a business under the leadership of the Carlsberg Foundation, implement a generational shift, and find more than merely acceptable solutions to the brewery's management situation. In hindsight, the story told in the following chapters, therefore, is the prehistory of the merger that was wanted since 1916 but, with ups and downs, not acquired until 1970.

3.3 Occupation and Postwar Settlement

The occupation of Denmark by Nazi Germany from April 1940 to May 1945 is not a parenthesis in Danish history. Life went on with few changes. On the other hand, Danish war conditions differed from what was seen in many other occupied countries. Denmark had accepted the German occupation after a few hours of armed resistance and, therefore, was not subjected to a war regime but retained its own governing institutions. Most people by far went on with their lives as they had done before. At the very least, that is what the breweries experienced. Danes drank just as much beer during the war as before, and an important job for Carlsberg's management, as usual, was to see to it that there was enough for these thirsty mouths especially on sunny summer days. However, a few things had to be adjusted with respect to the occupying power. There were also those who made a real effort to show that they were against the German presence in Denmark and began active resistance which in the last years of the Occupation led to a more serious confrontation with the Occupier, so that the Danish government ceased its functions by the end of August 1943. The breweries during the Occupation kept a low profile. Carlsberg harbored the underground student resistance organization but came out of the war physically intact. Tuborg, on the other hand, was subjected to so-called "*Schalburgtage*",[5] retaliation measures against resistance fighters organized by the Germans but carried out by Danish groups serving the Occupier towards the end of the war, which caused great destruction.

[5]Named for a Danish officer, Schalburg, who fought and was killed in battle in 1942, fighting on the German side on the Eastern front against the Red Army.

A supply problem that could become significant (particularly, in public opinion) was that German soldiers, who gradually became numerous in the country, also wanted to drink Danish beer when they could not get German products, and the breweries had as their part of maintaining a peaceful occupation to take this less welcome group of customers into consideration. After all, the Occupation led to a certain rationing of raw goods, and it might be difficult to get enough barley for malting. Carlsberg maintained that they should serve Danish customers principally and would not use rationed barley to service German troops. Therefore, they entered into an agreement for a special delivery of so-called "German barley" to be used exclusively for brewing beer for the Wehrmacht, which would not be allowed to buy "our beer" brewed on ordinarily assigned barley. Danish barley for beer for Danes and German barley for beer for Germans.

The public sometimes still harbored exaggerated conceptions of the extent of the production for the Germans. This could give rise to ill will against the brewery and accusations of economic collaboration even though it actually only came to a bit over two percent of the beer produced, which even then was brewed on a special delivery of barley. A fanciful rumor without any purchase in reality and a good example of the gossip of the time was published in the illegal newspaper *Information.* It went so far as to say that "the Carlsberg breweries are the only brewery that supplies strong beer to the Germans ... All the German breweries have suspended the manufacture of strong beer, and at the same time rations have been reduced drastically. Carlsberg's shipments go exclusively to southern Germany, where the beer is to be stored until the Nazis drink it during the final resistance. Even in Germany, these beer shipments have caused a great stir".[6]

Beyond the image problems that deliveries to the Wehrmacht might pose and isolated minor episodes, everyday life at the breweries was normal, ignoring the risk of sabotage or reprisals. Nor did the extraordinary circumstances affect the usual annoyances with Tuborg, which, as a rule, had to do with one or the other party trying to get a leg up on the customers to the detriment of the other party.

Carlsberg and Tuborg still fought about trifles, which may today seem curious; but, when serious problems arose, they showed solidarity in the spirit of the agreement of 1903. This was especially clear when, on the night of 5 January 1945, Tuborg was subjected to so-called "*Schalburgtage*", ordered by the occupation power. In this case, the action was carried out by a ill-reputed gang of Danish citizens in German service as a response to Danish

[6]INFORMATION no. 434 of 15 March 1945. NORDISK NYHEDSTJENESTE no. 399.

resistance sabotage actions—in this case, presumably, against a radio factory, which produced for the Germans and had been sabotaged three days before. That it was Tuborg, and not Carlsberg, that was hit might be due to the fact that one of Tuborg's directors, Einar Dessau, had a Jewish background and had fled to Sweden in 1943, but it might also have been without any specific cause or linked to the transport of Danish Jews from Tuborg harbor in October 1943 after the Germans started an action against Danish Jews. The attack destroyed Tuborg's boiler house and machine hall. Initially, however, they could continue production by a quick induction of steam from the outside and by the exploitation of the surplus capacity of a smaller brewery owned by Carlsberg. However, Carlsberg soon after stepped up and helped with the expert assistance of technicians and with malting and bottling until, after a few months, Tuborg was again completely back on its feet.[7] Later, one of the many complicated questions that arose in the mutual negotiations between the breweries became whether interest on the state compensation that Tuborg later received in connection with the bomb attack during the Occupation belonged under common operations. Carlsberg thought so, but Tuborg disagreed.[8]

During the Occupation, much information was disseminated of the type we today know as *fake news*. As mentioned, Carlsberg did not do anything special to get Wehrmacht shipments or profit from them, and no serous accusations could be made against the brewery for being eager to accept German orders. On the contrary. Nevertheless, there were rumors of major shipments to the Germans; and, even among the workers at Carlsberg, there were rumors that Carlsberg's CEO since 1934, Frederik Sander, who was known as a talented but not very diplomatic leader, had exposed himself by speaking sympathetically of the Germans. Various pieces of information about what people believed he had said and done had found their way to the so called Central Records[9] collected and kept by the resistance movement. These records gathered a wealth of accurate and—as it proved later—even more false information about great things and small, about persons who were considered unpatriotic or suspected of being so and whose circumstances, therefore, they wanted to investigate when liberation came. All this came out when liberation became a reality on 5 May 1945.

---

[7]In Jacobsen, reprint, p. 4; *Bryggeriforeningen Guide til det danske ølunivers* (2004), p. 55.

[8]Meeting 16 February 1949, case 27/49, box A 85.

[9]These records (called *Centralkartoteket*) were established by the resistance movement and led by a well-known professor of classical philology Carsten Høeg. The aim was to collect information about persons, companies, and acts considered suspicious from a 'national' point of view and which should be investigated in order to establish whether undue collaboration had taken place that should be prosecuted after the Occupation.

Unrest among the workers at Carlsberg in the days after the end of the Occupation was expressed in one of the era's most notable slogans—the desire to clean everything "from top to bottom", which never came to anything. Workers and clerks demanded as early as 15 May 1945 an investigation of a number of officials and demanded as a precondition for breaking off a strike that those involved be immediately sent on vacation. Events developed rather wildly and out of control, and a solution ultimately required police intervention. On 9 June, the brewery was 'occupied' by members of the former resistance movement, called freedom fighters, to press the demand to provide the names of the officials whose circumstances they wanted to investigate. However, with an intervention from the leaders of the liberation movement, represented by, among others, the resistance movement's minister Frode Jakobsen and Professor Carsten Høeg, who was a resistance fighter and the head of the Central Records, they were able to send the freedom fighters home. However, there was still dissatisfaction at the pace of the cleansing, and some days later the workers again went on strike, a protest march of around two thousand workers went through Copenhagen, and a declaration from a special investigative committee with Carsten Høeg as chairman could now no longer resolve the strife. There were demands for "death to snitches and informants", house-cleaning at Carlsberg "from top to bottom", and as a consequence an investigation of four higher staff members at Carlsberg with their removal while the investigation was taking place. Representatives for the workers negotiated at Christiansborg with Prime Minister Buhl and the two resistance movement ministers Mogens Fog and Frode Jakobsen. On 12 June, an agreement was achieved to go back to work and appoint a committee to investigate the circumstances of a number of people.

The anger of the workers was not only directed at work colleagues and staff but also to a high degree at the CEO, Frederik Sander, who was accused of being German-friendly without (at that point, however) being clear about what the foundation for the suspicion was. He had sometimes expressed himself undiplomatically, including about the effectiveness and timeliness of sabotage actions. Like many others, he had, especially in the first years of the war, expressed a certain admiration of what the new Germany could achieve. Sander was not the only one in the transitional justice phase after the Occupation who was accused on, at best, an imperfect basis and for attitudes or statements that might have offended someone but were not at all an expression of sympathy either for the occupying power or for its ideology, Nazism. Some got off with the support of conscientious leaders who dared to cut through the nonsense, while others were sacrificed. The Sander case ended in the latter category. It was clear that the workers wanted to get rid of Sander, and the dissatisfaction was so evident that it was decided by the end of May 1945 to send Sander on an unsought "vacation" in order to avoid strikes and interruptions of the work at the brewery. In principle, Sanders could have continued in contact from home with the remaining brewery management. It was, however, more or less in the cards that the vacation was the first step towards dismissal, and Sander complained in vain to the chairman, Johannes Pedersen, that he had been shut out of his position and his advice was no longer sought.

Whether, deep-down, Sander was a German sympathizer must remain unresolved. It stands with him rather like what Prime Minister Stauning said of the minister of foreign affairs and later prime minister during German occupation, Erik Scavenius, when Scavenius was accused of "German sympathies", that he was not sympathetic at all. Thus, many employees considered Sander as quite stiff and inaccessible and with a "Junker-like" attitude. He possessed a manor on the island of Langeland, and he spent his "vacation" there until a decision was made whether he would remain or not.

Through the intervention of Carsten Høeg, an "honor court" was appointed to investigate the case. It consisted of a Supreme Court judge, a prominent attorney, and the chief editor of a leading newspaper. The committee engaged in thorough interrogations to investigate the accusations made against Sander. The committee's report was ready shortly before Christmas on 17 December 1945.[10]

The committee took a position on a total of eleven issues that, as far as most are concerned, were based on uncertain information. The first three charges were accusations against Sander for having shown enthusiasm after shipments to the German Wehrmacht, accusations of private camaraderie with Germans, and accusations of Nazi contacts. On these three points, it was the committee's conclusion that they had no basis. Even when it had to do with other minor points, the committee found that the accusations lacked a basis. Some of the issues were more flimsy and, among other things, had to do with Sander's general attitude, sullenness or condescending statements. People had been taken aback by his blunt pronouncements about the resistance movement, circumstances around the general strikes of 1942 and 1944 of which Sander had not approved, an unfortunately-formulated encouragement (which obviously was not meant to be taken that way) for someone to join an armed corps collaborating with the Germans, and other so-called "unpatriotic behavior". Among those who willingly expressed their

---

[10]Account provided on 17 December 1945 by the Committee appointed by the Carlsberg Foundation for the investigation of the accusations against the administrative director for Carlsberg Breweries, Mr. Fr. Sander of unpatriotic behavior during the Occupation.

impression of Sander and his statements was his subordinate, deputy director Klintholm, who eagerly recounted to the committee what he viewed as Sander's admiration of Germany and German policies. He did not speak to completely deaf ears.

The committee acquitted Sander completely of the more serious charges but could not desist from expressing a more general critique of the way he behaved with and spoke to others. On the other hand, the committee believed, there were things that indicated that the antipathy against Sander was less grounded in his general attitude, which had been quite fixed in consideration of his not exactly easy position, but in a more general dissatisfaction with his management style. Workers were especially angry that, during the popular strike of 1944, Sander had followed the instruction of the Danish employers' association not to pay workers' salaries for lost labor time during the strike.

On this foundation, the committee's assessment could not lead to a clean slate for Sander, even though he had not "done" anything but talk. It was stressed in the report's conclusion that, for years before the Occupation, he had "been interested in Nazism in Germany and especially this system's political and social side, just as he had harbored respect and a certain admiration for the strength and firmness with which the leading men of the Nazi Party ruled Germany". The committee took the view that Sander's interest in Germany and Nazism had also found expression during the Occupation in such a way that "seemed wounding to Danish national sentiments and capable of arousing doubt about his patriotic disposition". This is not exactly rock-solid law, which one might have expected from a committee with this authority. On the other hand, the committee stressed that Sander had a temper and that he could express himself in a way that should not be taken literally. Basically, however, the committee's view was that, on a number of occasions, he had been "unnecessarily sharp and unsympathetic with respect to sabotage and other actions by the resistance movement". With this conclusion—which acquitted Sander on the material points but nevertheless, using the words "wounding" and "doubt" about his national disposition, expressed a not entirely unsympathetic attitude toward the accusations against him, Sander's fate was sealed. The three lawyers had done their work as they should and given the Foundation the necessary tools to part with the director even though there was nothing that resembled proper legal analysis in the case. With the use of the magic words "wounding to Danish national sentiments" and "doubt about his national disposition", any objective foundation was unnecessary.

The committee had done its job in a way that made it easier for the executive board of the Carlsberg Foundation to justify a dismissal that, in reality, had already been decided. Sander could not return without the threat of an industrial action by Carlsberg's workers, and that was to be avoided at any price in order to protect the Carlsberg brand. With the report from the investigative commission, the Foundation executive board believed it had a firm basis to expect that Sander himself would seek retirement, which he did reluctantly on 27 December. At the same time, it was reported that his successor as of 1 January 1946 would be an old friend of the brewery, a brewery council member of many years, and now former minister of trade, Halfdan Hendriksen.

The decision was made at a joint meeting with the brewery council on 18 December, where Sander's circumstances had been on the agenda. Chairman since 1933, the highly esteemed philologist of Semitic languages and historian of religion, Johannes Pedersen had directly asked Hendriksen whether he might think of taking over management of the brewery. Director Klintholm's eagerness to blab to the investigative committee when it came to Sander's more controversial statements had been noted by the Carlsberg Foundation and the brewery council, and there was agreement that, at any rate, he could not advance. The same was true of another director, so it was necessary to find a successor outside the executive board. Hendriksen had also responded positively that he would be happy to take up such a task, which he viewed as a transitional arrangement for the breweries and probably also for himself on his way to retirement. And thus the case was laid to rest. At the meeting itself on 18 December 1945, Hendriksen stated that, even though the report on Sander's circumstances during the Occupation was not as critical as one might have feared, any future collaboration between Sander and the staff and laborers would not work long without friction. Therefore, it was best that he withdrew. Hendriksen was quoted as having said directly: "Sander had been a German sympathizer the whole time".[11]

The Sander case had posed an unpleasant dilemma to the executive board of the Carlsberg Foundation. Basically, there was nothing to blame Sander for in the eyes of the Carlsberg Foundation. To the contrary. However, the workers were out for blood, and a return to his post as administrative director, it was foreseen, would lead to unrest and work stoppages that would harm the brewery. Therefore, no one showed the courage to stand by and support the

[11]CF meeting 18 December 1945.

director. A weighing of the Foundation's interests in the brewery and considerations of Sander as a person inevitably had to come out in this situation on the side of the firm. Therefore, it ended with a dismissal.

The events could later be boiled down by the chairman at the time, Johannes Pedersen, to a couple of discrete lines in a book about Sander's successor: "The autumn of 1945 was characterized by unrest. By the end of the year, the administrative director withdrew, and the Foundation had to find a replacement as quickly as possible".[12] At least, no secrets were revealed here, nor might anyone be offended or question the Foundation's dispositions. A later chairman, Kristof Glamann, provided an even briefer account of the Sander affair: "After the war, he withdrew…." This is, perhaps, such a fleeting example of history writing that it is not history writing at all or, rather, a form of writing history that does not want to relate any history. In a later *festschrift* for the Danish Brewery Association from 1999, we get a little closer. It is at least mentioned that Sander "was accused of 'unpatriotic activity' and had to step down from his position …."[13]

3.4 "The Transitional Figure"

It was neither an easy nor a pleasant decision for Johannes Pedersen and the rest of the Carlsberg Foundation executive board to dismiss Sander. As a director, he had led Carlsberg through years of German occupation; and, when there was occasion for it, he had stood quite uncompromisingly for the interests of the brewery and protected Carlsberg against any form of interference or expanded production with respect to the Germans. But the show must go on. Even before the dismissal was a reality, the Foundation sought refuge in a person considered a "rock in whom the entire Danish people had confidence and great expectations…."[14] Thus did his admirers characterize the Minister of Trade during the Occupation: Halfdan Hendriksen, who became Sander's replacement from 1 January 1946. In him, Carlsberg gained a talented, distinguished, and politically gifted businessman as a leader as well as a "survivor", who may not be the person to dig into every problem with the utmost thoroughness but who had a flair for flourishing and turning even the detrimental into an advantage. Hendriksen was born in 1881 and was since early youth trained in commerce: "I have been a merchant from the

[12]In Bølling et al. (1956), p. 236.
[13]Bryggeriforeningen (1999), p. 85.
[14]Bølling et al. (1956), p. 5.

time I finished school until today,"[15] he said about himself at an advanced age. As a 25-year-old, he became an office manager for the DFDS shipping line with responsibility for Iceland and the Faeroe Islands. He resided for a time in Iceland and became intimately familiar with the country. In 1910, with a business partner, he founded a company with a specialty in trading with Iceland, at that time still a part of the Danish Realm. Politically, he was an active member of the Danish Conservative Party and a member of Parliament.

In October 1940, he was encouraged by Prime Minister Stauning to step into the post of Minister for Trade. The general opinion during and after the Occupation was that Hendriksen had handled the difficult role of Trade Minister well and had administered supplies and rationing very well. He achieved significant popularity even though he stood for unpopular decisions and schemes, which he was good at presenting as unavoidable. His appointment is a good example of the brewery's ability to maintain good political connections that, over time, led to results that might not have been so easy to achieve otherwise. Hendriksen during his time as CEO of Carlsberg continued in politics and thus remained a man with real political connections as a member of Parliament from 1953 to 1957 and the Conservative Party's chairman from 1948 to 1957.

Hendriksen, who was 64 years old, was meant to be a transitional figure, but it turned into a longer transition than expected. He had stated in 1947[16] that he saw it as one of his most important tasks to find a replacement and, preferably, to test out the person in question for a couple of years to see whether he was suited to be CEO.

His time was a successful period in Carlsberg's history. Sales went well; and, in relation to Tuborg, Carlsberg was consistently on top with a sufficient economic and psychological surplus to deal with many small, everyday squabbles. The chairman of the Carlsberg Foundation later wrote about his era that "Carlsberg found a steady working rhythm, although there were still great demands when sales rose sharply both domestically and abroad until they achieved a high point that no one had previously imagined".[17] Hendriksen's style was probably the closest one could come (in a positive way) to the patriarchal conditions of earlier times.

[15] Bølling et al. (1956), p. 7.
[16] CFP 12, meeting on 19 April 1947.
[17] Bølling et al. (1956), p. 237.

3.5 Carlsberg and Tuborg

The increase in beer consumption in the postwar years benefitted Carlsberg especially. In the relationship between Carlsberg and Tuborg, it was not difficult to sense a feeling of superiority among the Carlsberg people, while Tuborg to the same extent felt somewhat pressed. Every brewery in the country in those years had to yield market positions to Carlsberg, which was Denmark's largest brewery concern. The total share of national sales of Carlsberg grew from 46.8% of the market in 1939–40 to 55.2% in 1950–51, while Tuborg's portion fell from 32% to 25% in the same period.[18]

It did not continue this way. Seen from Tuborg's side, what can almost be viewed as a "miracle" suddenly occurred.[19] The sales numbers turned. In November 1954, one could see in black and white that Carlsberg's earnings were going the wrong way in relation to Tuborg/DFB and that DFB was now clearly in the lead. Tuborg had already overtaken Carlsberg with respect to net profits, the chairman of the Carlsberg Foundation had to admit at an executive board meeting in November 1954. Carlsberg's net profits had that year fallen to DKK 12,664,302 against the previous year's 17,723,766. Tuborg's (or DFB's) net profits, on the other hand, had risen to DKK 21,581,806 from 14,237,899 the year before. In addition, Tuborg now seemed farther ahead in its production efficiency.[20] Glamann records in his book on the Carlsberg Foundation from 1950/51 to 1955/56 a decrease for Carlsberg from 55.2% to 34.3% of the total sales of the two breweries and a corresponding upturn for Tuborg from 25% to 46.8%.[21] The mid-1950s became a critical period for Carlsberg in which it had to accommodate itself to the role of recipient party in the collaboration. Carlsberg had grown used to being the stronger party. Hendriksen's successor as CEO since 1953, the less robust K. Skat-Rørdam, could probably sense where things were going, even if he was not personally and directly blamed for the falling sales. They were not simply due to structural causes but, to a large extent, stemmed from problems in brewing techniques, which, *inter alia*, caused a so-called foaming problem, which only after a great deal of searching proved to be due to poor barley quality. It was not a pretty sight when bottles were opened at the table, but it was visible problem to which customers immediately reacted. Customers began to avoid Carlsberg; and, as a natural consequence, it ended with the Carlsberg Foundation dismissing Skat-Rørdam.

---

[18] Thomsen (1973), p. 129.

[19] Hjejle (1982), p. 75.

[20] CF meeting, 12 November 1954, case 27/54, in box A 95.

[21] Glamann (1976), p. 88.

Skat-Rørdam's era, therefore, was one of the shorter terms in the history of the brewery. Skat-Rørdam himself was neither a brewer nor a businessman. He had been a loyal and efficient head of section and thus a public servant, whom Hendriksen had spotted in the Ministry of Trade, where he had displayed talent as an administrator in the handling of many complicated matters involving restrictions, etc., during the German Occupation and the years immediately thereafter. He might have sufficed in better times, but it became a problem that Skat-Rørdam's main competence was not business and that his sensitive personality could not handle the defeatist atmosphere in connection with the technical crisis in Carlsberg around their beer production. To grapple with that, nerves of steel were demanded; Skat-Rørdam therefore was dismissed, and the board even before he had actually left started the procedure to find the right substitute made of sterner stuff.

References

Bølling, H., Mikkelsen, H., & Clemmensen, E. H. (1956). *Halfdan Hendriksen. En dansk Købmand og Politiker*. Copenhagen.

Bryggeriforeningen. (1999). *Bryggerne og de tre store udfordringer*.

Drachmann, A. B. (1930–31). Kristian Erslev. Mindeord. In *Meddelelser fra Videnskabernes Selskab 1930–31* (pp. 85–90). Copenhagen: Videnskabernes Selskab.

Glamann, K. (1976). *Carlsbergfondet*. Copenhagen: Rhodos.

Hjejle, B. (1982). *Hof eller Tuborg – konkurrence og fusion 1895–1970*. Copenhagen: Nyt Nordisk forlag.

Thomsen, B. N. (1973). *Tuborg 1873-13. Maj-1973: Tuborg og bryggeriindustrien under skiftende markedsvilkår 1873–1973*. Hellerup: Tuborg Bryggerier.

4

1955—Towards Merger

4.1 The Dictator

With the appointment of A. W. Nielsen as new Carlsberg CEO in 1955, the brewery got a leader who possessed the required skills quickly to turn the relationship between business and the Foundation upside down. Until then, there had been no doubt about who was the boss and made the decisions. The Carlsberg CEOs up to that point had more or less known their place in relation to the Foundation even though Hendriksen may have dominated a bit and clearly belonged among those who believed that the Foundation was there for the sake of the brewery and not vice versa. As far as that goes, A. W. Nielsen also knew his place—only with the difference that he considered the brewery operations as primary and himself as indispensable. He did so to such a degree that he could make practically any outrageous demand he wanted and still expect that the chairman of the Carlsberg Foundation and others, to the extent he ever came into more than distant contact with them, would comply. This might all have been foreseen and was already foreseen by the Carlsberg Foundation's gray eminence, chemistry professor Niels Bjerrum, who represented the Foundation in the brewery council. But Carlsberg needed a new way of dealing with its technical and management problems and was willing to go a long way. What happened, therefore, was no surprise.

After the appointment as CEO in 1955 of the then 46-year-old A. W. Nielsen and his formal assumption of the role of managing director on 1 March 1956, things soon began to turn around. It was no longer a noble,

D. Tamm, *The Carlsberg Story*,
https://doi.org/10.1007/978-3-030-52670-2_4

slightly fragile former civil servant who decided but someone with a reputation for pure business acumen. The foam catastrophe at Carlsberg was one of the first problems to be solved. Professor P. Brandt Rehberg, later chairman of the Foundation, describes A. W. Nielsen's approach to the problem in this way: "Then comes AWN, and it is very characteristic of AW that he asks, 'what is it that's wrong?' 'Yes, it's bad barley. It probably got wet and had not dried enough'. 'How much is there?' 'Well, I can't remember whether it was for one or two million crowns.' 'Throw it out, sell it for fodder, get rid of it all, buy new barley, start over.' They already had a ministry civil servant as director, and it will be very rare that you can take a man who is a permanent secretary in a ministry and is used to a ministry's way of doing things and put him in charge of leading a business. He can never take any kind of decision. But AW could."[1]

A. W. Nielsen as Carlsberg CEO for the coming twenty years became a legend in Danish industry. He was a self-made man and proud of his background as a dairyman who had reached the top. His latest post before Carlsberg was as CEO of the Royal Greenland Trade Company, where he had earned a deserved reputation as a hard-working and difficult but very competent leader. Fears that his way of treating those whom he did not consider up to standard might cause internal problems proved to be absolutely real. He was also very accomplished when it came to his own business interest, but he earned the indulgence of the Foundation and his surroundings by working constantly and unconditionally for the promotion of Carlsberg and for achieving outstanding results even if a few blunders could also be counted. He also took a great interest in agriculture, he said himself, was obsessed with land, was the owner of an old manor, and actively took part in the production there and, in general, the promotion of converting moorland into fertile areas for agriculture.

After assuming his new post at Carlsberg, A. W. Nielsen turned the firm around in record time from being less profitable to once again one of the greats. In its collaboration with Tuborg, it was again the breadwinner and had to yield considerable sums of its profits to Tuborg. There was a certain prestige connected with this, and it was definitely better than being the loser; but, over the long term, it was not tenable to be the party, year after year, that was to pay a considerable sum to the other party. Especially in the context of the Carlsberg Foundation's desire for profits for grant money was it unacceptable in the long term that Carlsberg's profit went to Tuborg shareholders and not to science. For an ambitious businessman like A. W. Nielsen, the

[1]Minutes of conversation on 1 June 1975 between P. Brandt Rehberg and publisher Ernst Blædel, in the folder 'Historisk om C-Lab' in CF archives.

situation was unsustainable both in the short term and in the long term, and he was not very good at concealing his irritation from representatives of Tuborg. For him, the collaboration with DFB and the many considerations that constantly had to be taken for the other party and all the limitations that this implied with respect to acting on your own became more and more of an irritant. And it was not just about the equalization of profits but the whole structure of the agreement, which locked down so much between the parties and required incessant negotiations over everything, small or large. A. W. Nielsen wanted to move forward, to expand, and to build breweries abroad. He did not like the many commitments that followed from the agreement: not only that money was to be paid out but also the constant inquiries, negotiations, and consents required in the collaboration to get anything going. This tripped up expansion and, in particular, destroyed opportunities for a more and more critical international engagement.

The collaboration agreement of 1903 between the two breweries blocked the establishment of breweries in large markets outside of Denmark for which it was hard to get agreement between the parties. A. W. Nielsen asked as early as August 1956 about the Foundation's principled position on the establishment of a brewery in England. It came to nothing because of the difficulties stemming from the relationship and necessary negotiations and compromises with DFB; and this, in part, gave rise to great dissatisfaction. A. W. Nielsen early had an eye for the importance of the US as a possible future "prestige market" for Carlsberg. Heineken was there already. At the beginning of 1957, A. W. Nielsen was on an exploratory trip during which he quickly grasped that it was expensive to get into the American market and that, therefore, Carlsberg needed liquidity and, perhaps, even then, could not count on a large market share. Nevertheless, it would provide prestige that might strengthen sales other places.

By 1968, it was clear that the two parties could either separate or merge but something had to happen. In principle, they could also try to keep limping along in a collaboration based on the old agreement, but that option looked more and more unsatisfying.

4.2 The Great Beer Wedding

The history of the merger of Carlsberg and DFB (or, in fact, with Tuborg), known as the great "beer wedding" by the press, has so far mostly been told in pieces and by those who were there at the time and had their share in the events. The two leading figures behind the merger were A. W. Nielsen and the chairman of the board of directors of DFB, Supreme Court advocate Bernt Hjejle, who wrote in 1982 a more detailed account of the merger seen from his point of view.[2] Hjejle had a lifelong affiliation with Tuborg as an attorney, as a member of the board of directors, and from 1969 as chairman of the board. He became one of the protagonists in the negotiations and was, in reality, the person from DFB's side who could overcome resistance to the merger on his own executive board, where the intransigence was mostly based on some nostalgic reluctance to join Carlsberg (as the minor partner) and—probably more—the actual CEO's personal ambitions. Hjejle's book bears the stamp of his understandable pride about his own role. Even if the author possesses the kind of character which is reluctant to be publicly critical of anyone, it is apparent that he had no illusions about Tuborg's (at that time) economically and intellectually weaker position.

An important point is that Hjejle fundamentally respected A. W. Nielsen and the Carlsberg side more than his own and, presumably, would rather have been on what he must have considered the winning team than representing the losers. Kristof Glamann says straight out about Hjejle that he was "incredibly charmed by A. W. Nielsen", who could, therefore, get him to do almost anything.[3] He even seemed relieved to be able to turn over what (at that time) was a sickly Tuborg, led by a not auspiciously talented but avaricious director to Carlsberg's or, rather, A. W. Nielsen's professional hands.

The picture drawn in the existing source material does not deviate markedly from the protagonists' own view. In his account of the merger, A. W. Nielsen mentions that "foresight and prescience were prominent characteristics in the men who shaped the 1903 agreement between Denmark's two great brewery groups". He was especially thinking here that they anticipated developments in the beer market, which "since the Second World War has been in rapid development, characterized by mergers and concentrations of capital". He mentioned "the 1968 consolidation of the two great Dutch breweries Heineken and Amstel with a total annual turnover of around a couple of billion crowns and equity in the amount of a billion crowns and the huge capital concentrations within the British brewery industry, each representing annual sales up toward six billion crowns with equity exceeding five billion". It is interesting that the experienced CEO emphasizes how "these large Dutch and British groups introduced a huge expansion in the 1950s through the establishment of breweries outside their traditional market areas", which had led the major Danish breweries to "reconsider their previous line".

---

[2] *Hof eller Tuborg*, 1982.

[3] Conversation between Glamann and Martin Ottesen on 10 March 1993 in file Historical Doc. C-Lab (see note above).

This wise advice was apparently pushed into the background in the years after the merger of the two major Danish breweries when—as we shall hear—the "professors" decided to take over leadership a few years later.

A. W. Nielsen also mentioned how Carlsberg and Tuborg were each small in relation to the giants abroad and that, up through the 1960s, the managers of both breweries were clear that, at some point, they should join forces. A major problem, he stressed, was the equalization principle in the agreement from 1903. A continual imbalance between the size and contribution of the two firms had influenced the relationship in a way that the agreement had not foreseen. It is a part of the history that, with the increasing competition on the world market and the expected increased competition in the domestic market, it was necessary to look at the relationship between the breweries from a new angle. In A. W. Nielsen's view when he wrote his contribution to the history of Tuborg in 1973, they had "already come a long way toward the goal…." He foresaw that the merger agreement of 1969/1970 "will lead to the two great names of Carlsberg and Tuborg continuing to bloom both at home and abroad".[4] A. W. Nielsen actually seemed to be the first person who really understood the importance of being on the international stage in a changing world of beer, and it is somewhat surprising that his visions were only effectively implemented by Carlsberg in this millennium.

Bernt Hjejle understood that the hour was about to strike for Tuborg, and the time was ripe to find a new arrangement. With a dynamo like A. W. Nielsen at Carlsberg and consistently poor financial reports for Tuborg, things were just not working anymore, and Hjejle understood that Tuborg's team did not measure up to A. W. Nielsen. At his initiative, the negotiations with Carlsberg about a new way of cohabitation got started. In the spring of 1969, a committee was formed to discuss "the problems of the cooperating breweries". This was stated in a letter of 15 April 1969 in which the current chairperson of the Carlsberg Foundation Stig Iuul, a professor of legal history, followed up on the matter after a reference from Hjejle and asked A. W. Nielsen to be Carlsberg's representative along with himself and another member of the Foundation board. This introduced a sequence of events that eventually led to a merger of the two breweries and, thus, the first truly major consolidation in Denmark. The preparatory committee was discretely called the "Advisory Committee of 1 April 1969", and no one could guess from this designation that it was all about finding a lasting solution for the future relationship between Carlsberg and Tuborg.

---

[4]Loc. cit., p. 165 f.

The first meeting of the advisory committee took place on 28 May 1969, and its events were ominous. Fifteen minutes after the meeting started at 10 a.m., Iuul, who had just finished the introduction, felt ill and lost consciousness briefly. An ambulance was called. Before it arrived, 61-year-old Iuul once again lost consciousness and, upon arrival at the municipal hospital, he was pronounced dead.

As new chairman, professor of physiology P. Brandt Rehberg, known and respected as a former resistance fighter, was appointed. He was made of different stuff than his predecessor Iuul—robust, open-hearted, experienced, and direct in his dealings with other people. He was known for a retort he made as chairman of the Carlsberg Foundation: as an old resistance fighter, he had been interrogated under torture by the Gestapo in Shell House for some months in 1945 until he escaped when British bombers attacked the building (to destroy a German stronghold and to aid an escape). A remark kept in Carlsberg memory is how once, on his way out to a meeting with A. W. Nielsen, Rehberg said to the board members: "Well, ... it can't be worse than the Gestapo".[5] The meeting was to tell A. W. Nielsen about the designation of a new business-savvy member to the brewery council. Rehberg chose to start by telling A. W. Nielsen about his image in public opinion "as the strong, self-determining man who completely dominated the breweries and the Foundation ...." He also told him that it was to avoid Nielsen advancing objections that he had not been oriented beforehand on the designation. The Foundation board believed that it was better to present the director with a *fait accompli* than to make a decision against his will. In this case, it turned out that A. W. Nielsen was actually satisfied with the selection once he had gotten over the surprise of the ambush, which no former Chairman of the Foundation had dared.

In July 1969, the parties met again and agreed to continue discussions on intensifying the collaboration between the breweries and about appointing a work committee. The main point at the meeting of the Foundation in October 1969, therefore, was the state of the negotiations with Tuborg, and Rehberg spoke in this context about his conversations with A. W. Nielsen on the terms for a consolidation of the two breweries, whose economic conditions the director had studied thoroughly. A. W. Nielsen and Brandt Rehberg conducted the negotiations for Carlsberg and the Carlsberg Foundation. As it might be expected, the negotiations were entirely closed to the outside world and deeply confidential.

[5]Related by Niels Petri. The story is slightly altered in a version by Kristof Glamann (2002), p. 142, in a form that gives the impression that the line occurred in a conversation with him. See also CF 10 October 1969.

The key person and driving force was and remained A. W. Nielsen. Since May 1969, he had undertaken a number of investigations on the amalgamation of the two breweries and, in that connection, worked out a number of tax, financial, corporate, and other statements.

Another hurdle to overcome was the necessary changes in the charter of the Carlsberg Foundation. The decisive, new provision was article 14 of the charter, which became the basis for the Carlsberg Foundation's brewery policies for the next thirty years:

> The Carlsberg Foundation shall, at all times, own a holding of shares which gives an entitlement to not less than 51 percent of the votes in Carlsberg A/S, and The Carlsberg Foundation shall never, whether by sale or gift of shares or subscription rights, by voting for capital increases or by any other means whatsoever, act in such a manner that the aforesaid requirements are not fulfilled or in a manner creating a risk thereof.

The Danish words "at all times" (Danish: "*stedse*") and "never" (Danish: "*ingensinde*") sounded old-fashioned, and one could be tempted to believe that they derived from the original charter, but they actually originated in this draft from the autumn of 1969. It sounded like the Brewer's own voice, which would say 'to this point and no farther', but the provision was actually new and the formulation chosen in order to ease the approval of the amendment through the Danish Ministry of Justice. The word "*ingensinde*" could be found in the original Charter (of 18 October 1876, art. XIV) for the Carlsberg Foundation, but there it only had to do with a change in the purpose of the Carlsberg Laboratory and not the Foundation's capital. In the real world, of course, it turned out that "never" or "*ingensinde*" was not that long after all but rather 37 years before the requirement of ownership of shares in Carlsberg was radically altered—in 2007 and again in 2013. Never say never, they say; and they should not have done so here. But, at that time, it sounded comforting and helped get the consolidation and the charter amendment through. However, the requirement in the charter for the Foundation to own 51% of the share capital actually became a new obstacle to Carlsberg's development right from the start and long before it was abolished in 2007, just as the collaboration agreement had been until 1970.

Legally speaking, what happened was quite simple: Carlsberg contributed its breweries to DFB and received shares in return. DFB's share capital was expanded on this occasion by the necessary DKK 85,500,000, which was allotted to Carlsberg plus four million crowns in cash and a claim for 12 million crowns. Since the Carlsberg Foundation already owned a large number of shares in DFB, Carlsberg became the dominant owner of the consolidated firm. The winner was apparently Carlsberg, and it was really a takeover, carried out as gently as possible.

4.3 Ossis and Wessis

Even though there were those—especially at Tuborg—who believed (with justification) that this was a conquest, both sides tried to implement the consolidation in as *gentlemanlike* a manner as they could. Externally, both breweries preserved their peculiar character and good-will, and everything looked as if it were taking place in accordance with a complete equality principle, where no one was loser or winner. The two breweries still maintained their distinctiveness for a time, but the reality was a consolidation that had the character of a takeover. The situation may be compared to the German situation after the incorporation of the former DDR into the Federal Republic. Tuborg's people felt like Ossis ("Easties") in comparison with the Carlsberg Wessis ("Westies") who had taken over.

The merger, which became a reality in 1970, was followed by a quite demanding transitional phase in which it was all about getting the two breweries to function together and getting control of finances and an overview of the capital needs of the two breweries. A. W. Nielsen had retired as CEO in 1974 and had himself pointed to P. J. Svanholm, who was educated as a lawyer and whose capacity for work lacked for nothing, as his successor. Even though Carlsberg was central, he, like his predecessor, found time to attend to major board posts in other important Danish firms. He was, for example, chairman of the board of the leading Danske Bank and a member of the board for the largest Danish concern, Mærsk, at the same time he managed the breweries. And as member of the board of Volvo, he was the only Dane in such a prominent position in a prominent Swedish company.

Carlsberg had become a conglomerate firm with many activities, which might, every so often, divert attention from the core product (beer) and lead to the firm to close in on itself instead of being active externally. In those years, Carlsberg was a firm with interests in a number of other firms that belonged to the Carlsberg group. Particularly significant were interests in the Holmegaard Glass Factory, the Royal Copenhagen Porcelain Factory, and Tivoli in addition to a number of more minor commitments in the wine importer Vingaarden, silver retailer Georg Jensen, and Illums Bolighus, etc. It was not always easy to see from the books where there were losses and where there were gains or whether there were even profits. External communication and openness were hardly Svanholm's strength. Like his predecessor,

Svanholm became one of the country's most prominent and well-known businessmen with a place alongside shipping magnate Mærsk McKinney-Møller, and there was a close personal connection between the two.

With the historian Kristof Glamann's assumption of the chairmanship of the Carlsberg Foundation in 1976, there was a distinctive generational shift on the Carlsberg Foundation board. Glamann became an externally visible chairman for the Foundation and, as we shall hear, also for the brewery's board of directors. Glamann was a recognized economic historian and known internationally for his research in economic history. He knew his stuff about bookkeeping, finance, and business, albeit from the rather olden days.

A mandatory age limit of 70 was introduced to the Foundation's executive board the same year, and there was also a desire to introduce this age limit to the corporate board of directors. What was new for the Carlsberg Foundation was that ownership of the now merged Carlsberg and Tuborg/DFB was not a foundation-owned company, it was a shareholder company with an independent executive board. The Carlsberg Foundation could have chosen to let itself be represented here by one or more members of the Foundation board but instead chose to let the complete board of the Foundation also be members of the executive board of the brewery. The new age limit was said not to be aimed at the now 78-year-old brewery board chairman Bent Hjejle, who continued until it was determined by lot that he would step down at the end of 1977.[6]

When Hjejle left the brewery board, the Foundation's new chairman took advantage of the Foundation's position as major shareholder to take over as chairman of the brewery board, a very influential post in the management of the brewery. Thus, he united the posts of chairman of the brewery board and chairman of the board of the Foundation—actually, something of a coup. Since 1922, a professional brewery council and a brewery committee had secured an arm's-length distance between the Foundation board and the management of the brewery. It was, therefore, the first time a member of the Foundation board—probably not exactly what J. C. Jacobsen had in mind—took over such an important leadership post of the breweries instead of leaving the actual business to professionals, which was J. C. Jacobsen's idea. Since that time, it has been the custom that the chairman of the Foundation board as representative of the main shareholder is also chairman of Carlsberg Ltd. (Carlsberg A/S).

It is in itself unusual for a foundation chairman also to be chairman of a firm's board. In his day, the founder, Brewer Jacobsen, had given his

[6]CFP 36, meeting 23 February 1977.

brewery to the Carlsberg Foundation, but he had seen to it and conditioned the gift on the fact that there was a capable, professional management and had not thought that the Foundation would actively embark on managing the brewery. Jacobsen had selected the Royal Academy for his foundation, because its members were independent of other interests than academia and because, therefore, it could be expected that the members selected for the Foundation board would respect Jacobsen's ideas and see to it that his breweries were kept together and respected his standard to brew beer of high quality under capable management selected by the Foundation. The Brewer respected the academicians for their impartiality and their contribution to knowledge. He presumably would have been amazed if he had heard that the Foundation's chairman, a historian (even if his area of expertise had something to do with accounting and numbers albeit several hundred years ago) had assumed the chairmanship, which is normally occupied by someone with business experience. The merger of Carlsberg and Tuborg into one company in itself was a deviation from the Brewer's thinking. However, with a certain portion of good will, it could be imagined that, if he had lived, he would have accepted it as a move that would secure the future of his breweries and, thus, the production of quality beer in Denmark. However, whether he would have approved the Foundation taking over a central post in the management of his brewery seems more doubtful. J. C. Jacobsen trusted the Royal Academy and gave to the Foundation his breweries because he considered the members as independent of personal interests and did what they were good at. When it came to assuming the post as chairman of the brewery board, no one apparently asked what he might have believed. Nor did anyone openly raise the question and discuss whether it was the right decision.

Glamann's chairmanship period coincided with explosive developments on the international beer market. The merger of Carlsberg and Tuborg/DFB in the 1970s created one of the world's most powerful brewery conglomerations that almost had a monopoly of the Danish domestic market and possibilities of expanding on the international market, if the will was there. Nevertheless, it did not get off to a good start. For the new mega-brewery, it was not to be the period of expansion and initiative or the exploitation of the new business opportunities for which the merger of Carlsberg and Tuborg was to prepare the way. Instead, time was wasted on discussing internal structures, frustrations at Tuborg, and the many smaller businesses also run by Carlsberg under the name of the merged company. In 1987, it was officially decided to leave out any reference to DFB and name the company only Carlsberg A/S (Ltd.).

The almost two decades of the Glamann chairmanship of both the Foundation and the brewery board were, in many ways, a period of stagnation instead of the expected expansion. Too much time was wasted overcoming the differences in culture between Carlsberg and Tuborg that should have been spent on visions for the future. It was the period in the history of the brewery in which big changes were about to happen through concentrations on the international market. It was the time to expand and not to look inwards. Chances were missed, but something still happened, and it was very much worth noting that, for the first time in the accounting year of 1980/81, the brewery earned more from sales abroad than on the domestic market. But the opportunity really to expand abroad by acquiring breweries in other countries was gravely ignored.

For many years, the brewery's director Poul Johan Svanholm and the chairman of the Carlsberg Foundation and the brewery board Kristof Glamann were "Mr. Carlsberg" and "Mr. Carlsberg Foundation". Together, they provided an impression of continuity and stability, but they disagreed on decisive points—first and foremost, about the brewery's strategy. Their two opposing points of view illustrated what eventually became Carlsberg's fundamental problem, namely, the increasing need for capitalization in relation to the commitments the charter contained about ownership of the company. Glamann felt bound by the requirement in the charter of an ownership of at least 51% of the capital, which also in his view legitimized his chairmanship position, and he even boasted of his restrictive attitude when it came to the question of easing the charter's requirement of capital possession in order to free capital for expansion of the brewery.

Svanholm, the Carlsberg CEO, on the other hand, realized that something had to be done and that the resistance of Glamann and the rest of the Foundation board to adjusting the charter was not just a hindrance to moving on but directly dangerous to the firm's regional and international position over the longer term. There is no doubt that the CEO wanted to expand. Another question is whether there was actually a will in Carlsberg's management to overcome the resistance from the Carlsberg Foundation board to enter actively into the international brewery market and make purchases with an eye towards expansion. The actual initiatives were few, and there were no real, major proposals for purchases. It is difficult to decide today whether this was because Svanholm gave up in light of the Foundation's reluctance to relinquish ownership share or whether, in reality, there was no clear strategy with respect to international purchases and, therefore, insufficient activity because Carlsberg was content with the brewery's dominant position in the domestic market. What seems certain is that the management pushed to get the charter amended in order to have more ready capital and that the Foundation was not receptive. On the other hand, beyond an unfortunate purchase in Spain, we have no additional examples from the 1970s and 1980s that the brewery's management pushed specific projects or confronted the Foundation with the need for capital to realize them. That only happened much later. Carlsberg was in a stalemate in this period when one could have expected expansion, which is central to the relationship between the brewery management and the Foundation. We know today that the Danish Ministry of Justice as supervising authority was willing to allow a change in the Foundation charter to the effect that the Foundation needed only a majority of voting shares, which was possible according to Danish law, rather than 51% of the actual capital. And we know that the Foundation was unwilling to propose such a change with the result that Carlsberg had insufficient capital to enter the international brewing market seriously as a buyer of other breweries.

4.4 Carlsberg for 150 Years

In 1997, Carlsberg celebrated its 150th birthday. Carlsberg's CEO for the past almost twenty-five years, P. J. Svanholm, abided by agreement and stepped down at the end of 1996 as a 62-year-old. The anniversary, therefore, was celebrated with a new CEO, Flemming Lindeløv.

The Carlsberg board had wanted a candidate from the outside with a different profile as a clear signal that the relationship between management and board needed to be put on a new course. The chairman of the Foundation board since 1993, economist Poul Christian Matthiessen, who was also chairman of the Carlsberg Foundation board, was convinced that Lindeløv could take on the job and was the right man to lead the firm into the future. Lindeløv seemed both dynamic and attentive to the need for an international strategy, and this was presumably also a reason that he was the favorite of Erik B. Rasmussen, the vice-chairman of the brewery board. The new CEO was definitely not hired because his profile was reminiscent of departed directors. To the contrary. He fulfilled the desire not to get "a new Svanholm". He came from a minor firm, the Tulip Food Company, a firm and a type of firm that, with 5–6,000 employees and a quite different clientele, ranked significantly lower in the Danish business hierarchy than Carlsberg. Lindeløv was then 48 years old, trained as a chemical engineer, and had written an academic thesis on the durability of frozen food. He had been CEO of FDB, the Danish Consumers Cooperative Society, and, since 1989, CEO of Tulip (now, Danish Crown Foods). Coming from Tulip to Carlsberg was something of a career leap—improbable but not impossible if you held to the philosophy that, if you can lead one firm, you can also lead another. Whether that was true in this case, however, quickly became a good question. Lindeløv was not and did not appear to be the tough businessman type with the sort of authority people were used to at Carlsberg. His advantages were a winning and positive attitude and something that resembled good will in cooperating with others. He also understood that Carlsberg had to move in a new direction. The downside was his frank pleasure in talking too openly to the press and a deficient sense of how you should behave—including when your board should be kept informed.

The era was now over in which the director of Carlsberg with positions at Danske Bank and Mærsk belonged to the absolute pinnacle of Danish business life. Gone, too, was the time when a Carlsberg CEO was hired on a long-term contract and remained at his post until its expiry. In the future, CEOs would come and go. Lindeløv respected Svanholm but undoubtedly believed that his style had been somewhat old-fashioned, lacking modern management tools such as strategy and an organizational structure, and that he had spent too much time on his board posts at Danske Bank and Mærsk instead of concentrating his attention on the needs of the brewery, which might be a justified observation. The choice of Lindeløv, therefore, meant a shift in style from the form of management on which Carlsberg built its authority and stability to a new form with more strategic thinking and a concentration on brewing instead of being a conglomerate business. As a strategist, Lindeløv was on the right track in many ways. He seemed flexible and accommodating and had an eye for the need for innovative thinking. At first, the strategy was to sell off all business not related to beer, which was weighing down Carlsberg without generating sufficient earnings, and, instead, concentrate on core areas that had to do with beer and brewery operations. Carlsberg was not only a brewery; it was a conglomerate of many firms with interests in Holmegaard Glass Factory (which also produced beer bottles), the Royal Copenhagen Porcelain Factory (which did not really make money), and Tivoli as the most spectacular. In 1998, ownership in Rynkeby Juice (Rynkeby Most) was sold; in 1999, shares in the Odense wine company Vingården were sold as were 43% of the shares in Tivoli in 2000; and ownership in Royal Scandinavia was cut significantly. It was a sensitive area because national treasures were at stake, and there was criticism (not completely unjustified) that a company like Carlsberg failed in its national duty to keep this form of business in Danish hands.[7] In the longer run, however, this strategy, called "the Carlsberg way of doing business", proved to be right from a business point of view. Carlsberg became big through the sale of beer and not by wasting its energies on other forms of business.

Lindeløv acknowledged that Svanholm had created respect around his person and the firm and was good at maintaining discipline, but he had been too cautious when it came to purchases and expansion on the beer market. This sounded convincing to the Carlsberg A/S board. However, the choice of Flemming Lindeløv as new administrative director was a surprise to many—particularly, for the two other directors who, together with Svanholm, had constituted the top of Carlsberg's leadership. CFO Walther Paulsen and the head of international sales Michael C. Iuul, who had done well in England but did not appear to have any special success or credibility when it came to other international engagements, were disappointed. It is an open question whether the two had realistic expectations with respect to their opportunities for taking over together as coordinate bosses in the firm and now felt deceived, or whether their disappointment was especially due to the choice of Lindeløv, whom they had difficulties in recognizing as CEO and their leader. At any rate, the designation of the new CEO came as something of a bombshell for them. In his welcome speech to Lindeløv, P. C. Matthiessen spoke of ensuring "teamwork among Flemming Lindeløv, Iuul, and Paulsen". The board wanted to retain the two internal directors and tried to balance it like a sort of "tight-rope walk". It ended up not working for various reasons of which thwarted ambitions and the combination of a lack of respect for the new director and his own behavior were decisive. The management team could not agree. The two Carlsberg veterans were both disappointed to such an extent that the new CEO felt as if they were ganging up on him. It was mostly Iuul, who had his own agenda, while Walther Paulsen tried to live up to the board's desire for cooperation.

To that point, Carlsberg had mostly based its international sales on vulnerable license contracts and had not actively taken part in the aggressive buyouts taking place within the beer industry. Purchases by competitors of breweries all over the world, therefore, now threatened Carlsberg's position in the market. Other breweries were pursuing a proactive policy of purchasing foreign breweries in order to brew local beer, which, at the same time, gave their own beer label access to new markets. It was this last tactic that was dangerous because, if you did not join the race to buy up breweries, you

[7] See Ole Lange, *Information*, 2000, "Carlsberg i volumensyg rus" (Carlsberg in a blast of volume), and an article in the newspaper *Ekstrabladet* (from the year 2000) with the title "Tivoli solgt til røverpris" (Tivoli sold for next to nothing).

could lose access to foreign markets and end up a local brewery and, perhaps, even wind up by being bought out yourself. International investments made by Carlsberg up to that point had been scattered and random, and it could be fatal for Carlsberg to be overtaken by Heineken, which just a few years before had not been larger than Carlsberg. The person in Carlsberg who had done most in this direction was Michael C. Iuul, who, even if he used to repeat the mantra of "eat or be eaten", was rather unfortunate with purchases in Spain and Germany. Nor did his projects in the US work out. The reality was that the market was getting crowded without Carlsberg being there. If Carlsberg wanted to be more than "our beer", the bell was about to toll. If it ended up being just "our beer", there was a considerable risk at that time that Carlsberg would wind up being someone else's beer.

Under the two strong leaders, A. W. Nielsen and Svanholm, Carlsberg had very much been run by the CEOs, and the board of Carlsberg A/S played a minor role. Both the Carlsberg Foundation and the board of Carlsberg A/S had accepted the dispositions of the leadership without asking too many questions. With a powerful Palle Marcus (former CEO of several important Danish enterprises) as deputy chairman, the constellation had changed, and it was now expected that the director would inform the board of his own operations and adapt to the board's wishes to a far higher degree. Marcus also spent significantly more time at Carlsberg than a deputy chairman otherwise does; and, even though he harmonized his attitude regularly with the chairman and the two other business members of the board, it was clear that he had material influence on the decisions that were made. Svanholm had given Lindeløv the strategic advice never to say more in the presence of the company board than necessary and to stick to answering questions, but that was not the way Marcus wanted things to be done. From the beginning, Palle Marcus had been skeptical about the choice of Lindeløv as CEO. With the professional and talented Marcus as deputy chairman, the board was considerably strengthened and a rather weak CEO like Lindeløv had a harder time.

A flirtation in 1996 with the South American brewery Brahma had given Carlsberg what Lindeløv vividly called "a black eye". So, a certain caution was appropriate. In 1997, Carlsberg acquired the rest of the English Carlsberg-Tetley, but they got a new flogging when English competition authorities refused to approve a merger with the Bass brewery. Thereafter, Carlsberg could not gain a leading position in the large, beer-thirsty English market and, thus, achieve its expected international breakthrough. What Carlsberg actually had (ever since A. W. Nielsen's time) was the brewery in Denmark, a certain position on the English market, half of a brewery in Hong Kong,

25% of a brewery in Malaysia, a brewery in Malawi, and some low key breweries limping along in Spain and Germany. In 1997 and the following three years, Carlsberg purchased the entirety of the Finnish firm Sinebrychoff, Falcon in Sweden, and the Swiss firm Feldschlösschen. Sinebrychoff was the first Finnish brewery, founded back in 1819 by a Russian businessman in Helsinki. The story behind it was reminiscent of Carlsberg's history, but those types of considerations played no major role at that point. A brewery was a brewery, and it was not about history but the market. At the same time, Carlsberg expanded its ownership of the Italian brewery, Porretti, as well as in Malaysia, Nepal, Poland, Portugal, and South Korea. Carlsberg was on the way to becoming *worldwide*. However, Carlsberg still needed the big breakthrough for which the earlier restrictive capital policy of the Foundation had not prepared the way.

4.5 The Breweries' Game of Monopoly

Now it was all about how Carlsberg could technically equip itself without losing itself in a market where the principle of "eat or be eaten" rules and where the situation was changing all the time. "Carlsberg, which was historically first out on the major international export markets, has since been emphatically overtaken by, particularly, the Dutch firm Heineken and the Belgian firm Interbrew and is hanging by its fingernails onto the top of international beer", wrote the trade paper *Børsen*[8] in December 2002. As the beer industry was developing in those years, this could only be a snapshot. It was correct that both InBev and Heineken had been quickly out and were now bigger than Carlsberg. Carlsberg, however, succeeded in maneuvering in the almost promiscuous beer market over the coming years, so that it remained at the top.

Those who remember the game Monopoly will remember how important it is in the game to possess the right positions and always be buying and selling real estate. If you purchased a property too late, you suddenly had to pay every time you passed a spot, and the available space became very small. If you focused on capital instead of business, your capital slowly hollowed out while those who had purchased in time wound up winning the game and becoming magnates. That is a little like what happened (and is still going on) in the brewing industry in those years. In the Monopoly game, however, there is only one winner. In the struggle for the beer market, there are many;

[8]Executive DK500, 20 December 2002.

and, at the moment, Carlsberg is one of them. It has to do with buying your way into other markets, so you can have your products sold. In the literature about the beer industry, people have identified breweries with the houses they bought in the Monopoly game and the hotels with brands.[9] One may also use the game to illuminate how a collection of many breweries gradually falls into a few hands. Another game metaphor that can illustrate the situation on the beer market is the ancient Chinese strategic board game, the *game of go*, which has to do with strengthening your position by surrounding a larger area of the board than your opponent. Pieces cannot be moved but can be conquered. The game does not really end but stops when one or both parties resign. The territory of the individual players is reckoned by the number of pieces acquired and a particular point system indicating their individual value. This is not dissimilar to the tactics Carlsberg later used on the Chinese market when they chose western China to begin their expansion, leaving at first the populous and economicallymore-developed eastern China to others.

Early consolidations to acquire volume used the method behind the formation of Interbrew in Belgium: through the merger of the Artois brewery—with the popular label Stella Artois—and Piedboeuf. Heineken's acquisition in 1968 of the (also) Dutch Amstel occurred in the same way. This trend, along with the consolidation of Carlsberg and Tuborg two years later in 1970, meant that the consolidated firms acquired a dominant position in their domestic market. However, this position was not used to buy other breweries at a time when that was possible without too much investment. With the merger of Carlsberg and DFB, primarily the work of the far-sighted A. W. Nielsen, Carlsberg was otherwise well-equipped to enter the larger market; but, because of the inflexibility of the Foundation board, the reality was reduced to "all dressed up and nowhere to go". With some good will, one can see Kristof Glamann and his board as the last defenders of a vision of brewery management that belonged more in Jacobsen's time than the present. Reality was now different, and one could not just be satisfied with granting licenses and buying into limited markets such as the African state of Malawi or Malaysia with, at the time of investment, a low consumption of beer for which there was not too much hope of increasing it. However, that was also what Heineken did, and Carlsberg followed suit with the development of the so-called "Heineken model". "Build and brew", they called it, and Heineken simply did it on a significantly larger scale than Carlsberg.

[9]Germain Hansmaennel as early as 2006 was the first to see parallels with the game of Monopoly to the globalization of the beer industry.

The fall in 1989 of the Iron Curtain and the Berlin Wall played an important role in the development that began in the 1990s in which Carlsberg eventually joined. Brewery operations in the former socialist countries had been state-run. Now, they were privatized, and the Eastern European market was opened up to enterprising investors. A group of Finns and Swedes took over the Estonian brewery Saku, which was put up for sale, while three Icelanders together with the Swedish brewery Pripps and the Finnish firms Hartwall and Sinebrychoff entered the Russian market. They founded as a joint venture *Baltic Beverages Holding* (abbreviated as BBH) in St. Petersburg about which we shall hear more. It was a success. In the first ten years, production rose from 140,000 to 24 million hectoliters. The BBH-owned Baltika became Russia's largest brewery with a market share in 2001 of 30% and a production of 14 million hectoliters.

In South Africa, the disappearance of the apartheid government gave the South African *SAB* (an abbreviation of *South African Breweries*) an opportunity to enter into the international market and become very big. At the same time, there were reasons to be careful. In the 1980s, Spain was justifiably considered to be a potentially good beer market, but Carlsberg got off to a bad start there and suffered a financial blow in connection with a joint purchase of a number of local breweries virtually sight unseen and, therefore, acquired breweries with, in many instances, completely outdated production or distribution equipment. It was an unfortunate and unprofessionally executed disposition, which did not encourage additional purchases.

In 1990, the American breweries Anheuscher-Busch and Miller and the Japanese Asahi were among the world's four largest (with Heineken as no. three). Together, they were responsible for 25% of the world's beer sales, but they primarily sold to their domestic markets. At that point, Carlsberg was not even among the top ten. In 1999, AmBev was formed by a consolidation of two Brazilian beer firms, Brahma and Antarctica, and they soon acquired a dominant position in South America. In 1995, InBev crossed the Atlantic and joined the Canadian brewery Labatt. This inspired others—such as, for example, Carlsberg, which began to talk to the third-largest American brewery, Coors. With the acquisition of Labatt, InBev got the Mexican firm FEMSA in the bargain, but FEMSA was bought out again in 2004, and it merged with Heineken in 2010. In 1999, SAB, which had grown big in Africa, acquired the iconic brewery Pilsner Urquell; and, in 2000, the British brewery Scottish & Newcastle acquired the French firm Kronenbourg. Things were happening in the brewery market.

Through passivity in those years, Carlsberg missed the chance to grow big, even though the market opportunities were there. Carlsberg was too slow in discovering that the "build and brew" model had been replaced by another more aggressive one. Fortunately, it was still not too late, now thirty years after the consolidation of Carlsberg and Tuborg, to join in; but a lot had happened in the meantime on the international beer market—in particular, prices had risen. The new model, whose aggressive character Carlsberg had not acquainted itself with or taken stock of, was now "buy and build". Here, "build" no longer meant build in a literal sense but the building up of entire beer empires. The philosophy behind this is summarized as $1 + 1 = 3$ with the tacit sense that purchases and consolidations created increased value in themselves. A key word is "finance-led": the notion that purely economic considerations—i.e., earnings—are behind this strategy and not an ambition to achieve volume by selling more beer or less beer, much less beer of a certain quality. It was this form of strategy that Carlsberg was to pursue in the years after 2000.

In many ways, the Dutch-based brewery Heineken became (and remains) Carlsberg's closest competitor the moment it moved outside its own country. Both breweries had a solid anchoring in their respective home markets; but, outside and especially in European markets, they were competitors. What would have been worthwhile for Carlsberg to study a bit more closely was how Heineken had very early embarked on a strategy to enter into a number of foreign beer markets not only through license agreements but also by the purchase of local breweries that could give them a platform for expansion. Heineken thereby had a head start on Carlsberg, which, as it turned out, was not to change.

Otherwise, the "Heineken story" resembles the Carlsberg story. As a firm, Heineken is a bit younger than Carlsberg. The brewery's history goes back to 1863, when the then 22-year-old Gerard Adriaan Heineken acquired the brewery '*De Hooiberg*' (The Haystack) in Amsterdam. J. C. Jacobsen visited him during a visit to Holland. So, for the historically conscious, there was an old connection. As previously mentioned, Heineken senior had a German master brewer Wilhelm Feltman, who just like Carl Jacobsen, whom he knew personally, was sent abroad on a study tour to learn about beer production. In 1873, the brewery's name was changed to '*Heineken's Bierbrouwerij Maatschappij*'. As at Carlsberg, they were attentive to the importance of Pasteur's and later Emil Christian Hansen's research on beer production. Two researchers from Heineken's lab were sent to Copenhagen to study at the Carlsberg Laboratory: In 1886, Dr. H. Elion, another student of the French chemist Louis Pasteur, developed the so-called 'Heineken A-Yeast' at Heineken's laboratory, which is still said to be a key ingredient for Heineken's beer. In 1887, Heineken switched over to using bottom yeast.

It was mentioned how Emil Christian Hansen at the Carlsberg Laboratory worked with pure yeast and how Carlsberg's generosity in making it available to others helped Heineken's lab make progress. At the same time, technical progress with respect to machinery, refrigeration, temperature measurement, etc. occurred. The founder's only son, Henry Pierre Heineken, became leader of the firm as a 28-year-old in 1914; and, during his term, which lasted until 1940, Heineken developed a homogenous beer quality with large-scale production that made Heineken beer well-suited as an "international lager". This was what A. W. Nielsen wanted for Carlsberg in the 1960s but could not get going because of the 1903 agreement with Tuborg. After 1970, Carlsberg was no longer bound by that; but, once they were finally free, it turned out—as said—that the Foundation's veneration for the capital requirement in the charter was a problem.

In the Heineken family, the talent for brewery operations reached well into the first two generations. Third-generation Heineken Alfred "Freddy" Heineken, who began his career at the firm in 1940 and, in 1971, became chairman of the executive board, was the driving force behind Heineken's expansion into the world market in the following years. It was he who designed Heineken's characteristic green bottle and logo, and it was he who struggled to preserve the family's influence at the brewery. It was his point of view that beer is a product that can cross borders and need not be just a local product. Exports increased after the 1960s to countries such as the US, France, and Sweden. Heineken acquired a position as the largest beer exporter in the world; and, like Carlsberg, quality became a part of Heineken's brand. License agreements were established in France, Ireland, Spain, and Italy; and, subsequently, Heineken took a more active role in the operation of these breweries. Outside of Europe, the Caribbean in particular received licenses.

In the same way as Carlsberg, Heineken also found out that they had come late to the buying party. After having achieved a permanent position in the 1970s and 1980s in a number of markets, Heineken tried after 1992 to introduce its beer to the German market, which is traditionally reckoned as complicated with its many breweries and strong local anchoring. Heineken did this through licenses or partnerships with an existing brewery or by establishing its own brewery, depending on local circumstances. In 1995, a brewery was established in Thailand. In 1998, Heineken bought two Polish breweries and, in 1999, the Spanish firm Cruzcampo. In 2001, Heineken joined a German brewery group (*Schöngruber*) in the same way that Carlsberg the year before had joined Orkla about which we shall hear more. In 2007, the paths of Heineken and Carlsberg crossed unexpectedly and surprisingly (about which we shall also hear) in connection with the acquisition of the

Scottish and Newcastle (S&N) brewery in the UK. Today, Heineken owns approx. 170 breweries and has a global distribution network. Heineken still is controlled by the Heineken family while the rest of the shares are publicly traded. Freddy Heineken's daughter, Charlene de Carvalho-Heineken, holds the largest single block of shares in the firm.

Thus, Heineken and Carlsberg are old competitors. In September 1965, it was reported that Heineken was preparing a push into the Swedish market. This was a breath of fresh air and a warning of future but still somewhat distant times. The tough Dutch business methods were feared. A. W. Nielsen visited Heineken to discuss Scandinavian business methods, and an agreement was entered into with Heineken, the practical effect of which was to keep Heineken out of Denmark. This agreement lasted until 2002 after which Heineken was distributed and marketed in Denmark by Royal Unibrew. In the spring of 2007, the agreement was expanded with a production license agreement for Heineken beer at the Royal Unibrew brewery in Aarhus and, later, the brewery in Faxe. The first Danish-brewed Heineken beer came on the market at the beginning of 2008. The fact that Heineken entered the Danish market so late gave rise in 2002 to charges in the press against Carlsberg and Svanholm, the director at the time, of having agreed with Heineken to keep Carlsberg out of Holland if Heineken stayed out of the Danish market. However, that is not the way it was, Carlsberg maintained. Both parties respected each other's home markets. The explanation was that it was "in the air" and something both parties understood without need for a formal agreement. The case was investigated by the EU Commission, which ended up shelving the matter without taking a position. This was not considered entirely satisfactory for the proud Danish brewery, which had expected a straight out "acquittal".

Beer, as opposed to most other foodstuffs, is local in the sense that every country has its typical labels, which are consumed locally and often preferred to international labels. Local affiliation and pride in the local brewery means something else and more than it does with respect to razor blades, batteries, paper towels, or other products that are part of ordinary housekeeping and are quickly consumed and, thus, rubricated as FMCG, fast moving consumer goods. The purchase of leading national breweries, therefore, meant control of a national beer market and access to earnings from the sale of beer in addition to an opportunity to launch one's own beer label alongside the local. On this point as well, times had moved from Jacobsen's ideas about the perfect product, but Carlsberg had not. The quality of the beer is still a top priority even though, naturally, it is simpler to keep track of that with a brewery in Denmark than when you are running more than a hundred breweries spread out all over the world. That was the reason Jacobsen preferred the sole proprietorship or foundation construction. Breweries run as shareholder companies are more difficult to control; shareholders want their dividends; and, as a brewer, you are no longer master in your own house. Jacobsen's way of thinking was now considered obsolete. The world looked different, and beer brewing was an endangered business. Since the end of the 1990s, Carlsberg chose to change strategy and ambition and also strove to attain a high position in the international beer market.

The originally Belgian Interbrew has, without doubt, been the most aggressive and, with respect to volume, the most successful player on the international market on a scale that could only be dreamt of in Carlsberg. Starting as a minor Belgian brewery, it later merged with the Brazilian AmBev and the American Anheuser-Busch, whose top label is the iconic American beer, Budweiser. It is a fascinating story how, in 2008—the same year Carlsberg and Heineken bought S&N, the energetic Brazilian-dominated management of InBev acquired, through a surprising hostile takeover, Anheuscher-Busch, which was otherwise known as "the lone constant in the industry, as it has remained the dominant brewer in the United States since 1957".[10] The purchase price was the net sum of $52 billion, but the top had not yet been reached because, in 2016, AB-InBev also acquired for a price of $130 billion the number two brewery giant at the time, SABMiller, thus attaining the uncontested position as the world's largest beer producer.[11] It was once predicted that SABMiller would take the winner's slot. Today, however, it has passed from the saga as an independent brewery and as a name. The three brewery giants, AmBev, Anheuser-Busch, and SABMiller were now one unit, representing over 30% of the world market, and their value in 2016 was estimated to be over 200 billion dollars.

In 2016, the magazine *Business Insider* wrote that, back in 2004, "10 breweries controlled 51% of the global beer market, calculated by volume. Ten years later, five breweries, Anheuser-Busch InBev, SABMiller, Heineken, Carlsberg, and China Resources Enterprise controlled pretty much the same amount". Whether it would continue this way or Carlsberg would enter into this super-league was not to be predicted at this point. We find as numbers two and three today the family-owned Dutch Heineken and the Danish foundation-owned Carlsberg. This is a distant third-place, far behind AB-InBev, and closely followed by the two Chinese breweries China Resources and Tsingtao and the American MolsonCoors, which had the opportunity to acquire full ownership of what came with the Miller brand

[10]Tremblay (2005), p. 75.
[11]See MacIntosh (2010).

after the consolidation of SABMiller and AB-InBev in accordance with requirements from American antitrust authorities. In the meanwhile, the Japanese brewery Asahi acquired Peroni, Grolsch, and Pilsner Urquell, among others.

It is no accident that the desire of the Heineken family and the Carlsberg Foundation to preserve a determining influence in their breweries has protected them from takeover. Buyouts and consolidations are about money, not the quality of the product. The driving force on the world market in recent decades has been in conflict with old Jacobsen's thinking. Neither Jacobsen senior nor junior would have wanted his brewery to be run with others. Now, it was a matter of gathering up as many breweries as possible and earning enough to buy others: "buy and build." These are also the conditions for Carlsberg today, if it wants to be a part of the international market. At the same time, however, Carlsberg has had the advantage that the shares of the Carlsberg Foundation are not for sale. The rationale behind the charter amendments, as we shall learn in the following, was to secure possibilities of expansion for the brewery and to provide an opportunity to keep up in a world market that is run by this form of economic thinking in which it is all about becoming bigger and bigger. Still, Carlsberg's construction as a foundation-owned business is a safeguard against being bought up.

Reference

MacIntosh, J. (2010). Dethroning the king. The hostile takeover of anheuscher-busch, an American Icon. US: Wiley.

5

2000—From Regional Brewery to the International Top

5.1 Going West or North?

The year 2000, the turn of the millennium, marked the point at which Carlsberg decided to expand and become a serious player on the international brewery market. Carlsberg was still primarily a regional brewery, and the choice could have been made to remain so or, rather, to try to remain so, because markets and survival have been and are uncertain for businesses that do not choose to expand. Carlsberg had learned the lesson in the 1990s that it was necessary to be more active and make an effort to expand on the international market. To attain that goal, a modification of the Charter of the Carlsberg Foundation was prepared to make it possible for Carlsberg to enter into a more advanced economic collaboration with other breweries. To this point, the Carlsberg Foundation had refused to change the charter. A possible change in the charter to allow the Foundation to give up holding the majority of shares counted as capital had been discussed since the 1980s, but nothing came of it until new strategies were discussed at the end of the 1990s. This led to negotiations with the Danish Ministry of Justice, which willingly allowed the charter to be modified in order to make it possible for Carlsberg to establish subsidiary companies in which Carlsberg did not have a majority of capital or votes. This was a first legal step towards loosening up the charter to permit more capital to be syphoned from the Foundation into the brewery business. Being run by a Foundation was a blessing since it made the brewery resistant to takeover, but it could also be a problem as

D. Tamm, *The Carlsberg Story*,
https://doi.org/10.1007/978-3-030-52670-2_5

illustrated by the history of Carlsberg in the last decades of the 20th century by hindering the supply of necessary capital.

Carlsberg CEO Flemming Lindeløv's goal at that time was to build Carlsberg into one of the five largest breweries in the world. On this, he was backed by Michael C. Iuul, who as the person responsible for international relations said at a brewery board meeting in August 1997 that "an ambition of merely belonging among the 5–10 largest was the same as saying that Carlsberg's role as an international brewery will be phased out". He also said that "there should be a focus on fewer markets ... with the overall aim of making Carlsberg into one of the 3–5 largest in each market".[1] At that point, this might have sounded completely unrealistic, but the goal was actually achieved much sooner than expected. At first, however, Carlsberg bet on a number of horses and searched for partners toward the west in the US and toward the north in Norway. In order to proceed and have sufficient flexibility, however, the above-mentioned changes of the Foundation charter were necessary. Negotiations with the Ministry of Justice were kept secret as the news of Carlsberg going for more capital might raise suspicion among other breweries. Project Charlie was the name of this whole series of negotiations and preparations.

At that point, Carlsberg A/S had an internal organization based on three main business areas. Carlsberg Finance owned properties at Tuborg in particular. Carlsberg Soft Drinks had been placed in a shareholder company of which Carlsberg owned 51% and Coca-Cola Nordic Beverages 49%. Coca-Cola, originally feared as an international giant bringing new and aggressive ways of doing business to Denmark, had proven to be quite a good partner for Carlsberg. The beer division was divided into a Danish and an international division. The international division was further divided into a number of units for each country. Carlsberg A/S functioned as a holding company for these businesses. The person primarily responsible for the international division was Michael C. Iuul. Even if he was probably the person in the old management who caught the scent earliest of the direction things were going, he turned out not to be the most loyal or diligent executor of these ideas, when it came to the question of how it should be done. At his initiative, Carlsberg put feelers out at the end of the 1990s about a collaboration with the large North American brewery Coors. Coors was a recognized, traditional, family-owned brewery somewhat the same size as Carlsberg; and, on the surface, it looked like a partner you could work with if you wanted to enter the American market and get more volume into the English market, which had long been a Carlsberg priority. Strengthening efforts in the English

[1] Board meeting at Carlsberg A/S, 28 August 1997.

market together was, therefore, an important issue. Internally in Carlsberg, these secret conversations with Coors were talked about as the *Coldstream Project* directed toward a common acquisition in England, while the American project, which aimed at a broader collaboration giving Carlsberg access to the US, was called *Project Monarch*. In the beginning of November, the Foundation's chairman, P. C. Matthiessen, and representatives of Carlsberg went on a negotiation trip to the US. The time was not wasted, even if the outcome was different from what was expected. Palle Marcus describes the journey in this way: "PCM and I were together on a trip to Coors in Colorado in a stretch from Kastrup Airport to London, on to New York in 3½ hours with the Concorde, and then by plane to Denver, where the first meeting started in the middle of the night (Danish time). After a morning meeting the next day, the trip home went via Detroit and London. For a businessman, this was not unusual".[2] After their visit to Coors, Marcus and Mattiessen were not as convinced as before about the move. Both had gotten cold feet. The same was true for Carlsberg CFO Walther Paulsen, who did not believe that a connection to Coors would benefit Carlsberg. The Americans wanted to do business and so, in a way, did Carlsberg; but Carlsberg was unsure whether the American counterpart understood Carlsberg's special legal construction and the brewery's anchoring in the common Danish national consciousness. Nor were they sure that an agreement with Coors would provide the desired entry into the US market. Still, they continued negotiations and contemplated the matter internally over the coming months, even going so far as to draft an agreement in February (though they were far from convinced they would take this course). An agreement based on a parity of influence—that is, 50–50%—created a risk in the event of disagreement that initiatives might not be able to be realized. In Carlsberg's view, the cooperation also entailed a risk that Carlsberg itself might be acquired by the other party in the long term if, at some point, they became the weaker party of the two. The many years of cohabitation with Tuborg and the complications such an agreement raised were not forgotten completely.

Thus, there was good reason to be cautious and to abandon negotiations if something better came along. On 1 March 2002, the Carlsberg Foundation conferred with its attorney; and, in the afternoon, they talked to the Danish Minister for Justice Frank Jensen. On 3 March 2000 at 8 a.m., another meeting was held with the Ministry of Justice to elaborate on the conversation from two days before. Fisch-Thomsen had gone through the draft agreement with Coors and discussed the problems it might raise with

---

[2] E-mail 11/4 2018.

respect to the charter. The Danish Ministry of Justice was willing to accept an arrangement in which Carlsberg would have fewer than 50% of the board seats in a collaboration with another brewery if they could not agree on a 50–50% arrangement.

A greater "psychological" problem in this connection (but it was the Foundation's and not the Ministry's) was the location of the headquarters: London was being discussed as a compromise between Copenhagen and some American city. There were also some unresolved issues such as whether the chairperson of a joint board would have a decisive vote and what should be done if it all went wrong.

The management of the American brewery had evidently believed there were good prospects for an agreement. In April 2000, both the Carlsberg Foundation and the brewery board decided not to pursue the American opportunity and alerted Coors of this. They had found another, better partner and did not want to cut the strings to Coors completely until that was ascertained. The negotiations and the earlier visit to the site, however, had apparently created expectations for their host. The CEO of the American brewery, Peter Coors, wrote a letter to P. C. Matthiessen on 5 April 2000 about the "shock and great disappointment" at hearing that negotiations had broken off. Carlsberg had probably gone "a bit too far" in the negotiations as P. C. Matthiessen says today.[3] More letters were exchanged between the parties, and the North American brewery asked its Danish attorneys to sound out Carlsberg about the reason negotiations had been broken off. Also disappointed was Michael Iuul, the man who had initiated the whole thing and had reckoned it would be a breakthrough for him and pave his way to a new position as an international leader with an important role in London. Now, he was left as someone who had lost the confidence of the chairman of the board, having once again produced a failure.

5.2 Ashlad and the Norwegian Troll—Orkla

In Norwegian folktales, there is a character named Ashlad (sometimes called Boots in English translation). He is the youngest of three brothers and appears to be nothing but "a klutz who stays at home rummaging in the ashes",[4] but—against all expectations as in Hans Christian Andersen's fairy tale about Clumsy Hans—he ends up running off with the princess, the gold, and whatever else might be worth getting. Often, he tricks a troll or

---

[3]Conversation 1 March 2018.

[4]Gyldendals store danske encyklopædi, "Askeladden".

some other imaginary creature. In the fairy tale named "The Boy Who Had an Eating Match with a Troll," Ashlad challenges a troll to an eating contest. One has to be careful with this sort of thing, because trolls often have a more or less hidden agenda to eat the challenger at some point—usually as dessert. However, here, it ends with Ashlad fooling the troll and "getting all the silver and gold to be found in the mountain and going home with it." In the business fairy tale that is to be related below, the carefree Ashlad with the initiative and optimism is actually Danish and called Carlsberg, and the troll, who ends up feeling cheated, is named Orkla, hailing, as real trolls should, from Norway.

In the history of Carlsberg, the tale of Carlsberg and Orkla is a decisive chapter, which has to do with how, in 2000 after much searching, Carlsberg found what for a time was believed to be its 'true love' but—as can sometimes happen—encountered serious problems in the relationship. Mostly, Orkla did not entirely understand that Carlsberg meant it as more of a non-obligatory alliance than a serious lifetime commitment. The cohabitation with Orkla dissolved, and Carlsberg kept what it wanted of its partner's property, which is what it was after all along. It cost money, of course, but it was still seen as a smart move for Carlsberg, which was and had always been happier with the community property than with its partner. The Norwegian variant of this tale is slightly different. It has to do with how a serious profit-oriented business conglomerate ("*storselskabet*", as Orkla called itself with characteristic Norwegian modesty, meaning 'giant company') embarked in good faith on a serious "business" venture with what they considered to be a solid, reliable partner, a professor-run brewery—and was "hoodwinked" by someone they had trusted, who then ran away with its gold and the family silver.

To put it more prosaically, at the end of the 1990s, Carlsberg was well on its way toward becoming an international business with around 90% of its sales from abroad. The charter amendment in the spring of 2000 was an important piece in the game, which both psychologically as an incentive and in practice had to do with moving on and establishing a more binding cooperation with another major firm. That firm ended up being a regional partner, the Norwegian Orkla, the owner of just the sort of breweries that fit Carlsberg's profile, and it is this story we shall tell here.

Orkla's business history was actually far older than Carlsberg's. It went back to the 1600s, and its origins were in copper and iron pyrite mining.[5] The old firm reckons its founding from 1654, while modern Orkla was established

---

[5]Orkla's history since 1974 is exhaustively described in the anniversary publication *Brytningstider 1654–2004* (2004) by the three historians Trond Bergh, Harald Espeli, and Knut Sogner. The time after 1991 is described by Harald Espeli, pp. 319 ff.

in 1904 under the name *Orkla Grube-Aktiebolag*. However, it was actually only in the 1980s that Orkla became a major industrial enterprise, a so-called conglomerate with a number of consumer and brand goods, creating a comprehensive financial business. It was this "new" Orkla, which appeared in the 1990s as a multinational company in which the brewery operations were simply a smaller part of the business, that Carlsberg began negotiating with.

Orkla was a large firm with many interests, and beer was only one of them. However, when it came to beer, Carlsberg and Orkla complemented each other rather well. Carlsberg was dominant in Denmark and had major interests in England. Orkla for its part could contribute breweries in Sweden, Norway, and especially Russia, which for Carlsberg was the market of the future. Among its assets, Orkla had the Norwegian brewery Ringnes and the Swedish Pripps. Pripps was acquired in 1995 by Orkla from Swedish Volvo as a part of the Procordia Food company. Orkla already at that time owned Ringnes, which merged with Pripps, and Pripps owned half of BBH, Baltic Beverages Holding, which in turn owned an economically attractive Russian brewery, Baltika, along with several other breweries. This was the largest purchase in Orkla's history to that point, which resulted in Orkla owning at first 51% of the shares in the merged Pripps-Ringness and, in 1997, also the rest of Pripps-Ringness bought from Volvo for SEK 4.4 billion. This agreement with Volvo for the takeover of the breweries had been a "quantum leap" for Orkla, said Orkla's chairman of the board Jens Heyerdahl at the time.[6]

Thus, Pripps brought along 50% of Baltic Beverages Holding (BBH) into Orkla and, with that, promising interests and opportunities in Russia, where things were going quite well in the 1990s with a growth of 90% in 1997 and an income that year of SEK 1358 million. BBH was originally established in 1991 by the Volvo-owned brewery concern Procordia Beverages, which owned the Swedish Pripps and the Finnish Hartwall, with a view toward selling beer in the former Soviet Union. It also had a majority share in other breweries in the Baltic region, including, first and foremost, Baltika in St. Petersburg. BBH was a company that relied on local managers and the extension of local markets.

On the whole, Orkla was in a period of growth during the 1990s and undertook extensive purchases of other firms. Orkla also had an ambition to gain control over the Finnish-owned Hartwall brewery concern, which owned the other half of BBH, so that they could gain full control over BBH. It is understandable that Carlsberg could see possibilities in a cooperation with Orkla that might provide access to developments in the Russian market,

---

[6]Espeli (2004), p. 319 and pp. 331 ff.

which was geographically just down the street. Quite simply, Orkla had something to bring to the table. While Carlsberg's earnings in these years were unsatisfactory, BBH's income was high, but the same was true of the risk. A devaluation of the ruble in 1998 had led to a great loss of value, but the growth in volume continued.

Like Carlsberg, Orkla, too, was now on the lookout for expansion opportunities, and the next step was the deal with Carlsberg about which we shall now hear. Orkla's strongest card on the global market was its share in BBH, which also became an important part of Orkla's stake in the collaboration that was established with Carlsberg. Already in 1997, feelers were sent out between Carlsberg's Flemming Lindeløv and Orkla, but nothing came of it.[7] That same year, Carlsberg bought 60% of the Finnish brewery Sinebrychoff, which owned a share of the Swedish company Falcon. Here, Carlsberg already had 50% of the ownership and now gained control of the entire brewery. Thus, Orkla and Carlsberg were competitors in the Nordic market in which, together, they were dominant and over which each wanted hegemony. Carlsberg was strongest in Denmark and Orkla in Norway and Sweden. A consolidation, therefore, would have great advantages for both parties and substitute collaboration for competition. In addition, Orkla was ready since another (and for Orkla) obvious possibility for cooperation—a merger between Pripps-Ringnes and Hartwall—had been rejected by the Hartwall family in 1999, which feared that the company would only have a minority position. Hartwell also sounded out Heineken, which, however, was only interested in a full acquisition.

A central figure in the negotiations with Orkla was Nils Smedegaard Andersen, whom Lindeløv had brought back to Carlsberg in 1999 in a leading position with special responsibility for sales in the Nordic countries. He, who proved to be a future star in the Danish world of business, had come to Tuborg in 1983, and he later proved his competence with success in the Middle East, which is not exactly known for its beer consumption. Later, he somewhat rectified a few failed Carlsberg investments in Spain and Germany. After a short time as CEO of a Swiss staples goods business, which he got on its feet in a mere two years, he was now ready for Carlsberg—for a time.

Contact with Orkla was renewed in Nice in September 1999, when Nils Smedegaard Andersen met Paul Bergquist from Orkla. The two men agreed that a collaboration between the two competitors in the Nordic market was the way forward, and they discussed a business agreement based on 40%

[7] Espeli (2004), p. 363.

to Orkla and 60% to Carlsberg. In December 1999, Orkla's leading directors, CEO Finn Jebsen and Paul Bergquist spoke to Lindeløv while in transit through Copenhagen after having had a meeting with Heineken, which at that time was Carlsberg's biggest competitor with significantly better earnings and a positive trend on the stock market, while Carlsberg was at a standstill. Lindeløv took things farther, organizing a meeting in Oslo between Nils Smedegaard Andersen and Bergquist at the beginning of 2000.[8]

A collaboration with Orkla was a far more attractive agreement than the one with the American brewery, which Carlsberg had been pursuing up until then. Thus, the breakthrough with Orkla was a primary reason for the definitive break in the American negotiations. Presumably, Carlsberg would not have reached an agreement with the Americans on the terms given, but with Orkla they were well on their way toward what would be "the best deal ever for Carlsberg", as the Danish architect behind the arrangement, Nils Smedegaard Andersen, put it. He was the one who exploited the contacts that led to cooperation with Orkla, which in the long term became the path to an international position for Carlsberg. The more official negotiations with Orkla kicked off in April and May 2000, and on 31 May of that year, they signed a number of agreements. One agreement was on the establishment of a joint subsidiary named Carlsberg Breweries, which gathered all the brewery activities in the two companies. This agreement was made public on 31 May 2000; and, upon the announcement of the new brewing company, the stated value was DKK 23 billion with 27,000 employees. Orkla contributed its beverages firm, that is, Pripps-Ringnes, including its share of BBH, while Carlsberg contributed its breweries. Carlsberg received an equity interest of 60% as opposed to Orkla's 40% of Carlsberg Breweries, the first chairman of which became Carlsberg A/S's board vice-chairman Palle Marcus. The construction was that a new established company, Carlsberg Breweries, purchased the breweries of Carlsberg and Orkla for shares in Carlsberg Breweries. Carlsberg CEO Lindeløv became the head of the board of directors with Bjørn Erik Ness and Paul Bergquist as the Norwegian members in addition to two additional Danish members. The shares could not be divested in the first two years. There were mutual preemption rights and a right to demand an IPO after three years. The intent in establishing the subsidiary was to avoid intervention from antitrust agencies, but the Finnish competition law authorities proved especially hesitant. The agreement with respect to its consequences for the Carlsberg Foundation was approved by the Danish Civil

[8]E-mail of 6 May 2008 from Smedegaard to Krogsgaard, which corrects his statements in the newspaper *Jyllandsposten* the Sunday before and recounts the sequence of events prior to the Orkla agreement.

Law Directorate—the supervisory board for foundations—in August 2000. In January 2001, the Danish competition authorities gave their approval, while the Finnish competition authorities, which believed that the Carlsberg-Orkla consolidation created too dominant a position in the Finnish beverage industry, imposed some important conditions.

The parent company Carlsberg A/S continued as before. At that point, the Carlsberg Foundation owned 55% of the share capital of Carlsberg A/S. Legally speaking, the construction established a subsidiary in which the parties contributed brewery operations, but in practice Carlsberg Breweries was run as a joint venture with an independent board.

A decisive point for the Danish supervisory authorities was that Carlsberg did not give up in advance its controlling influence, i.e., it did not allow its equity share to drop below 51%. Article 14 of the charter only allowed deviation from the requirement of controlling influence under the special condition that itwas demanded by a business "necessity", and such controlling influence could only be surrendered after a concrete evaluation. This was an important limitation, and it could have been a problem threatening the whole agreement, since it turned out that Lindeløv had not informed Orkla that they might face this situation: that additional permission by Danish authorities was needed before important dispositions could be made. At Orkla, they saw this as a "deal breaker". Suddenly, the whole transaction with Orkla was in danger, but it ended with Carlsberg accepting (with the consent of the Danish Civil Law Directorate) the original formulation of the agreement, which said nothing about being able to go below 51% with regard to influence.

The Nordic countries, Great Britain, Eastern Europe, and Asia were designated as core markets for the new company. The strategy was to establish a base with strong local brands of beer and to use Carlsberg as the international brand. Since the 1970s, Carlsberg had been sold internationally under the slogan: "Probably the best lager in the world". Carlsberg was the most prominent Nordic brand, and its share in BBH was the entrance to Eastern Europe and Russia. Part of the package was a Pripps-Ringnes' collaboration with Pepsi Cola. The new brewing company, Carlsberg Breweries, would have its headquarters in Copenhagen and its top leader was to be Carlsberg A/S CEO Flemming Lindeløv, while Nils Smedegaard Andersen, Michael C. Iuul, and two Norwegians, Paul Bergquist and Bjørn Erik Næss, constituted the rest of the management. The philosophy behind the cooperation was to ensure controlling influence for both parties and—just as important—a right of first refusal for the other party if one of the parties were to put its shares up for sale.

After the launch of the collaboration between Carlsberg and Orkla, it turned out that it was not only the North American company Coors that had believed in Ashlad and now were disappointed at suddenly being left on the road to the altar. The Hansa Borg brewery, a local Norwegian brewery located in Bergen, had conducted detailed negotiations with Carlsberg for several years. Papers were ready for signature when the announcement was made public about the new collaboration. The Bergen company's CEO Tor Andersen said to the press: "Our entire agreement with Carlsberg was in place. We had signed the documents, press releases were sent out in Norway and Denmark. Therefore, we are sitting here with the feeling of having been used in a larger game …." He added: "I understand completely that Carlsberg is choosing the far larger agreement with Orkla. But I would never myself use the sort of methods Carlsberg exploited in this case. We were kept in the dark until the last second. This is not good business practice …."[9]

Nobody, not even in Carlsberg, would deny that he had a point. The Danish Ashlad was not someone you could trust. Carlsberg's negotiations with Hansa Borg had been ongoing for three years ever since Hansa Borg was sold by Orkla on its acquisition of Ringnes. Lindeløv admitted in an interview in a Norwegian business paper that the story was not flattering: "We have a bad conscience that the management may feel we have cheated them", he said, while the head of Carlsberg's Nordic activities at the time, Nils Smedegaard Andersen, would only go so far as to say that there were people at Carlsberg who were "a bit sorry about how things went"; yet, he was not among them. He was rather satisfied. Business is business. Hansa Borg was quite simply a pawn in the game, and "if you can choose between a huge business and a tiny business, you choose the big one". This was neither the first nor the last time Carlsberg followed that rather cold piece of advice by keeping as many doors open as possible until it became clear whether you could go in through the largest gate with the right partner and come out on the other side with the spoils. Perhaps, not flattering but effective. Orkla, which had entered into the collaboration with more realistic intentions, soon learned first-hand that Carlsberg looked out for its own interests first and only thereafter—if at all—its partner's.

[9] Bent Højgaard Sørensen and Michael Olsen, *Berlingske Tidende, Erhverv* (18 August 2000), p. 5.

5.3 BBH—First Act

Carlsberg was never sincerely interested in Orkla itself. What was attractive and decisive for the alliance was not Orkla but what Orkla brought with it—particularly the breweries, the silver and gold in the fairy tale's language. The consolidation of the Nordic market and, particularly, the possibility of entering into the Russian beer market through BBH was the most important part of the rationale behind the agreement with Orkla. The second part of the story of Ashlad and the Norwegian troll, therefore, has to do with BBH of which Ashlad now owned half in a partnership with the 'troll' and how Ashlad avoided becoming a party in a *ménage à trois* with yet another partner, so they would have to share BBH with even more partners. Thus, Orkla was in possession of the key to the Russian market, which looked more than promising at the time, and Lindeløv was impressed by the great business opportunities in Russia. In addition to vodka, plenty of beer was consumed, it appeared, and the possibilities for expansion were significant. But everything was quite more complicated, due Russia's unpredictability, and the so-called BBH case came to haunt Carlsberg for years thereafter.

At that moment, the Finnish antitrust authorities made their conditions clear. They found that the agreement between the Carlsberg and Orkla breweries created a dominant position in the Finnish market. The Finnish authorities, therefore, required Orkla to sell off its 20% share of the Finnish company Hartwall or, in the alternative, Carlsberg to sell its interests in Finland if, together, they wanted to acquire the half of BBH owned by the Hartwall family. Orkla's desire, which Lindeløv supported, was for Carlsberg Breweries to acquire the half of BBH owned by Hartwall. The plan was to avoid some of the demands by Finnish antitrust authorities by taking Hartwall in as a third co-shareholder in cooperation with Carlsberg Breweries. With respect to Orkla, Lindeløv stated that there was a "common understanding" about the acquisition of full control over BBH, the complete details of which, however, his own board had not yet approval. As the requirements of the antitrust authorities were formulated, this would mean, among other things, that Carlsberg had to sell its interests in the Finnish brewery Sinebrychoff. On the other hand, Orkla was in the situation that, if they did not get Hartwell into the collaboration, they would have to sell *their* interests in Hartwall.

Orkla's Finn Jebsen had negotiated with the chairman of the Hartwall brewery, Gustav von Hertzen, who represented the Hartwall family. Jebsen had worked out an outline of a deal with Lindeløv. What Orkla's management found as "the best solution" was a merger between Carlsberg Breweries and Hartwall. They spoke about giving 10% to Hartwall with Carlsberg and Orkla each relinquishing 5%.

Carlsberg still wanted a majority with 50–55%, but after a stock issuance in connection with the IPO, they had to expect to drop under 51%; and, thus, this solution could lead to loss of controlling influence. Hartwell with its 50% of BBH would be part of the collaboration between Carlsberg and Orkla with a share that would not immediately change Carlsberg's dominance in Carlsberg Breweries, but which, in the long term, might mean that Carlsberg would lose control. It also implied that Carlsberg had to sell the Finnish brewery Sinebrychoff. A proposal in this direction was on the table at a board meeting at Carlsberg Breweries on 12 June 2001. Palle Marcus, chairman of the board of Carlsberg Breweries, stated that the negotiations were being conducted without his orientation. Of this approach, the chairman diplomatically used the word "inexpedient". Lindeløv did not have his support base behind him.

Palle Marcus and Poul Christian Matthiessen considered this sort of venture to be entirely too risky for Carlsberg. At that point, the remaining half of BBH could have been acquired for approximately DKK 7–8 billion, but both were reluctant to put such a large part of the company's assets into hazard-filled Russia, and they would certainly not be part of an arrangement that might lead to Carlsberg losing controlling influence and ending up in a minority position. Therefore, Carlsberg would not give its consent to something that could lead to a drop below 60% influence.

At the decisive board meeting at Carlsberg Breweries on 12 June 2001, therefore, Carlsberg's members rejected the proposed merger with Hartwall. They did not want to increase exposure in Russia; they wanted to retain 60% of Carlsberg Breweries. The result was that Orkla, therefore, had to sell its shares in Hartwall. The Carlsberg side prevailed with three votes against Orkla's two votes, cast by Finn Jebsen and Roar Engeland. Finn Jebsen, understandably from his point of view, said that Orkla was "uncomfortable with the decision-making process". What they considered to be a really good business opportunity was passed up, and their good relationship (to that point) with Hartwall turned ice-cold after negotiations failed. Hartwell felt they had been conducting futile negotiations to no end; and, in Orkla's view, Carlsberg was too fixated on its ownership structure and spoiled good business opportunities.

At a meeting in Oslo on 20 June 2001, the decision was confirmed; and, on 6 July 2001, Finn Jebsen wrote in reaction that Orkla's management was "very disappointed in Carlsberg A/S's response...." Orkla's head, Jens P. Heyerdahl, also said at a meeting at Carlsberg Breweries on 7 August that he considered the decision not to expand the commitment in Russia as "a dramatic and historic decision for Carlsberg Breweries A/S with unanticipated consequences". He was right about that although in a different way than he may have thought. This time, Orkla had to sell its shares in Hartwall in order to accommodate the Finnish competition authorities. Next time, even more had to be sold.

Whether the rejection was ultimately wise or not when it came to control of BBH can definitely be debated, and opinions will vary, depending on the side from which it is seen. Seen from Carlsberg's side, the concern for the outcome was understandable. In a 2007 letter to Poul Christian Matthiessen, Palle Marcus—much later—wrote that he was "convinced that the decisions we made in the 4½ years we worked closely together will be discussed very positively in the history of Carlsberg and the Foundation when it is written".[10]

Viewed in hindsight, this assessment is entirely understandable. The letter was written before Carlsberg in 2009 acquired the other half of BBH for a far larger sum than in 2000. But Marcus and Matthiessen simply did not dare take the plunge at that decisive point, and it was from this perspective the decision not to take on Hartwall as a partner must be seen. Had they done so, Carlsberg would have been one of three partners and would not have received a push in the direction of an independent development that we shall hear about in the following. The Ashlad in the fairy tale is a carefree soul who survives by luck and cunning, but it was presumably also a piece of luck that two more cautious relatives in this case could set a limit to his conduct. These two were worried about the risk of having such a large stake in a single market and especially at renouncing Carlsberg's controlling influence, which would have been an obvious result of taking in Hartwell as a partner. The risk was real enough that, by absorbing Hartwall into Carlsberg Breweries, Carlsberg might, in the not so long run, lose its dominant influence in a collaboration with Orkla and become the object of acquisition by others. At any rate, the opportunity was passed by. The Hartwall family shortly thereafter sold its shares as a part of a generational change. As a result, the Scottish brewery, Scottish & Newcastle (S&N), took over Hartwall and thereby the other half of BBH. Carlsberg Breweries then had to adapt to a new sort of cohabitation

[10]Marcus summarized the situation at that time in this way: "We made 3 bold decisions: Changed out the executive board and hired 2–3 serious managers, we rejected some partners, but chose one who could add value without being able take the majority away from the Foundation against our will, and we rejected a development that could have robbed the Foundation of its majority vote, which was very risky business-wise especially in light of the relatively poor economy in traditional Western European markets and in light of the insufficient/weak management we had then", see his letter of 8 May 2007.

in relation to BBH with someone with whom they only shared a table but not a bed.

The events surrounding BBH had serious consequences for the relationship between Lindeløv and the chairman of the board for Carlsberg Breweries. Marcus was already irritated at Lindeløv's conspicuous pleasure in expressing himself to the press; but even worse, in his view, was the fact that Lindeløv embarked on negotiations with Hartwall and Orkla without having his support base squared away. He was on his own in an understanding with Orkla's Jebsen and had gone around the board chairman much too far in discussing influence in Carlsberg Breweries with Hartwall. He had given an impression that he was negotiating on Carlsberg's behalf, which he was, in fact, actually doing but without a mandate to do so. Already in February 2001, Palle Marcus aired the possibility to Orkla that Carlsberg might part with its CEO. Marcus had begun to doubt whether Lindeløv was mostly Carlsberg's or Orkla's man. Perhaps, he was just his own person; but, for Marcus, he had negotiated too much as Orkla's man and, therefore, had committed, in Marcus' view, a "gross breach of confidence".

At Orkla, they looked—for good reason—more positively on Lindeløv's efforts. Orkla's Jens Heyerdahl, therefore, wanted to give him one more chance. Palle Marcus and Poul Christian Matthiessen then had a serious conversation with Lindeløv about the framework for future collaboration. In June 2001, however, Marcus reported to Orkla's management that they had lost confidence in Lindeløv. At Orkla, they understood the meaning of breach of confidence, but they wanted to keep Lindeløv, whom they understood and knew how to deal with better than with "the professors", as they called the Carlsberg A/S board. They asked for a postponement without getting into burdensome negotiations around Hartwall.

At Orkla, they were worried about disruption around the collaboration, but Orkla reluctantly accepted the resignation of Lindeløv with effect from 31 August 2001. The relationship with Orkla was shaken, first, by the rejection of the Hartwall collaboration and, now, by the dismissal of Lindeløv; but things were not made right even though Poul Christian Matthiessen recounted in a long, detailed letter to Finn Jebsen the many angles in his and Palle Marcus' considerations. Here, he pointed out, among other things, the central place in Danish society that Carlsberg A/S occupied and what a hefty obligation it was to maintain and promote this business in a way that respected the national Danish expectations as to Carlsberg. Therefore, they could not take on the risk that a commitment in Russia would entail or accept a diminution of ownership share and, thus, influence. Even this letter could not heal the wound. Carlsberg had forsaken some important business opportunities that Orkla was busy with, and now Carlsberg even fired the CEO who guaranteed good contact between Orkla and Carlsberg. A disappointed Finn Jebsen wrote back on 9 October about the opportunities Russia offered and the concern that Hartwall's BBH share—as it also happened—might come into "hostile hands". The collaboration had received its first dents and scratches, and confidence between the parties was never fully restored if it had ever actually been there.

In addition to the negotiations around Hartwell and BBH, it was on Lindeløv's debit ledger that Carlsberg's engagement in the East, Carlsberg Asia, went completely off the tracks. Once again, the board believed that Lindeløv had let them down. It turned on an agreement into which Michael Iuul had entered on Carlsberg's behalf with the colorful Thai "whisky king" Charoen, an agreement that proved to be very unfavorable for Carlsberg. Iuul had previously been good at finding partners in the East, but now things had gone wrong. Disappointed at being passed over after Svanholm's departure, Iuul chose, instead of slamming the door and leaving the firm, to stay on and build up his own empire with its own policy in London and, later, in the East as a more or less independent counterpart to the headquarters in Valby. A bit like the French cartoon figure Iznogoud, whose job description is grand vizier and who is known for saying: "I want to be Caliph instead of the Caliph", which in France is a standing expression for people who, without obviously being qualified, want to be supreme leader.

Poul Christian Matthiessen had already lost confidence in Michael Iuul after the experiences in the US. In Matthiessen's opinion, he had been far too eager to enter into a risky collaboration; and, gradually, the international work was taken over by Smedegaard Andersen, but Iuul had kept Asia. The idea here had been to find an influential, strong partner. Iuul succeeded to some extent, but the terms and conditions had been completely opaque. The deal for a joint venture into which Iuul had entered on Carlsberg's behalf proved not to live up to the requirements that Carlsberg had set and the board chairman, Palle Marcus, in his time had approved.

The intention was that, beyond paying a larger sum, Charoen was supposed to build a brewery in Bangkok and provide a profit guarantee; but, in the summer of 2001 when Lindeløv met their Thai partner, he discovered that the profit guarantee was missing. He had put his name to an agreement that was different from what was originally agreed to, relying on Iuul, who—it later turned out—was also on Charoen's payroll list, receiving a significant sum from Charoen. Thus, he was playing a double game. It all ended up being expensive for Carlsberg, which had to go through an arbitration case and pay compensation to Charoen.

On 1 September 2001, Lindeløv was replaced as CEO by Nils Smedegaard Andersen. Shortly thereafter, in 2002, Palle Marcus stepped down from Carlsberg's board for health reasons, and Carlsberg Breweries got a new chairman of the board, Jens Bigum, a well-known figure in Danish business and a successful CEO of the Arla Food Company. A part of the new strategy after 2000 had been ongoing replacements in Carlsberg's leadership. In 2000, CFO Walther Paulsen had to leave Carlsberg. In 2001, it was Lindeløv, and soon after (at the end of 2002) it was Michael Iuul's turn. After his departure, it became clear that things were even worse with Carlsberg Asia than first indicated. When, in 2003, Nils Smedegaard came to Bangkok to have a look at things, he discovered that their Thai partner Charoen had not invested the value they had agreed with him. He decided to cut off all connection with Charoen. The whole affair gave rise to considerations about Iuul's personal role in Carlsberg's commitments in Thailand. The word "fraud" was mentioned in this context. Beyond letting Carlsberg down in the negotiations, Iuul occupied paid posts on other boards with Charoen and had received large gifts, free vacation stays and other economic benefits. An arbitration tribunal was appointed; but, in order to avoid involving Carlsberg in a scandal, it ended with a settlement in which Iuul admitted receiving significant sums and paid Carlsberg compensation of around DKK ten million.

The adventure in Thailand wound up costing Carlsberg almost DKK 1 billion, an influential collaborative partner, momentum in Thailand and the rest of Asia, and its good reputation. On the other hand, they were now strategically free in Asia and could keep working in other directions on this huge potential market. Smedegaard was personally without blame for the turn of events in Thailand, but he had to deal with bad press as a result of this case and other problems such as the closing of breweries in Norway and Sweden. Smedegaard's answer to the question of how things were going was, at that time, a bit of a diversion: that they were making good headway and following the planned strategy, which was "necessary to be able to take on all competitors".[11]

5.4 Half and Half

The 2001 courting of Hartwall, which came to nothing, had left behind a Hartwall family that felt Carlsberg had treated them badly. Once again, Carlsberg had acted the part of carefree Ashlad and given the impression of not respecting the other party with whom they were negotiating. The Hartwall

[11] *Politiken*, 7 August 2003.

family was forced to sell for other reasons, and in the end the Hartwell half of BBH was bought by the Scottish brewery Scottish & Newcastle (S&N) for what corresponded to DKK 15 billion of which a part was paid as shares in S&N. Thus, one of their competitors on the European market had become owner of half of Baltic Beverages Holding (BBH), which Carlsberg had not dared to acquire in 2001 on the given conditions. S&N now possessed the other half of the golden nugget, and possession of full mastery of it became more and more tantalizing since it seemed that the Russian thirst for beer was insatiable as in Ukraine and other former Soviet states, including the Baltics, where BBH's largest asset Baltika was the dominant brewery. Therefore, the third act has to do with Ashlad's frustrations at having to share BBH with others even though he had not dared to get it all in the first instance. Ashlad went for the gold, or—to put it more prosaically—an important strategic goal for Carlsberg was now getting control of the Russian market by acquiring complete mastery of BBH. Therefore, Scottish & Newcastle became the next "target".

Seated in Edinburgh, S&N was one of the biggest brewery enterprises in Great Britain. S&N was also an old brewery with roots back to 1749, when William Younger began brewing beer in Edinburgh. There was even an ancient connection with Carlsberg. During a study tour in England and Scotland in 1868, Carl Jacobsen visited this brewery for six months. The report he gave his father on it confirmed, wrote J. C. Jacobsen to Carl, that "the impression I had formed of Younger's breweries was quite correct, and it cannot be anything but an elementary school for you. This is, at base, regrettable, but for the moment there is nothing to do but use it to learn what can be learned".[12] J. C. Jacobsen actually doubted whether Carl should stay in Edinburgh for the six months he had paid for, "because time is far more precious to you than £ Sterling." On the other hand, Carl was happy about the more cheerful sides of life in Edinburgh, while his father warned against "strong English drink" and asked him to consider going somewhere he could learn malting and the rudiments of brewing. Carl's stay was a sort of refined industrial espionage masked as a paid guest visit. His father expected detailed information from Carl about the brewery and the opportunities for exporting to the British Isles and colonies.[13] At the end of the 1860s, J. C. Jacobsen considered exporting beer to Edinburgh but gave it up, among other things, because his son's visit to Younger had shown that a competitor,

[12]Letter to Carl of 8 December 1868.

[13]Do. 9 December 1868. On Carlsberg's export to England, which was begun in 1869, see Fraenkel (1897), p. 356 f.

albeit at minimal scale, "would hardly be welcomed by brewers there".[14] Since then, a lot had happened. Younger's brewery grew over the years; and, after a merger in 1931, the brewery now was called Scottish Brewers, which again in 1960 joined with Newcastle Breweries and thereby got its name. The brewery had purchased other British and foreign breweries and, at that time, was the leading brewery in Great Britain. In addition to half of BBH, they owned the French Kronenbourg 1664 along with Foster's, John Smith's and the cider factory Strongbow in Great Britain, the Portuguese Sagres, and the Finnish Lapin Kulta. Just under half of the turnover was in Great Britain, approximately 17% in Eastern Europe through BBH, and the remainder in the rest of Europe. The turnover in 2005 was around GBP 4 billion. This was about the size of Carlsberg. Thus, S&N should not be seen as an entirely impossible mouthful for Ashlad.

S&N would have liked to enter into a closer collaboration with Carlsberg more than just around BBH. In 2002, the chairman of the Scottish brewery Sir Brian Stuart sent out strong feelers, which were discussed at Carlsberg before they were ultimately rejected. The risk once again was that, with a merger, Carlsberg might lose influence and identity. S&N and Carlsberg were reminiscent of each other in size but, if Orkla was also a part, Carlsberg's ownership share and influence would be so much reduced that it could end up with Carlsberg having neither controlling nor significant influence. The possible collaboration with S&N was discussed under the code name *Drive*. Keeping the Foundation's status as a unique Danish institution with an important social role in culture, art, and science was the first priority. It was an issue whether Danish "society" would accept Carlsberg being run by non-Danish owners even if such ownership would give the Foundation a better return. In the long run, S&N's owners could hardly guarantee "controlling" or "significant" influence to Carlsberg. There was a risk that the breweries and the main office would not be located in Denmark. It would be a purely financial investment in a foreign brewery.[15] At a board meeting on 27 September 2002, Poul Christian Matthiessen, as chairman, concluded that "a realization of the Drive project could not be recommended". This point of view was supported by the other foundation board members and by Carlsberg's external board members. The main reason was that the necessary 'significant influence' would not be effectively ensured. In addition, there were considerations of insecurity about new EU rules governing takeover attempts, competition law problems in Great Britain, and risks around requirements for material sell-offs in Great Britain.

[14]Do. 17 November 1868.

[15]File 402. Carlsberg A/S—Board meetings 2002, in G 273.

A particular problem connected with the 50/50 ownership of BBH by Carlsberg Breweries and S&N was that they could not just let time go by. The rules of the game included a so-called 'shoot-out' (or 'shot-gun') clause, which meant that, if one of the owners of BBH wanted out, a written offer to sell was to be submitted and the other party could then choose to buy at the offered price or, vice versa, sell its shares at the same price. Thus, the offerors had to be prepared to sell or to buy for the offered sum, and the latter might be a problem if they did not have the necessary capital or the possibility of raising it. On the other hand, Carlsberg knew that S&N had significant debt, and the risk that S&N would take the initiative by exploiting the clause, therefore, was deemed limited. Ultimately, the assembled board rejected the idea of a merger between Carlsberg Breweries and S&N but noted that Carlsberg now had an understanding as to the structure of the collaboration with S&N and an insight into its plans that might be of use when a position had to be taken later.[16]

The amendment of the Carlsberg Foundation charter in 2000 and the initiation of a close collaboration with Orkla had been a step in the right direction. Nevertheless, it was soon clear—at any rate, for Carlsberg—that the business collaboration between the two could not function over the long term. It had quickly turned out that the encounter with Orkla was also an encounter with a somewhat different business culture. There was no foundation behind Orkla or professors on the board. It was and is all about business. Orkla might even have had the intention to acquire Carlsberg at some point, while Orkla was too big and too differentiated a mouthful for Carlsberg. Carlsberg was exclusively interested in getting its hands on the former Orkla-owned breweries, which were now in Carlsberg Breweries. For Carlsberg, the collaboration between the two was strategic and, first and foremost, had to do with access to new markets. Seen from that angle, the years with Orkla were a breakthrough for Carlsberg with respect to its self-image, its understanding of Carlsberg as a business, and its insight into what it would mean to be on the global market. The Orkla era was also an eye-opener with respect to the opportunities to stand on their own.

For Orkla, on the other hand, it was difficult to understand and accept the decision-making process at Carlsberg, but it was not a decisive matter for Orkla, which could live with the "professors" as long as they did not interfere too much, as they did not. Much later, Palle Marcus described the Foundation's other members and their participation in board work by saying that they "were good at asking questions" but that they "did not or only very

[16]Case file 402. Carlsberg A/S—Board meetings, in G 273.

rarely contribute constructive proposals".[17] That was just not the way they did things at Orkla, where they were used to thinking business was business, run by professionals. For them, it was a strange thought that respect for the mindset behind a more than hundred-year-old foundation would stand in the way of good business. Respect for the professors as business leaders was limited at Orkla, and the Carlsberg model was not something they wanted to emulate. But the Norwegians had no desire to leave the collaboration for this reason as long as it was profitable in other ways.

The relationship did not get better when, in March 2003, Orkla opposed Carlsberg CEO Smedegaard's desire to purchase the Peroni brewery in Italy, which would have given Carlsberg a leading position (along with Heineken) in the Italian market. A purchase agreement was ready when Orkla suddenly pulled out. Later in 2003, however, Carlsberg acquired the German Holsten brewery for DKK eight billion. But it was still not the really big score, and Carlsberg's management was up for much more. The Peroni disappointment was probably the triggering event for the later break with Orkla. Not that a possible purchase of Peroni was accompanied by great expectations, but it was a part of the strategy to take Carlsberg further.

In August 2003, stock analysts stated that Carlsberg Breweries was doing more poorly than its competitors. Stuart Price from the financial house West LB Panmure had some fun rewriting the brewery's slogan as "Probably the Worst Brewer in the World". On 16 August, an irritated Nils Smedegaard said of the analysis to a Danish newspaper that "it was a little too smart-alecky and, anyway, West LB is Probably the Worst Bank in the World with what you hear about them out in the world".[18]

5.5 Ashlad Runs Off with the Gold

Carlsberg had entered into a collaboration with Orkla to strengthen its own position and not because they had any particular desire to collaborate. Afterwards, people talked about a sort of "clash of cultures", but this could not cover up the reality that, from a very early point, Carlsberg was waiting for the right moment to get out of it again. The concern was to get it done before it was Orkla's turn to occupy the chairmanship post of Carlsberg Breweries, which, by agreement, rotated between the parties. Since the middle of 2003, with Nils Smedegaard at the helm, Carlsberg's management was not inclined

[17] Letter from Palle Marcus to P. C. Matthiessen of 18 November 2017.

[18] Lunde (2008), p. 132.

to give collaboration any more chances. Smedegaard was supported by Carlsberg A/S's new deputy chairman Jens Bigum, whose blunt philosophy was that, once a decision is made, it should be implemented as quickly as possible. Thus was launched the fourth and final part of the story of Ashlad and the troll, which has to do with how Carlsberg had the troll thrown out and ran away with the gold.

Since entering into the collaboration with Orkla, a number of changes had taken place. The Foundation's chairman was the person who, externally and internally with respect to Carlsberg, pulled the load. As chairman, Poul Christian Matthiessen had understood and wanted to accommodate the brewery's needs in a completely different way than his predecessor and far more actively than any previous chairman. Together with the deputy chairman at Carlsberg (in this case, Palle Marcus), he had taken part in crucial decisions about the brewery and its operations. With the establishment of Carlsberg Breweries as a subsidiary, with a businessman as its chairperson to run the breweries, and with the Carlsberg Foundation's chairman as chairperson for the board of Carlsberg A/S, leadership had been distributed in an expedient manner. Business know-how had been made a priority, and this was noticed.

Poul Christian Matthiessen would turn 70 in 2003. As his successor on the board, another distinguished professor of economics was chosen, Professor Niels Kærgaard. A pharmacy professor, Povl Krogsgaard-Larsen, who at that time had become rector of the School of Pharmacy, was elected as new chairman. He could sometimes be loose-tongued from a business perspective when it came to spilling information about Carlsberg to the press. This was noted, commented on, and sometimes criticized, but he was tough on decision-making. The big issue was getting out of the collaboration with Orkla as best they could, and the new chairman soon realized this. The desire to break with Orkla was entirely on Carlsberg's side. The Norwegians were at first surprised and later became quite embittered. Orkla saw the advantages the collaboration brought and had no desire to break off the relationship in an untimely way even if there were disagreements. At the end of May 2003, the designation Omega was given to a Carlsberg project, the aim of which was to buy Orkla out of Carlsberg Breweries as quickly as possible. On 27 June 2003, a meeting was held at Carlsberg's initiative in Oslo at which Carlsberg declared its intention to stop further collaboration and offered to acquire Orkla's shares for approximately DKK 10 billion.[19] In the alternative, they would push for an IPO. At Orkla, the decision evoked consternation. Orkla's Danish attorney was called home from abroad to a crisis meeting. Orkla was

[19]Mentioned by Krogsgaard-Larsen (2011), pp. 173 ff.

inclined to forget that such a meeting had taken place or, with yet another Norwegian troll metaphor, "to put the troll in the bottle again". Orkla would like to go on and did not want to sell, but, if the parties inevitably had to split, Orkla preferred for each party to take back its original assets. Of course, that was not an option for Carlsberg, which wanted to get its hands on the breweries. Orkla had brought into the relationship breweries that now belonged to Carlsberg Breweries, and Carlsberg's standpoint was that the parties must respect the common ownership with Carlsberg owning 60%. Thus, Carlsberg was in a position to buy out Orkla. The price in the end was high. Carlsberg raised the offer to DKK 11.5 billion, while Orkla demanded DKK 16 billion. In December 2003, Carlsberg threatened to call an extraordinary general meeting, where it would make use of its rights as majority shareholder. The matter was decided in meetings at Copenhagen Airport on 26–27 January 2004 and again on 18–19 February, when a sales price of DKK 14.8 billion was agreed.

It all ended in 2004, much to Orkla's surprise, with Carlsberg running off with the Orkla's assets. The price was formidable in the terms of the day. A few years earlier, Orkla had paid far less for the breweries. The price was also more than Carlsberg had imagined but still a trifle in relation to the sums that would later be on the table with new acquisitions. Carlsberg had to go into debt. The financing required a share issue in which the Carlsberg Foundation bought Carlsberg B-shares for over a billion Danish crowns, and the equity interest in Carlsberg A/S fell from 55 to 51%. In the history of Orkla,[20] the last round in the collaboration was described in this way: "A little before 1 p.m. on 18 February 2004, Orkla's board voted, over the objections of the employee representative, to sell Orkla's 40 percent equity interest in Carlsberg Breweries to Carlsberg AS. The sale represented the largest single transaction in Orkla's history. Orkla's net compensation was under DKK 15 billion or NOK 17.5 billion. The financial yield was very good".

At Orkla, not surprisingly, there was great dissatisfaction at being bought out in this way by "the professors". Yet, it was not them but Carlsberg's executive board of directors that had spun the web. Still, it was more fun to have "professors" as the object of hate. Orkla's Finn Jebsen put it this way in the newspaper *Berlingske Tidende*: "Of course, we have respect for the Foundation's role in Danish society and cultural life, but, commercially, the Foundation is sparsely equipped ...." He may have been right, but behind the Foundation was a professional Carlsberg management that was at least as determined as the management of Orkla.

---

[20]Espeli (2004), p. 349.

Worse from a Norwegian national point of view was that, upon the dissolution of the collaboration, Carlsberg ran off with the arch-Norwegian brewery Ringnes, one of the country's crown jewels in public opinion. Orkla had simply sold off one of its core areas, the beverage business, and even though there were still breweries in Norway, they were not Ringnes. The national brewery Ringnes was lost forever and, suddenly, the mega-company Orkla was not so mega any more. The loss of the Ringness brewery, founded in 1876, was described in the Norwegian press as something along the lines of a national catastrophe. During a press conference in a full concert hall in Oslo, Finn Jebsen had to make the admission that it "is a sale we undertake with a heavy heart, but cold intellect and sound reasoning dictate that this is the right move. This is in our shareholders' interest ... Orkla wanted to buy all of Carlsberg, but since that was not possible, we had to settle for this, instead. We sold it at what we believe is a good price ... The parties have moved away from each other, and conflict has been a growing".[21]

The Norwegian paper *Finans* quoted Christian Ringnes, a descendant of the brewery's founders, saying: "You can put it this way: a country without its own brand of beer is like a man without his potency." The Norwegian historian Espeli probably hits close to home when he explains Orkla's defeat in this way:

"The point is rather that, in the view of Orkla's management in the spring of 2000, the Carlsberg Foundation was not assessed as any significant risk factor".[22]

Orkla simply had not done its homework well enough and become acquainted with Carlsberg's special foundation structure or understood that, in reality, Carlsberg was playing a game that resembled their own folktale of Ashlad, whom no honest troll could trust. After the breach of agreement, people at Orkla were bitter and angry at Carlsberg. Of the "professors" on the board, Finn Jebsen had already said that, commercially, they were "very sparsely equipped".[23] In those circles, 'Denmark' became a dirty word. Danish business methods were compared to the Dutch, and this was not a compliment. The anger between Carlsberg and Orkla about terminating the collaboration was expressed in two particular provisions in the final agreement. One aired the possibility of a compensation claim, and the other established a special penalty for the injury and inconvenience that the termination of the collaboration had meant for the proud Norwegian concern: In this case, DKK 80 million.

[21]NRK 19 Feb. 2004.

[22]Espeli (2004), p. 367.

[23]Espeli (2004), p. 378.

It might be that Orkla had—or gave the impression of having—an ambition to take over Carlsberg at some time. At any rate, there were those at Orkla, who figured, as it appears in the minutes from May 2000, that "Carlsberg would probably not be an independent company in 2–3 years".[24] Statements by Orkla boss Jens Heyerdahl had been interpreted to indicate that Orkla was probably harboring conceptions of an imminent takeover. At any rate, Orkla felt "duped" by the Carlsberg Foundation, and they may have been right. Carlsberg breached a collaboration agreement that had been intended to last a longer period of time. Orkla was outmaneuvered by people who were not suspected to being capable of such a brutal course of action. Orkla had placed too much confidence in Flemming Lindeløv and also accepted a minority status in the collaboration without securing a better position for itself. It was an advantage for Orkla to merge its beverage business with Carlsberg since Pripps-Ringnes was not in a strong position and a competitive relationship with Carlsberg could easily have developed in a threatening direction. Pripps-Ringnes worked well as a part of Carlsberg Breweries, but it was felt all the more as an industrial setback when they were left empty-handed in 2004.

The architect behind it all was Carlsberg CEO Nils Smedegaard Andersen, who, when asked whether he was happy that Carlsberg was once again in Danish hands, coolly replied: "Whether Carlsberg is in Danish hands or not, I don't think is very important. Many of our shareholders are foreign anyway. My chief pride is in the fact that we have created a strong firm and that we could afford to buy Holsten and Orkla's shares and, thus, create a simple structure. This was not in the cards three years ago".[25]

5.6 In Search of a Partner

"They're all in bed with each other", wrote the German journalist and observer of the beer industry, Ina Verstl, about the incessant consolidations and mergers on the global beer market in recent years.[26] Carlsberg was not reticent and wantonly leaped into the mix. Sometimes, they remained at the edge of the bed; but, at other times, as we shall hear, they threw themselves into the great escapade—albeit, it had more to do with money and influence than love and sex. Partners such as Orkla, who had done their part, were pitilessly cast aside, so Carlsberg could be free to pursue another. The affair

[24] Espeli (2004), p. 368.

[25] In Carlsberg's personnel magazine *Kilden* and quoted by Lunde (2008), p. 325.

[26] Quoted by Swinnon and Briski (2017), p. 60.

ended with Carlsberg—of course, with appropriate compensation—unilaterally ending the relationship, having absorbed Orkla's share of the estate, the breweries. In the agreement with Orkla ending the affair, however, there was a condition that, if Carlsberg were to sell the breweries Orkla brought into Carlsberg Breweries within a three-year period from March 2004 to December 2006, Orkla would get 40% of the profits. This was especially dangerous in relation to S&N, the co-owner of BBH, which could trigger the shoot-out clause.

Such clauses are entirely customary, and it meant in this case that Carlsberg, if it didn't want to pay out a huge sum, had to control itself for a long period of time and hope that the other party would do the same. This was a little thing in relation to the main result achieved by buying out Orkla, namely, that the complex ownership structure was dissolved and the parties no longer had to consult each other. Carlsberg was now sitting at its own—considerably larger—table and was free to enter new relationships. The main thing was for the table to be bigger with room for more, and Carlsberg could not have done this without a detour around Orkla. And, as it often happens, they also learned something about themselves and their own values in the confrontation with the talented Norwegian businessmen from Orkla. Carlsberg came out of the relation self-conscious and strengthened in many senses. Confidence in the firm was approaching 100% after they had shown they could flex their muscles and win. Materially, Carlsberg came out of it owning half of BBH and thereby possessed a key to the Eastern European and Russian markets, and *that* was what they wanted much more than they really wanted the Norwegians. It had been expensive, and now Carlsberg had to work to bring down the debt and discuss the most obvious next goal, namely, a closer connection with or an acquisition of S&N. The next battle, therefore, had to deal with the half of BBH that was now part of a joint venture with S&N. Feelers from S&N on a closer collaboration or a merger with Carlsberg had been rejected. The two were now together in the ownership of BBH, and the question was whether they were just going to continue in this way or whether one of the partners would try to gain control of it all. Another risk was that another large brewery would look longingly at one of the partners and buy either all of S&N or their share of BBH. Here and now, however, the acquisition of BBH was still too large a mouthful for Carlsberg. In 2006, therefore, closer cooperation with either the American brewery, Coors, or with the somewhat larger and still growing InBev was also discussed. Here, the danger was not just becoming the minor partner but being swallowed up entirely in the long term. InBev was, apparently, an inexhaustible purchaser of breweries against whom one had to be on guard.

The most obvious possibility in reality was to stick with S&N. Everything would be fine if the parents could work out the common custody rights over their daughter BBH. Back in 2002, the Carlsberg Foundation had investigated the legal ramifications of such a collaboration, including English law, and had come to the conclusion that S&N was too big to absorb. Carlsberg would not be able to count on having a majority and thereby ultimate control in the same way as with Orkla. But they were still tied to each other, and Carlsberg's chairmen P. C. Matthiessen and later Povl Krogsgaard-Larsen, therefore, conducted more non-binding conversations privately with S&N's external gentleman-chairman, Sir Brian Stewart, about the possibilities.

The shoot-out clause, in principle, could be activated at any point by one of the two parties to force a purchase or sale of the other party's share of BBH. It was like a ticking time bomb that could blow up at any moment. And as long as the agreement to compensate Orkla was valid, it was important not to provoke an activation of the clause. Carlsberg's economic latitude after the purchase of Orkla's breweries was markedly reduced, and the options for activating this clause offensively with a purchase offer, therefore, were limited. In a letter dated 24 November 2004 to the chairman of the Foundation, CEO Nils Smedegaard Andersen predicted as a realistic possibility that, if some action was not taken, Carlsberg would lose its half of BBH before too long and that it would soon be reduced to a regional brewery. He found it crucial, therefore, to retain BBH and worked for a closer collaboration with S&N. The joint overall management of BBH was going quite well, and both parties agreed that they should have Russian management to an appropriate extent at the local level, people who had the necessary contact with the somewhat unpredictable Russian politicians and authorities. For Carlsberg, it was now a matter of deciding among various scenarios in relation to S&N.

The opportunities for another expansion were limited in the beer world as it looked at that time. Entrance on the American market, which was dominated by other beer giants, was difficult. The negotiations with Coors in the 1990s had been broken off when the opportunity for a collaboration with Orkla became a reality in the spring of 2000. Nor did Heineken succeed in building up an international distribution network. China, on the other hand, became a new target area. Here, in 2005, Carlsberg owned a brewery in Hong Kong and in Dali and shares in Lanzhou Huanghe Brewery, Wusu Brewery, breweries in Xinjiang, Lhasa, and Guangdong, and a newly-built brewery in Qinghai province. At that point, about 10% of Carlsberg's earnings came from these and other Asian breweries in Southeast Asia. Carlsberg did not choose the central part of China, which was well-covered, beer-wise, but areas in which there was an opportunity for expansion. In 2002 and 2003, breweries in Bulgaria and Serbia were also acquired. The strategy in western China was reminiscent of what Carlsberg had learned in Eastern Europe, where they acquired (as a rule) cheap, local brands that could be developed into something bigger. The chosen strategy in which the preference was to be leading in a local area rather than invisible in a larger area led to the prominence of Carlsberg in the less affluent—and therefore also less beer consuming—western China with a market share of 60%. However, it was still, first and foremost, Eastern Europe and Russia that were considered to be the growth markets. There were a number of opportunities in China; two breweries were bought in Yunnan province. Still, the average citizen annually only drank four liters of beer compared to the 97 liters consumed in Denmark. But demand in China was developing, and Smedegaard correctly believed that it was a growth area.[27]

After the expiry of the dissolution agreement with Orkla at the end of 2006, it became quite pertinent to get on with the relationship with S&N. Here, it was necessary to go quite far. A genuine collaboration with S&N was still a possibility, but the Scottish brewery had become so large that Carlsberg did not have a chance of acquiring the brewery alone. Therefore, if they wanted the other half of BBH for themselves, the only possibility was for Carlsberg to get capital and, if possible, find a partner with whom to share expenses and plunder. And it would inevitably be expensive. Financially, S&N had long been too much of a mouthful, and it was feared it might be the dominant party in a closer cooperation. In the intervening years, however, Carlsberg had worked its way up; and, in 2007, Carlsberg was financially ready to match the Scottish side. They were now again relatively equivalent in size and, thus, equally matched players on the unsettled beer scene.

As late as 1 March 2007, the Carlsberg Foundation's chairman, Jens Bigum, and CEO Nils Smedegaard Andersen met at Carlsberg with Sir Brian Stewart and CEO Tony Froggart from S&N. Krogsgaard-Larsen expressed his assurance about the advantages of a collaboration between the two. On the other hand, he did not downplay the difficulties of potential charter amendment requirements, the involvement of the Danish Royal Academy, the approval of the authorities ("probably, the prime minister will be involved"), that all these parties had to be presumed to be conservative and less "supportive", and that "the window will probably be narrow". He outlined as the Foundation's "flag issues" or fixed conditions for a closer cooperation that the name of Carlsberg must be retained with its principal place of business in Copenhagen. S&N, on the other hand, wanted a main office to be located in London or Edinburgh. The brewery management with the cosmopolitan

---

[27] *Børsen*, 12 April 2004.

CEO Nils Smedegaard Andersen at its head could accept that and even see the advantages of a head office outside Denmark. But this was a deal-breaker for the "professors", who considered it their job to preserve a Danish business in Denmark, as it was also said at the meeting on 1 March 2007.

Once again, Old Jacobsen was 'consulted'. With some good will, it might be thought he would have accepted his brewery's international expansion but, with respect to the location of the head office, he was supposed to have said: "This far and no further". Moving away from Denmark would be a slippery slope. Or as Krogsgaard-Larsen later put it: "Throughout my time as chairman of Carlsberg, it has been decisive for me to have Carlsberg remain in Danish hands".[28] Carlsberg was Danish, and it would remain domiciled in Denmark. If S&N could not go along with that, then they had to think along different lines. With respect to S&N's Sir Brian, therefore, it was a matter of keeping up appearances for what soon afterwards proved to be a really wicked play, namely, to go *after* instead of going *with* S&N.

Yet, Carlsberg kept the option open for a more wide-ranging collaboration with S&N—or feigned to do so—in March 2007. In a letter as late as 19 March 2007 to Sir Brian Stewart, the Carlsberg Foundation's chairman explained evasively that the opportunities for a charter amendment to pave the way for a "merger" between Carlsberg and S&N were even narrower than they reckoned. In particular, it turned on the location and name of the headquarters. The Carlsberg Foundation stood firm on this. Therefore, a consolidation was no longer considered "a realistic possibility", but meetings and talks could still continue.

Whatever the solution might be, it was necessary to raise more capital, and the demand that the Carlsberg Foundation should own 51% of the shares was an obstacle. A charter amendment was legally necessary. Sir Brian knew that Carlsberg was not big enough to threaten S&N by itself. What he did not know or, perhaps, had not entirely realized was that behind this peculiar construction of a scientific/cultural foundation with a professor as board chairman hid a hard-as-nails management strategy: once a decision was made, it was purposefully put into motion without unnecessary sentimentality or rumination. Nor did he know that, for some time with great secrecy, Carlsberg had already been preparing a charter amendment, which was to be the tool to realize Carlsberg's expansion strategy. Moreover, the amendment might not even cause major difficulties with the supervising authorities as Krogsgaard-Larsen had intimated at the meeting at Carl's Villa on 1 March.

---

[28] Krogsgaard-Larsen (2001), p. 158.

5.7 First Countdown

The most recent charter amendment in 2000 had been far too cautious, and the question was now how to loosen the requirement that the Foundation had to own 51% of the capital. The Carlsberg Foundation had to prepare an amendment to the charter, which permitted it to raise capital of sufficient size to proceed aggressively as a buyer on the brewery market. The next step, therefore, was of a legal nature. If the charter amendment in 2000 was viewed as a test of how far Carlsberg had been able to get the Royal Academy and the Ministry of Justice to go, this was something that might be thought to go against what the Brewer in his time had written or could be presumed to have believed to an even higher degree. It was not just about merging with others or establishing joint subsidiaries but, quite simply, giving up the fundamental requirement of owning a majority of share capital in Carlsberg. Today, we know that this would hardly have been a problem if they had only noted what the Danish Ministry of Justice had already approved in 1981; but this important piece of information had been lost at the time in the Foundation chairman's struggle to "keep the gold".

In 2007, the goal was to get so much money into the till that more breweries could be acquired with the aim of getting a consolidated position on the international market. The thought process behind it had nothing to do with Jacobsen but more to do with growth, dividends, and distributions. This required capital and presumed that shares should be sold to raise capital and not kept in a box by the Foundation. The question, therefore, was how far the Carlsberg Foundation could be permitted to go in reducing ownership in Carlsberg A/S. The Foundation's chairman contacted the Ministry of Justice about this in the late summer of 2004. At a meeting with representatives of the Ministry of Justice in September 2004, Povl Krogsgaard-Larsen, who turned up alone in order to stress the deeply confidential nature of the inquiry, had sounded out the possibilities for approving a Carlsberg Foundation charter amendment that would make it possible to raise enough capital to enter into new markets. The charter amendment in 2000, it was plainly obvious, was insufficient for this purpose. The argument was principally that, if Carlsberg wished to retain its position as an important beer label, as Jacobsen had wanted, a charter amendment was necessary. At the same time, Krogsgaard stressed that the Foundation wanted to keep control through a majority vote as was possible according to Danish law, which allowed different classes of shareholders with different votes, e.g., up to ten times more. This meant that the Carlsberg Foundation could be in the minority as to capital but still retain its dominant influence by possessing a majority of shares in a class with higher voting rights.

The meeting with the Ministry was informative. Nothing was written down, nor was any statement made by the Ministry, but they had heard and understood the message. Carlsberg's lawyers, therefore, prepared a series of memos to illuminate various legal possibilities and risks. What they did not do was look into the old minutes or dossiers in the Carlsberg Foundation's archives. Had they done so, they might have discovered that, already in the 1980s, the Ministry of Justice had sanctioned an interpretation of the 51% ownership requirement as voting shares instead of share capital, but no one knew that in 2004. No one mentioned that, in reality, the Ministry of Justice had long ago given the green light.

At the meeting in September 2004 with the Ministry of Justice, the Foundation submitted a declaration of the need for a new charter amendment, feeling that the Ministry of Justice would take a sympathetic position.[29] In May 2005, the chairman again met alone with the Ministry of Justice, and it was agreed that the Carlsberg Foundation need only maintain a stake of at least 51% of the votes in Carlsberg A/S. The reason given for the change in the charter's requirement was to maintain Carlsberg's position as a leading beer label. Thus, in addition to referring to developments in the beer market, the board pointed out an essential connection to the "golden words" about achieving the highest degree of "perfection" in beer production.

A desire for confidentiality was obvious. On one side, there was a risk that someone might discover that Carlsberg was strengthening its capital resources and begin to wonder why. That would pose a problem in relation to the secret negotiations for a takeover of S&N. On the other side, there was also a risk that someone with veneration for foundations and foundation law and respect for old charters would begin to write about the case and thereby create difficulties.

Many people had to be convinced, but that turned out not to be so hard after all—at least, not as difficult as they had given the impression of. The first and most difficult hurdle had not been, as some believed, getting the Ministry of Justice to approve such a significant amendment of the charter. Even though the old permission to do so was forgotten, they could, in addition to the important business reasons, refer to the fact that other foundations—for example, the Novo Nordisk Foundation—had previously been allowed to change their ownership conditions. The task really was just to add more words and build up the argumentation, so the Ministry of Justice

[29] Undated memo, *The Carlsberg Foundation* (in folder Strategy 2011–12).

could officially grant its permission. At first, it was decided to maintain a requirement that the Foundation should at least own more than 25% of the capital. The 25% idea was inspired by the so-called breakthrough rule in EU directive 25/2004, called the EU takeover directive.[30] According to this rule, an owner of more than 75% of the shares in a firm—without respect to voting rights differences—could require the calling of a general meeting and require the installation of new management. If you owned at least 25%, you were protected against such an attack. This limit was entirely redundant, as it depended completely on the Foundation whether shares in such an amount would be sold. It is difficult to see other motives from the consulting lawyers' point of view than keeping a reason for another change of the Charter later.

Changes in the charter had to be approved by the Danish Royal Academy. It was necessary to explain how the latest charter amendment had not been far-reaching enough. Confidential material had been sent to members of the Royal Academy, which discussed the matter on Thursday, 12 April and Thursday, 26 April 2007. At the first meeting, the need for capital expansion and the legal considerations with respect to the charter amendment were explained. No one in the room even asked a question. The Academy is a knowledgeable assembly. Despite great learning within more specialized disciplines and, as a rule, even with a very rudimentary understanding of big business, it can also understand that it is a serious matter when the Carlsberg Foundation asks for a charter amendment enabling it to acquire necessary capital. At the second meeting with the Royal Academy, however, a single voice[31] pointed out that the amendment was apparently not in agreement with the phrasing of the charter's §14.1, which stated that the capital requirement must "*ingensinde*" ("never") be deviated from. This was quite rightly spotted. What was not answered, however, was that the "*ingensinde*", even though it sounded old-fashioned, was not placed in the charter until 1970 and, therefore, did not require the same veneration one would have for the Brewer's own words.

That next day, Carlsberg issued a press release that a charter amendment was being sought to make possible a doubling of Carlsberg's share capital at the same time that the Carlsberg Foundation retained the majority of votes in the firm. It was stressed that "the Foundation's preservation of a majority vote will ensure that Carlsberg may continue as an independent business with the values and well-known brands that are an essential part of the firm's heritage and identity."

[30]Directive 2004/25/EU of 21 April on takeover bids. The directive is not implemented in Denmark. So, here, too, they were unnecessarily cautious, as it turned out.

[31]Krogsgaard-Larsen (2001), p. 198. The member in question was Professor Lene Koch.

On that same day the application was submitted, i.e., 27 April 2007, Carlsberg CEO Nils Smedegaard Andersen announced that he would step down from the management of Carlsberg A/S. He had accepted a position as CEO of the major Danish firm Mærsk, ranked as number one in Danish business. It was an offer he could not refuse. At first, this news was kept between the parties, but it was clear that a new management board would be appointed before long and also that Carlsberg had to inform the public about it very soon. Krogsgaard-Larsen and Bigum agreed on the strategy, and the goal was still clear. It was still a matter of bringing Carlsberg into the elite of global brewers through growth and about achieving this without losing the brewery's historical and traditional anchoring in Denmark. Therefore, it was still a requirement for the headquarters to remain in Denmark and for the brewery to be named Carlsberg. That was, after all, the reason they had refused approaches from S&N.

On 15 May 2007, the Ministry of Justice approved the requested amendment. The Ministry had stressed that the amendment was a means to maintain the purpose provision of the charter, which in turn was to ensure the quality of Carlsberg beer. It was also emphasized how the previous charter amendment had not met the desire to acquire capital to a sufficient degree and that an amendment was necessary for the foundation to meet the quality requirement and maintain the brewery's place in the international beer market.

The fundamental break with J. C. Jacobsen's ideas and values was the 1970 amendment that enabled Carlsberg to become a shareholder company. We might—justifiably—be skeptical about any hypothesis as to what J. C. Jacobsen's position might have been, had he lived. It was now established that the main concerns were not how to run an independent quality brewery but ownership shares, voting rights, and the danger of falling behind economically on the market. The most important thing was that Carlsberg and the Foundation were now legally equipped to go hunting for new partners.

5.8 Going Dutch

"To go Dutch" or "going Dutch" is an idiom that means that each party pays for themselves when they do something together. The expression in some way implies that the Dutch are considered stingy and do not like to pay for others. In this respect, Danes may easily be mistaken for Dutchmen. Both peoples are known for dividing restaurant bills and other accounts down to the last cent, and this is what happened when the Danish Carlsberg and the

Dutch Heineken went "Dutch" in 2007. Or, if we were to use more daring metaphors with sexual undertones such as are common in describing the beer world, what was happening now was that both Carlsberg and Heineken were "sleeping with the enemy" in order thereafter to go on the prowl together. If anything really big were to come out of it, it would require an expensive solution that involved a lot of money and, therefore, could only be implemented with the charter amendment in their pocket, which was approved in May 2007.

The idea of the collaboration with S&N had been given up by the Carlsberg side. Now just two months after they had last talked to S&N, an opportunity appeared to go a completely different way that was just as titillating, namely, exploiting an already established contact with an archrival on the European market, the CEO of the Heineken brewery, Jean Francois Boxmeer. The 46-year-old Boxmeer was educated as an economist and had been with Heineken since 1984—as CEO since 2005. The then unlikely idea of a collaboration with Heineken had arisen with Nils Smedegaard and CFO Jørn P. Jensen shortly after the break with Orkla. At that time, a rumor was circulating that Boxmeer had expressed interest in a "breakup" of S&N; but, shortly after his accession as CEO two years earlier, he had rejected a feeler from Nils Smedegaard at the otherwise festive and somewhat fabled World Beer and Drinks Forum in Munich.[32] Smedegaard had asked Boxmeer directly to collaborate in a takeover of S&N, but Boxmeer denied having earlier heard about such an idea in which, at that point, he had no strategic interest. However, the contact was still there, and Boxmeer had certainly not forgotten the conversation. When the 2007 charter amendment was in place, it was suddenly a signal that Carlsberg, which was now well on its way to strengthening its capital resources, might be strong enough to participate in an attack against S&N. That realization pushed Heineken onto the field,[33] and suddenly things went very quickly.

Probably in mid-May 2007, Boxmeer contacted Smedegaard.[34] Soon afterward, a new project with the name INCA was set up with the intent to acquire S&N and split the firm up. The pre-Columbian Incan culture in Peru was destroyed by Spanish conquest in the 1500s, and this may have been the basis for the name, which would have sounded intimidating to the modern Incas at S&N, if they had known that conquerors were coming in the form of a well-equipped and hostile, uncompromising and cold blooded Danish-Dutch consortium.

---

[32]Lunde (2008), p. 2017.

[33]See e-mail from Nils Smedegaard Andersen dated 6 August, which recounts events.

[34]Lunde, loc. cit., p. 239.

S&N was suitable prey as a rather loosely conjoined group of brewing firms owned by a large number of smaller shareholders. Carlsberg was especially interested in breweries located in Russia and France, while Heineken wanted to consolidate in England. INCA was launched in August 2007, when the partition plans were discussed. Internally at Carlsberg, people spoke of Project INCA in connection with conspiratorial plans for the takeover and financing of the purchase. The name with its somewhat brutal allusion, however, was substituted during the process by the gentler term *Rainbow,* which provided the possibility for linking different colors to the parties and, of course, Carlsberg got the color green.

Already at the end of June 2007, the news was out that "the five Professors who run Carlsberg are preparing to bid for Scottish and Newscastle…."[35] It sounded funny talking about the five professors even though most of them were not really part of it. The professional leadership at Carlsberg A/S had conceived the plans and steered the process. During a dinner following a meeting in Amsterdam in August 2007, Carlsberg's top echelon—a professor of pharmacology unknown to the Dutch, a Danish businessman they might have heard of, and a CEO on his way out (i.e., Krogsgaard-Larsen, Bigum, and Smedegaard)—succeeded in convincing the Dutch brewery that they meant business and that money would not be an obstacle. The Reuters news bureau heard about the charter amendment, but they did not yet know about the negotiations with Heineken. The surprising international beer news in the fall of 2007, therefore, was that intense negotiations were going on between two competitors, Carlsberg and Heineken, to acquire S&N through a "hostile take-over" with the intention later to split up the 269-year-old Scottish brewery's assets between the two buyers.

Unlike the Danish corporate structure in which shares in many major Danish firms are often gathered into a few hands, the English model is built on a wide dispersal of shares. With many small shareholders who have less influence, it is, as a rule, easier to buy into the company or offer tempting takeover conditions. This advantage was exploited by the consortium of Carlsberg and Heineken. It had to do with money and keeping at it until your opponent's shareholders were ripe for the picking. In light of its earlier amicable consolidation negotiations, Carlsberg's attack could be deemed hostile, and it was also meant that way. Already in September, S&N leadership had gotten wind that something was brewing; and, on 13 September, Sir Brian Stuart wrote to the chairman of the Carlsberg Foundation what would be the last friendly letter from that corner: "We have had

[35] *RPT—Carlsberg professors brew big bid*, 29 June 2007.

a very constructive and fruitful relationship over the years, and I certainly expect that to continue. I am happy to negotiate any time...."

In the so-called consortium agreement entered into with Heineken, Carlsberg had informed the Danish Department of Civil Affairs as supervisory authority that a major transaction was on the way that was to be financed by a significant capital increase. The Department of Civil Affairs had no remarks in a letter dated 10 October 2007, since the transaction would still remain within the framework of the 25% ownership share and a majority vote requirements. At approximately the same time, news came out that the large North American brewery Molson Coors had entered into a joint venture with the brewery concern SABMiller. There was every possible reason now to think big. Carlsberg had earlier considered the consequences of and possibilities for a merger with Molson Coors, which was especially strong in the US. In August 2007, Carlsberg had also received an inquiry from the largest Spanish beer chain Mahou-San Miguel (MSM), which was interested in acquiring shares in Carlsberg and, perhaps, also some other form of collaboration. There was real activity going on in brewery circles, so there was every possible reason for Carlsberg to explore opportunities with its new partner.

Smedegaard was the person who had contact with Heineken, and he had conceived a plan together with Jørn P. Jensen and representatives of Heineken. They were utterly aware that going after S&N would be a challenge and that it would spur both national and EU antitrust authorities to intervene. However, they believed in it and now considered themselves sufficiently strong with a turnover in 2006 of DKK 41.1 billion, and profit after taxes of DKK 1.9 billion. Heineken's turnover was almost twice as large with €11.8 billion and a profit of just under €1 billion during the same period. They also knew it was a matter of playing your cards close to your vest.

In August 2006, Nils Smedegaard spoke to the CEO of the large American brewery Anheuser-Busch, which also had a feeler out and had spoken of the danger that a competitor, SABMiller, would take over S&N's half of BBH. Smedegaard wrote to his management and board in strict confidence on 24 August 2006 to tell them he had replied that "it seemed a little out of proportion for us to execute a hostile and expensive takeover of Scottish & Newcastle for the sole purpose of changing one 50% partner in BBH with another". He also wrote that Anheuser-Busch's Pat Strokes did not understand the threat of being taken over by InBev "as real at that point"; but, not long afterwards, it, too, happened. Just two years later in 2008, Pat Strokes' brewery was acquired as a part of the beer giant that is today abbreviated as AB InBev. For Carlsberg, the advantageous thing about the inquiry might be that, if Anheuser-Busch bought its way in, it would increase capital for the takeover of S&N. The question was how serious the inquiry really was and whether it was worth the risk to get involved with such a large partner. Nothing came of it.

A lot had happened in the six years Smedegaard led the company. From being a regional brewery with a slightly worrying future, Carlsberg had entered into the brewery elite with the big boys and girls and delivered its best annual report ever. This was the result of successful efforts in Eastern Europe and Asia. In his farewell speech for Smedegaard at the end of August 2007, Krogsgaard-Larsen highlighted Smedegaard's intelligence, the sharpness of his analysis, and "a formidable ability to assess strategy and, at the same time, keep a handle on a sea of details". The board and management functioned according to a strict set of rules, said Krogsgaard, and he spoke of a confident collaboration. Smedegaard was quite funny, said Krogsgaard, but to reproduce his witticisms "requires NSA's dry humor and unique voice".

Carlsberg could have recruited an outside CEO to lead the firm into the future in an interplay with the current CEO and CFO, who were strong on sales and finances. A headhunting firm was brought in on the case, and even if they proposed several good external candidates, it was decided to recruit internally, perhaps, to avoid a situation like the choice of Flemming Lindeløv as CEO in its time. The whole process took a bit too long with accompanying uncertainty; and, particularly seen in hindsight, doubt was raised about whether appointing Jørgen Buhl Rasmussen was the right solution. They wanted as new CEO, the board chairman Krogsgaard-Larsen said, "the best in the West", and he praised Buhl Rasmussen, who was already a member of management and "an internationally-oriented man who had worked with staple consumer goods". Jørgen Buhl Rasmussen was seen as quite talented in sales, but to move him from there to being CEO was a significant step, and not everyone was convinced that the new team was the best one. The story behind it was that, in 2006, Jørgen Buhl Rasmussen had been headhunted for Carlsberg. He had had responsibility for the brewery's international sales in Eastern Europe and saw immediately that, in the years since he had traveled abroad at the beginning of the 1990s, Carlsberg had shifted its position quite a bit. Jørgen Buhl Rasmussen's strength was sales. He came to Carlsberg from the international firm of Duracell/Gillette, where he had worked in London for twenty years selling batteries and razor blades. Thus, his experience derived, first and foremost, from the sales of so-called FMCG, "fast moving consumer goods", products that are sold quickly and directly to the consumer, where the brand is decisive for what products consumers end up preferring among the many different choices. The new CEO, the chairman noted in his speech, was also "analytical and creative", could "handle large, demanding tasks", could delegate and listen, and foster engagement among the employees.

Buhl Rasmussen was designated as the next CEO, while CFO Jørn P. Jensen was upgraded to deputy CEO while retaining his position as CFO. Jørn P. Jensen had come to Carlsberg in 2001 after the dismissal of Walther Paulsen. In the opinion of the deputy chairman Palle Marcus, he had done an excellent job as CFO of Nilfisk, a major supplier of cleaning products, and more recently making Carlsberg's complicated accounts more transparent. Even though, in principle, Jørgen Buhl Rasmussen was the leader, the two were considered from the outside as a team that worked together. The press wanted to play it as though there was a winner and a loser for the post of CEO, but the reality was that the two directors were more or less equal, received the same towering salaries and advantageous retirement packages, and were otherwise in agreement with the division of the posts and competencies internally. It was generally known that the main skill of the driven numbers analyst Jørn P. Jensen was not communication either internally or externally, while Buhl Rasmussen was open and extroverted with abilities more in the direction of sales than numbers.

Whether this way of organizing the Carlsberg top echelon was a suitable construction and whether it was the right form of leadership remained an open question. For the more historically conscious, it was evident that both new directors were distinctly oriented toward markets and the bottom line and directed their attention only to a lesser degree toward Carlsberg's heritage, special history, and culture. At his first strategy presentation on 18 September 2007, Buhl Rasmussen stated as the first of "my Carlsberg management beliefs" that "it's all about building brand and company value", that "cost and quality are compatible", and, third, a good piece of advice: "Keep it simple". It was hardly a confession of faith that could expect great resistance, invoke great enthusiasm, or get anyone to feel anything close to the wings of history.

In the fall of 2007, focus was on the Rainbow Project directed toward Scottish & Newcastle. There were now rumors in London about Carlsberg's role in a takeover bid for S&N. In England, there is a special professional Takeover Panel, which had heard about the hostile takeover. In August, Carlsberg received a confidential inquiry from the panel about the seriousness of the takeover plans with a so-called "lay down the tools" order, which meant that they should declare themselves by manifest actions in the course of a few weeks whether they were up to something or otherwise stop completely. It was the task of the new management team, Buhl Rasmussen and Jørn P. Jensen, to prepare for the takeover of S&N. Even before this inquiry, a top-secret task force was set up of trusted employees from Carlsberg and Heineken including their bank connection, Lehman Brothers, so they were armed to the teeth when the order came.

The above-mentioned inquiry eventually had a sequel. On 17 October 2007, the panel demanded an answer to the rumors: "confirm or deny". At that point, Buhl Rasmussen also spoke to an angry Sir Brian Stewart, who felt betrayed by Carlsberg. The collaboration on the joint venture of the two breweries had gone well, said Sir Brian. Buhl Rasmussen had to explain that, even though it went well, it could not continue that way. Carlsberg had far too much of its sales in Baltika to be able to live any longer with the constant risk of being bought out. The consortium between Carlsberg and Heineken (tellingly, called *BidCo*) confirmed the rumor of a takeover bid; and, on 25 October 2007, the consortium submitted its first joint purchase offer of 720 pence per share, corresponding to a total price of DKK 73 billion. However, it was not enough.

After 17 October 2007, negotiations in relation to S&N and Heineken were directed on the Carlsberg side, primarily by Buhl Rasmussen and Jørn P. Jensen but, obviously, in close contact with Povl Krogsgaard-Larsen and Jens Bigum, who was not directly involved but as deputy chairman of the Carlsberg A/S board had to be kept informed. The new CEO and CFO both led the difficult negotiations with Heineken with great energy and skill, and they were the ones to implement the takeover of S&N after Smedegaard had left Carlsberg. All significant steps were approved by Carlsberg's board; but, as the economic expert, Jørn P. Jensen was given wide latitude.

On 25 October 2007 at an extraordinary board meeting, the Foundation confirmed a decision to enter into a so-called Rights Protection Agreement. Present at the meeting were the monetary institutes that guaranteed the means for the purchase. At the same time, Lehman Brothers International, BNP Paribas, Danske Markets (Danske Bank), and Nordea Bank Danmark submitted a declaration to Carlsberg A/S about the purchase. This had to do with the so-called bridge financing that was needed before the new shares that were to finance the purchase were sold. This sort of thing is quite profitable when it goes well. With a yield of 1–1.5%, it would mean a round billion in Danish crowns to the banks. These banks also entered into an agreement to guarantee the difference if the Carlsberg Foundation did not achieve the necessary yield in connection with the sale of shares to maintain its ownership and voting share pursuant to the charter.

For Carlsberg, the goal the whole time had been to gain control of BBH and the Russian market, which was still very attractive with high growth. There was now only one way forward, namely, the takeover of S&N's half;

and, if they could not get it the easy way, it had to go the hard way. It was all a bit reminiscent of the agreements in the 18th century between Prussia's Frederik the Great, Austria's Marie-Theresa, and Russia's Catherine the Great on the division of helpless Poland. S&N was not completely defenseless but had probably underestimated the drive in the management of the two breweries based in smaller countries. In particular, it might have underestimated Carlsberg. S&N probably smirked at what they called the professor-run brewery, doubting they would embark on such a large enterprise as an attempt to take over one of the crown jewels of British beer. The English press, provided with negative information about Carlsberg by a willing S&N, took note of the Carlsberg Foundation's lack of business experience. An anonymous source was cited by *The Telegraph* on 19 November 2007 as saying: "This is a bid driven by a bunch of professors", and it was not kindly meant.

Perhaps, it might not have been entirely clear that behind the not so absent-minded professor with experience from the pharmaceutical sector as chairman was, first and foremost, a professional business panel with an executive board but also a business-oriented deputy chairman, Jens Bigum, who knew how to expand and whose hands did not shake when a decision was made. At a meeting of Carlsberg's board on 8 October 2007, Jens Bigum had also foreseen that "the process can be both difficult and, from S&N's side, carried out in a hard and unsympathetic tone …."[36] He was right. The management of S&N held firm, and they had to increase the offers from 720p to 750p, then 780p, and finally to 800 pence per share. In this sort of situation, you pull out the big bag of tricks; and, as a rule, they all get used. It is all about maximizing the pressure by tempting the shareholders with an attractive offer and putting pressure on the board to sell and, thus, satisfy the shareholders' desire for immediate profit.

S&N was a different kind of brewery from Carlsberg. The Scots were happy with their large brewery, but it was not, like Carlsberg, a national treasure. In addition, the one-tier structure of governance was different from the way Carlsberg was run with a separate board and executive directors. When it came down to it, S&N's shares were for sale and could be bought in a hostile take-over. Both the chairman of the board and the CEO of S&N liked their jobs and preferred to hang onto the brewery, but the economic pressure from the shareholders became so strong that they had to give in. This sort of situation could not have arisen at Carlsberg, where the Carlsberg Foundation had decisive influence, and that was Carlsberg's strength. Their weakness was that they were not always willing to take a risk, but that is not where Carlsberg was

[36]Board meeting on 8 October 2007 of Carlsberg A/S.

at the beginning of 2008. Now there was will to action; and, after a complicated bidding procedure, it was officially reported on 25 January 2008 that a bid of 800p per share was proffered to S&N. This offer, which was perhaps somewhat over the edge of the value, was finally accepted on 31 March 2008 by the brewery's shareholders, and the brewery was then sold for a total price of £7.8 billion.

This was all very expensive for Carlsberg, which had no way back once they had started down this road. In relation to Heineken, Carlsberg was stuck with the greater part of the additional price for the S&N shares but also got the desired prize, BBH, while Heineken for its part achieved a leading position in the English market. Heineken might claim that Carlsberg got the best part of the bargain, namely, the expansion into Russia, where they were already involved, while Heineken's share was a position in a more flat English market. But Heineken knew what it was doing and had every reason to be satisfied with its booty. Just a year later, Carlsberg ran into problems in Russia, and these problems, which were linked to the Russian market, cast a shadow over the future CEO's leadership tenure. In the spring of 2008, however, the future still looked bright, and the consortium was convinced that it had been a good deal.

Seen from S&N's side, this sequence of events was economically beneficial, but they also felt they had had a tough opponent who would not engage in dialogue. At any rate, that is what they said to the press when they were asked: "They could have said to us, can we have a chat about this, please?", said S&N's CEO John Dunsmore, who had been in charge of negotiations on the share price and rejected some very high offers until the final price was reached. He also said that he would rather lead S&N as a business than just press up the price for sale.[37] It is not like in sports, he said, where "if you play a better match, you win". However, he acknowledged, S&N had too many eggs scattered in too many baskets.

Carlsberg's situation was that they had to buy at almost any price since they were otherwise obligated to sell its shares in BBH to S&N once the battle had begun and they had gone hard at the other firm, which had until then collaborated well with them. The purchase of S&N had taken place as a "hostile" takeover, and this is to be understood literally. There was no prior friendly contact or warning but a direct, hard showdown in which, apparently, anything was permitted in terms of aggressive conduct and brutal rhetoric. If Orkla had felt "lurt" (or "cheated"), the Scots believed Carlsberg was guilty of bad sportsmanship. S&N's chairman of the board, Sir Brian

[37] *The Sunday Times*, 6 April 2008.

Stuart, conducted a number of negotiation sessions in an apparently good atmosphere with Povl Krogsgaard-Larsen at the same time that plans for a hostile takeover were being devised behind his back. Actually, in style, Carlsberg and the Scots at S&N were probably more like each other than the ice-cold Dutch Heineken with whom they ended up in alliance. The Dutch had a tough but clear strategy and a purely business approach to the takeover. Perhaps, it was just that Heineken and Carlsberg had understood a bit sooner than S&N that the time for gentlemen's agreements in the beer industry was over. Now, you went directly for the throat. You no longer engaged in solemn beer weddings, you waged a dirty beer war.

Carlsberg and Heineken took over S&N in April 2008 for an overall purchase price of about DKK 105 billion (around 14 billion euro, 1 euro corresponding to 7.5 crowns) of which Carlsberg paid approximately DKK 57 billion and Heineken approximately DKK 48 billion, which was later adjusted somewhat. Among other things, as mentioned, Carlsberg had to bear the lion's share of the additional expenditures by raising the offer to 800p per share. The consortium between the Danes and the Dutch was a "marriage of convenience" and not a "marriage for love", but it was about neither love nor convenience, for that matter. It was about power. The connection between the two breweries had been made with a view only toward the task to be done. It was "the perfect match" but only for one night. Subsequently—and, naturally, in such a huge deal, some additional questions arose about who was to pay what, which were later to be resolved by a settlement in 2010. Otherwise, the parties each went their own way; but, of course, they kept an eye on each other's results in subsequent years.

The takeover of S&N was, in Povl Krogsgaard Larsen's words, the biggest business deal in Danish history. As chairman of the Foundation, Povl Krogsgaard had proven to be good at his role in dissolving the collaboration with Orkla. The acquisition of S&N was also something of a triumph for which Carlsberg's earlier and present management (as well as chairman and deputy chairman) could share credit. Carlsberg was now strong and earning money, so it was an optimistic firm that the new management took over and one that was also in the process of a completely new venture.

Carlsberg and Heineken had been almost impertinently lucky in their timing. A few months later, the economic situation looked entirely different, and it would probably have been impossible to carry out the takeover of S&N. In fact, everything might have gone wrong with the financing if it had just been a little later. Carlsberg's main bank, Lehman Brothers, which was one of the guarantors of the stock issuance, unexpectedly went bankrupt just a few months later in September 2008, and the other banks in the support consortium could hardly have stepped up.

The purchase itself was financed, in part, by a comprehensive increase in the number of shares in May and June 2008 with a yield of over DKK 30 billion, which now left the Carlsberg Foundation as owner of 30.3% of the share capital and, thus, significantly below the prior 51%. Carlsberg, however, was still dominant as it retained a voting share of around 76%. The rest of the purchase price was financed by loans. Still, even gold can be bought too dearly. The question was whether the overall price paid by Carlsberg of DKK 57 billion for the other half of BBH was too high, when it came right down to it even if Carlsberg, in addition to BBH, got the French brewery Kronenbourg with more than 3,000 employees and a French market share of 35%, the Grimbergen label, and the rather small Mythos brewery in Greece, which in its homeland had 10% of the sales and a total of 250 employees, as well as some minor breweries in China and Vietnam. Now there was a worldwide economic crisis, and it changed many of the preconditions.

Carlsberg's new management was optimistic and saw good opportunities for further growth and earnings. It was a venture, and the risk that was connected to it might have been underplayed in the general euphoria around the purchase. As mentioned, a portion of the purchase sum was procured by loans, and Carlsberg now had debt of around DKK 49 billion. Yet, even that could be turned into something positive: "Debt has gone onto become a powerful driving force in Carlsberg's development. The board is relatively comfortable with this debt", related an apparently satisfied CEO Jørgen Buhl Rasmussen to the business paper *Børsen* on 1 February 2008; "debt is not in itself undesirable as long as it is a tool to create activity …," he said. He was correct, but debt also requires interest payments and instalments and, therefore, requires money to come in again.

Heineken had acquired other parts of the earlier Scottish beer empire. Along with their share of the purchase of S&N came the cider producer Bulmers with the Strongbow label. Heineken got Forster's in addition to the Finnish Lapin Kulta and interests in Portugal, Belgium, the US, and India, where Heineken was already represented. The British part of the brewery, which was acquired by Heineken, took the name Heineken UK Limited.

In an unusual, almost devilish alliance, innocently called in the professional jargon a consortium, Carlsberg with Heineken had purchased S&N and had become the sole owner of BBH and, thus, a major player in the Eastern European and Russian markets. Carlsberg was also left with a gigantic debt. On the other hand, they had become big and had entered into the super-league of large breweries. This had a cost, and the big question to which only the future contained the answer was, of course, whether it was worth the money. At that point, the sale of beer in Russia, which in recent years had been growing at a furious pace, still looked bright. A year later, the situation did not look as bright as in 2008. Developments in Russia were turning, and Carlsberg's management was to face great challenges.

5.9 The FMCG Era

In 2008, Jørgen Buhl Rasmussen spoke about the Baltika brewery in Russia as a "fantastic firm". He began as an optimist with respect to the Russian market, but he soon had to acknowledge that the value of the Russian market share, which was originally estimated to be around half of the overall business, was not as large as reckoned and that commitments in Russia had to be toned down considerably. By getting full control over BBH and over a number of other foreign breweries in the purchase, Carlsberg had really become a global business and grown from being middle-sized to large. This created a whole new dynamic in Carlsberg, and there was no longer any doubt at Carlsberg that the 2008 expansion had been the right move—not even when, shortly thereafter, earnings from Russia began to go downhill. With the acquisition of the entirety of BBH in 2008 and with new management at the brewery since 2007, a new chapter in the history of Carlsberg as a leading brewery on a world scale began. In 2011, a future chairman of the Foundation, Flemming Besenbacher, expressed the connection between Jacobsen's enterprising spirit and the developments in the previous decade by saying that it was "true that Carlsberg in the 1990s was falling behind. Therefore, something radical had to happen. That was why the Orkla buyout, the charter amendments, and the later purchase of Scottish & Newcastle were necessary. It was entirely in the spirit of brewer Jacobsen to create something big, to want to achieve something with his business. Much of what Carlsberg succeeded with in the last decade was indeed due, in part, to talent and, in part, to luck. But that's how it is to run a large business, you have to gamble".[38]

J. C. Jacobsen would probably have had a hard time recognizing Carlsberg in 2008 as the same brewery he donated to the Carlsberg Foundation. Therefore, there was good reason to mention him again even though he probably would not have liked the talk of FMCG and would have stressed more that beer brewing was about quality and not just selling in big quantity. It was a different firm than before, and there was a lot to hold together. Carlsberg

[38] *Berlingske Tidende*, 28 November 2011.

was now one of the biggest on the international brewery market. Seen in hindsight, the history of how it had come to that might not all look very pretty. In many instances, there had been something like double-dealing, leaving behind disappointed partners in the US, Norway, and more recently in Scotland. Not entirely without justification, Orkla felt that Carlsberg had embarked on an alliance for which they would not accept the full consequences when it came down to it. Now, together with an archrival, Carlsberg had taken over a friendly, iconic British brewery, carved it up, and divided the booty. Militarily, it was well executed but also brutal and over the line, even though there were good business reasons for Carlsberg to act as it did. The foundation model had not only passed the test, it had proved to be an instrument you could play on.

It is interesting to observe the encounter between an academic culture and a business culture. It is often thought that "professors" or university people in general are less hard-hitting than businessmen and -women. That is not necessarily so. The academic culture is highly selective and tough as nails. Researchers often go ruthlessly after results and money and are disloyal to colleagues, while people in business to a higher degree tend to take into account that tomorrow is another day, and we may want to work together some other time. In business, you cannot often afford to destroy a good network. These roles combined in an apparently amicable academic as manager of the Carlsberg Foundation, who was at the same time somewhat of a tough and uncompromising businessman and backed by a team of hard-core businessmen. This combination, therefore, could be deceiving. A large American brewery, Orkla, and S&N learned the lesson that professors are not necessarily absent-minded, kind, or starry-eyed theoreticians. They are actually willing to go a long way to achieve their goals and also to destroy friendships or other kinds of relations on their way. When it came to the Carlsberg side, the goals and the aggressive ideas did not, however, stem from the 'professors' as a group. The strategy and the goals were conceived in the Carlsberg A/S headquarters in Valby. Mostly, it was the chairman of the Foundation who was also chairman of the board of Carlsberg A/S alone who took an active part in the game and its implementation. He was not just acting as a marionette but deeply involved in the action and expected to take on the tough role of front man when the storm troopers marched out.

Gradually the change in the position of Carlsberg as a global firm had consequences for the recruiting of board members. An initial change took place when, in 2007, Jens Bigum stepped down as deputy chairman of the Carlsberg A/S board and replaced later by the top man at Mærsk, Jess Søderberg. Carlsberg and Mærsk had swapped seats, almost. Again in December

2008, one of the business members of the Carlsberg A/S board, Henning Dyremose, aired the idea that it was now the time to recruit not only Danish but also international board members with a broader experience with this type of firm. Along with the transition to international board members came a transition of the board language to English in 2009, another necessary step away from the tradition.

In the history of Carlsberg's most recent decade, there is an obvious tension between the concept of beer as a quality product and a good brand and, at the same time, the more unsentimental look at beer as a FMCG, a fast moving consumer good, to be sold in great quantities. Replacing a consideration of quality, which J. C. Jacobsen had stressed with his "golden words", was now a cold-blooded sales mindset. In fact, the word quality seemed to have disappeared from this view of Carlsberg's products. CEO Buhl Rasmussen's slogan, formulated after the takeover of BBH, became that Carlsberg should be "the fastest growing brewery in the world", and it actually looked that way for a brief time. With Buhl Rasmussen and Jørn P. Jensen at the helm, respectively, as CEO and CFO, there was less history, tradition, and talk of quality and more of a concentration on business that was customer- and consumer-oriented. Emphasis was placed on sales, the overall beer portfolio, and, in this connection, the construction of central units that were responsible across all the local breweries for purchases, IT, production planning, and, to a certain degree, marketing of international brands such as Carlsberg, Tuborg, and Kronenbourg.

In organization and management theory, an important question is how you create a firm's own identity. After the purchase of S&N, Carlsberg went through a process of transformation, which raised the question of the extent to which Carlsberg's history, the Carlsberg story, should be the story that bound the whole organization of breweries together combined with their own histories. In management language, *organizational historicizing* and authenticity are words that indicate how the real history and real values can be useful in branding a firm, not just as morsels used for rhetorical purposes without reflecting any actual history.[39] Creating such a cohesive narrative is a work of art that would demand much of the new Carlsberg management, which also had to recognize that they could no longer be borne by the wave of euphoria that had accompanied the Russia adventure. Now, instead, they were struggling with poor results in Russia and disappointed expectations about what should have been the purchase of the century.

[39]Hatch, Schultz, and Skov (2015), Hatch and Schultz (2017).

A serious blow came to Carlsberg after 2009 when the Russian economy, like the rest of the world economy, was hit by recession after the financial crisis. At the same time, beer taxes were raised in Russia along with other obstacles to beer sales, which promoted the consumption of vodka, a strong alcoholic drink far more dangerous to health than peaceful beer drinking. It was like what happened with Danish 'schnaps' in the 19th century. This new alcohol policy, which benefitted the traditional vodka, was influenced by local Russian business interests and was accompanied by the general economic downturn, which helped make the grand venture far less attractive than it had appeared in 2002 and 2007. In subsequent years, earnings stagnated even though the Russians still drank a lot of beer, and the business in Russia expanded in terms of volume. It was necessary to readjust expectations significantly downward for yields in Russia. Time and again, Jørgen Buhl Rasmussen negotiated with Russian authorities and met personally with the country's political leader Putin, but it was difficult to achieve results in the impenetrable Russian political system, which was not exclusively governed by the desire to change Russian alcohol habits or promote beer sales as a good product in a country with extensive agricultural areas.

The big question for "the twin regime" (or "J and J" as the 'twin set' of the CEO and the CFO was called) was whether they were capable of, first, implementing innovations after the 2008 expansion and, then, leading quickly and efficiently the transformation process after a downward adjustment of expectations in Russia. This turned on finding new strategies, when it proved that the Russian market was not the golden egg it was believed to be in the longer term. Buhl Rasmussen told the board about the merits of their competitors InBev, Heineken, and SABMiller and mentioned such parameters as efficiency, premium branding, and the ability to translate words into real action on the markets, but they were also in a tight spot to come up with a word for what Carlsberg was especially good at. "Cash is king" was a bit paltry in this context but entirely realistic, since the point of reference was that Carlsberg had taken on debt on which interest and instalments had to be paid, something they would, preferably, get rid of. EBITDA (earnings before interest, taxes, depreciation and amortization), primary operating income, and EBIT (earnings before interest and taxes) were given pride of place.

A great many new managers and employees with experience from other international FMCG firms such as Unilever, Nestle, and Coca-Cola were hired in the coming years to implement Carlsberg's transformation into an international FMCG business. Under Smedegaard Andersen's leadership, Carlsberg's management pyramid had been quite steep. Jørgen Buhl

Rasmussen relaxed the top management of the brewery through the establishment of a new ten-man management group (ExCom) immediately beneath the CEO/CFO level and tried to find a new balance between being global and local (i.e., *GloCal*). But it only partially succeeded in constructing an overall new vision for the firm or a common identity for the firm's executives and employees, who were, first and foremost, loyal to their local brewery and had a harder time seeing the advantages of the many centralization measures and the constant focus on short-term earnings. The transformation process meant in many places that various "cultures" or mindsets clashed, and many local and regional executives were dismissed, their place taken by others in those years. So, in many ways, it was an entirely new staff that led the breweries from then on.

Buhl Rasmussen's mantra was that it was all about how to execute or carry out decisions; and, by that, he meant getting things done and done in the best possible way. In the eyes of some, it could look as though there was less interest in what you were actually doing. Such a view reflected a lack of interest in the firm's own identity or in the construction of an overall identity for such a large organization and that the Carlsberg management was concentrating on profit and centralization, while leaving it more to the individual breweries locally to be proud brewers and exploit their history. Buhl Rasmussen placed the emphasis on the balance between brewing techniques, on one hand, and selling FMCG, on the other.

"Beer is local" was another mantra neglected. An academic study showed that Carlsberg's business management created certain frustration around the local breweries, which felt that central management did not always show sufficient interest in the individual breweries' own particular cachet.[40] Therefore, some had a hard time finding their identity in a firm that focused one-sidedly on quick growth without looking back to its fundamental values sufficiently. On the other hand, some breweries in the Carlsberg group wanted to do things in their own way. A large brewery like Baltika was not necessarily interested in the Carlsberg brand as such, trusting that they could do things better themselves in keeping their own identity.

In many ways, the European market was at a standstill, so innovation had to come from Asia, especially China, Southeast Asia, and India, where there were more and more thirsty palates—in the millions—to quench. New thinking was needed to keep up the tempo, and this was not so simple in an international beer market that, slowly and quietly, closed itself off to new players. This often happened through expensive purchases of not always

[40]Hatch et al. (2015), Hatch and Schultz (2017).

entirely efficient breweries in China but also in Vietnam, India, Myanmar (Burma), Laos, and Cambodia. In Thailand, they even tried a new partnership. A good foundation for expansion in Asia was also created in those years, especially in the Chinese market, even though Carlsberg did not achieve a leading position, remaining number three or four, which was considered a precondition for implementing a proper market strategy. In China, the strategy was to buy a large number of breweries in order to develop a taste for beer in less populated and consolidated western China.

5.10 Second Countdown: From Capital to Votes

After the 2007 charter amendment, the Foundation continued to own a now reduced 25% of the share capital. It was superfluous to bind the Foundation in this way, but there had been reasons, which—as usual—were grounded in an exaggerated caution accompanied by the desire to establish bullet-proof protection against the risk of hostile takeover. Now, the time was finally ripe to move on. Since 2012, the Foundation's new chairman, Professor Flemming Besenbacher had particularly pressed to get a charter amendment that removed any requirement for the Foundation to own a specific amount of the share capital, so they would be ready the day opportunities for expansion appeared. It would be expensive if they were still to have a chance in either the US or China, where the market was not yet closed, and it could hardly be done for less than DKK 18 billion, which could be raised with the issuance of new shares if they maintained a 15% share. Since the 2007 amendments, it had also happened that the danger from the so-called breakthrough rule, which was the reason for the requirement of a 25% ownership share in the charter, had shown itself as exaggerated. The EU Commission stated in a report from 2012[41] that there did not seem to be a need to make this rule obligatory; but, even under other circumstances, the Foundation could just have held onto the necessary number of shares over which it had control in order to avoid risk, whether they wanted to divest or not.

Flemming Besenbacher, a professor in nanoscience at Aarhus University in 2011, was elected as chairperson of the Carlsberg Foundation and, as a consequence, also to the Carlsberg A/S board with effect from 2012 with four votes and one abstention. The choice of Besenbacher as chairman for the Foundation proved to have great significance for the balance between the brewery management and the Foundation. As chairman, Besenbacher

[41]COM no. 347 of 28 June 2012.

was significantly more active in the brewery's daily activities than had been seen before, and he intervened directly in the brewery management and its decisions. One of the first initiatives undertaken by Besenbacher was getting the charter amended, so that the Foundation was no longer bound by a superfluous requirement to possess a certain share of capital. At a Carlsberg Foundation meeting on 25 September 2013, a draft for a charter amendment was discussed, which aimed at dissolving the requirement for the Foundation to own more than 25% of the share capital and, instead, concentrate on the majority vote by simply maintaining that, in the future, Carlsberg was to own shares with the right to at least 51% of the votes in Carlsberg A/S. The purpose was to secure an immediate economic tool if an opportunity to collaborate with a foreign brewery suddenly turned up. Now, the chairman of the Carlsberg Foundation was on the forefront as opposed to his foot-dragging predecessor in the 1980s. The charter amendment was a proactive measure without any specific occasion, intended to increase the brewery's financial flexibility and to make the company stronger by providing the option of striking on short notice and participating in the global consolidation of the beer industry:

> The Carlsberg Foundation shall forever be owner of a block of shares that gives the right to at least 51% of the votes in Carlsberg A/S, and the Carlsberg Foundation must in no way (*ingensinde*) by divestment or gift of shares or subscription rights, by the gift of votes for capital increase, or in any other way act so that the aforementioned requirement is not fulfilled or so that a risk therefor arises.

Business was going badly in Russia, and the brewery now needed to be able to act without unnecessary fetters. The main reason for the amendment was a current and urgent need to be able to obtain additional, very significant equity though the issuance of B-shares (one share, one vote shares) in Carlsberg A/S without the Carlsberg Foundation thereby losing its controlling influence. The amendment, as the Carlsberg legal consultant explained it, "even if it were exploited to issue new shares to its full extent, would not mean that the Carlsberg Foundation would lose its so-called negative control of Carlsberg A/S. They could still prevent unwanted amendments to the Charter and determine the selection of the board even if they still did not have so-called positive control, which required a majority of 2/3 of both votes and capital." The central content in article 4 of the original charter was the intention to develop beer production "to Perfection", and the purpose of the capital resources requirement was to ensure the fulfillment of this provision if an opportunity appeared, which, however, has not yet been the case.

At the turn of 2013/14, the value of the Foundation's shares in Carlsberg was DKK 28.6 billion. In 2014, Carlsberg was the world's fourth-largest and is today, after a couple of spectacular mergers, the world's third-largest beer concern. Any position after numbers one and two is vulnerable; and, therefore, Carlsberg's strategy has been to buy its way into a position as number one or two (at least) in other markets in connection with the so-called consolidation of the beer market, which occurs in the form of buyouts or, to use the professional term of art, acquisitions.

It was not an easy exercise to lower expectations in the coming years. In the autumn of 2014, Buhl Rasmussen and Jensen had been in place for seven years. That was longer than the two most recent CEOs and more than the six-seven years that is considered the normal span for business leaders. It was no secret that the CEO and the chairman of the board had different approaches to many issues. The chairman wanted more dynamism in management and a closer cooperation between brewery and foundation. He wanted to use Carlsberg's history as a part of the company's "brand", recognizing that they had to orient themselves in different directions after the losses in Russia and that they were not stuck with stereotypical FMCG concepts. It had to do, in particular, with the management of the brewery and the vision of its fundamental values. The time had come when the board with its chairman in the lead wanted a change. Externally, it appeared as though Jørgen Buhl Rasmussen was trying to resign; but, in reality, it was a firing. Over the course of the summer of 2015, the twins, CEO Jørgen Buhl Rasmussen and CFO Jørn P. Jensen, stepped down within an interval of a few months. They both had retirement compensation agreements that amounted, in a Danish context, to dizzying sums for the two leaders, who, after all, had not even been brought in from the international market but were already employed, recruited from within. A golden handshake of just under DKK 24 million and DKK 32 million from ongoing share-based salary programs was in a Danish context considered excessive, bordering on the immoral. Upon his retirement, in addition to a salary of DKK 11.6 million for first three quarters of 2015, Jørn P. Jensen received over DKK 25 million and almost the same amount from his stock option programs.

5.11 Beer and the Science Behind It

Since 1875, one of the Carlsberg crown jewels was its own research laboratory, which had produced such tremendous scientific results both in the 19th and the first decades of the 20th century. The Carlsberg Laboratory operated from the beginning with two departments that were, in effect, two separate laboratories with only little interference. In addition, there came a third, the Biological Institute of the Carlsberg Foundation. A growing problem for the Carlsberg Foundation to which a solution was only found in the 1970s after the merger with Tuborg was that the operation of the Carlsberg Laboratory had become an economic burden for the Foundation as more and more demands for equipment were made. Wages rose even as the Foundation's income stagnated or, at least, did not rise at a corresponding pace, and it could be foreseen that nearly all of the Foundation's income would be spent on the laboratory to the detriment of other purposes. A solution was found by transferring most of the laboratory activities to the brewery after the merger of Carlsberg and Tuborg/DFB. The initiative for this organizational change came from the dynamic CEO of Carlsberg in 1972, A. W. Nielsen.[42] He and others had spotted the problem of a laboratory that was not focused on beer-relevant research and, therefore, wanted closer contact between brewery and laboratory. Nielsen wanted the new beer giant to be competitive on the international market and needed research that helped improve the quality of beer. The brewery, therefore, was willing to take over the financing of the laboratory. The transfer to the brewery itself required restructuring, which in turn required some diplomacy. A number of researchers were worried about working directly under the brewery and in directions laid out by the brewery. Many of the researchers could be moved to the Biological Institute, which was an independent unit on Tagensvej. The head of the Institute, Professor Erik Zeuthen, stood strongly for the right to research freely and could not see himself as the employee of a laboratory under the management of the brewery. The chairman of the Carlsberg Foundation, Professor P. Brandt Rehberg, was in favor of the arrangement on the Foundation's side. Together with A. W. Nielsen, he was good at finding solutions to the structural questions. Ebba Lund, a member of the board of the laboratory and the Foundation, said much later in 1991 about the transfer to the brewery that "Carlsberg A/S has brought Carlsberg Laboratory from a stage close to a technological museum to an institution in scientific flower". The chairman of the Carlsberg Foundation at the time, Kristof Glamann, also believed that the 1972 agreement to transfer the laboratory from the Carlsberg Foundation and subordinating it to the brewery (still with certain support from the Carlsberg Foundation to secure a certain independence) was beneficial to the Foundation and should be considered "a great gift to the laboratory".[43]

[42]A part of the laboratory was transferred to the Carlsberg Foundation's second research institute, the Biological Institute of the Carlsberg Foundation, which existed from 1932 to 1981.

[43]CFP 44, meeting 18 October 1991.

The brewery's interests had a natural influence on the laboratory's future research and development work even though there continued to be a right to free research in order to recruit the best researchers. The Carlsberg Foundation still provided sufficient financial support to ensure that such research could continue. The scientific members of the Foundation's board were still supervisors of the laboratory management. As a rule, one or two representatives of the brewery's management or other beer brewing specialists were appointed as members of the supervisory board. From the brewery's point of view, one of the tasks was also—preferably, to be done with a certain finesse—to push research in a brewery-oriented direction. At the same time, it was to be respected that the laboratory's attractiveness as a place for research and its international position with respect to basic research was dependent on its reputation as a laboratory open for free research. A Carlsberg Research Center was now established as an overall institution with the Carlsberg Laboratory as a department in addition to biotechnological and machine-technological departments. A new laboratory building was erected in connection with the old, and it was completed in 1975–76 to host the many activities of the growing research institution. Obviously, the new structure gave rise to countless administrative problems in which the laboratory wanted to retain its special position, and the Carlsberg Foundation board had to take a position on many of them in those years.[44]

It was a great lift for the laboratory's international research profile that the transition to the brewery was linked to the appointment of an international star, the geneticist Diter von Wettstein, to the laboratory as a professor. Thus, the laboratory's international fame was secured for many years. Wettstein was a mentor of huge dimensions with an enormous network around the globe. Under his management, the laboratory attracted researchers from all over the world within the disciplines with which Wettstein was associated. He also saw to it that promising young Danish researchers got training at foreign universities where specialists in the specific field were found. His biological research program in the years up to his departure from the laboratory in 1996 was a continuation of Øivind Winge's barley refinement studies. Wettstein seemed to master to a higher degree, perhaps, than his immediate successors the balance between basic research and research more directly relevant to the brewery. He and his research team occupied themselves with a number of important topics for the brewery—*inter alia*, plant breeding and genetic variations of barley and barley mutants. These topics have had great significance for the brewing process and constitute even today a most important core of

[44]CFP 36, meetings on 1 October and 8 October 1976.

the lab's research. Yeast refinement was also favored in those years. The initiative and creativity at the place was at such a level that the researches often manufactured themselves the necessary instruments for the execution of the highly-specialized research, which created international attention around the laboratory in those years.

The internationally-renowned Wettstein was highly regarded among his research colleagues and students, but the enthusiasm for his efforts for the laboratory was more tempered at the brewery. Carlsberg CEO Poul J. Svanholm, in particular, was less impressed by his efforts to further brewery interests. Good results, however, were achieved to improve the shelf life of beer by removing sediment; and, with a tenure from the beginning of the 1970s to the end of the 1990s, Wettstein is remembered with gratitude by his many students, and his research today is venerated as basic for the present activities at the laboratory. Unfortunately, it all ended less decorously when a disappointed Wettstein, who wanted his employment extended, had to leave the laboratory with legal fallout concerning seeds that Wettstein had taken with him to the US for his own commercial exploitation.

New rules for the laboratory from 1997 stressed that it was still a primary task for the ongoing research to "procure as complete a scientific foundation for malting, brewing, and fermentation operations as possible". In this connection, studies of seed types that are suitable for brewing, genetic and other matters related to yeast, proteins, and carbohydrates, and the relationship of these materials during brewing operations were especially stressed. At the same time, CEO Poul J. Svanholm's wish was fulfilled, namely, that the Carlsberg Charter expressly established that, in agreement with practice, patents on research results could be taken out even as they maintained the requirement for the publication of research results. The Brewer's original and idealistic notion—for results to be made available free of charge to others—might have been workable in his time, but in a new and competitive era it had to be abandoned. Today's somewhat harsher economic conditions do not allow an individual institution to renounce necessary income from its discoveries, which were achieved by costly research.

For many years, the history of the laboratory was the history of a series of more or less well-known star researchers surrounded by a circle of students and other researchers who came to Copenhagen, attracted by the international environment and the quality of the people who worked together there. Therefore, it is not entirely easy to find a common thread in the laboratory research, which was led by individualists with their own teams and their own ideas of what was important for them to live up to the requirements of the Charter. For long periods, it was difficult to formulate and maintain an overall objective for the laboratory's work in compliance with Brewer J. C. Jacobsen's intentions, and it was actually only in very recent years that it has become clear where the laboratory has been heading.

Wettstein's appointment as head of the laboratory's physiology department in 1972 was a clear boost to the laboratory's research at the time. On the other hand, the relationship between the chemistry and the physiology departments was tense. At the same time, a special department of yeast research, the yeast genetics department (established in 1987; since 2001, a part of the department of physiology), was managed (since 2004 as a research group) by Morten Kielland-Brandt until the end of 2007. In a continuation of a strategy set by Dieter von Wettstein, this department worked with issues surrounding the synthesis of the amino acids of yeast cells. It succeeded in the use of classic genetic methods to refine brewer's yeast, so that they could shorten the maturation time for beer after its primary fermentation and, thus, save costs in connection with the production, which had great significance in the longer term. Another brewery-related topic in this department was the transport of amino acids, where the work was of less significance for the brewery but contributed to the understanding of the physiology of yeast.

In 1988, the chemist Klaus Bock joined the laboratory as leader of its department of chemistry. From 1993, he had the title of research director and, in the period from 2001 to 2007, was the overall research director of the laboratory. In the following years, he took over the CRC's research council (CRC is an abbreviation for *Carlsberg Research Center*) after Wettstein. In these years, Bock was a talented and powerful laboratory head. His special area of expertise was nuclear magnetic resonance used on low molecular weight carbohydrates. He was highly respected in the brewery's management and, together with Morten Kielland-Brandt, one of the advocates for a more brewery-oriented direction in the laboratory's research, which came to affect the department of chemistry less than the departments of physiology and yeast genetics.

At times, the work at the laboratory after Wettstein's time had been plagued by conflict, an often less than optimal relationship to Carlsberg's research laboratory, failing cooperation between the various departments, and the lack of an overall vision for the laboratory's work. In the years after 2000, the brewery's good economy at the time of its collaboration with Orkla benefited the laboratory as well. Special agreements were entered into on the research center, and the affiliation with Carlsberg A/S and Carlsberg Breweries was strengthened, while the person responsible for laboratory finances was the brewery's economic wizard, CFO Jørn P. Jensen. During Bock's management period, carbohydrate research was given priority, and the work continued on refining barley and yeast. In the 1980s and 1990s, the laboratory worked on gene-splicing and transgenic organisms; such research later came into certain disrepute. The "gene policy", therefore, was changed in the following years by achieving important results on plant breeding with other means. A fruitful cooperation was introduced in 2001 with the Heineken Supply Chain, so-called ABIN I and II, (ABIN being an abbreviation for *Applied Barley for Industrial Needs*), which continued to 2008. In a time, when neither brewers nor consumers want products made with gene-modified organisms, it is noteworthy that the laboratory succeeded in adapting the most modern high-technological methods to find new barley plants and yeast cells, the functionality of which was often the equivalent of corresponding gene-modified organisms, and plant breeding by traditional methods (without gene splicing) are today the laboratory's flag ship.

At the same time, a number of biotechnological projects were launched that were farther from the topics that the Brewer in his time had mentioned as central for laboratory research. Some part of Bock's carbohydrate research was also on the periphery with respect to applications for the brewery. This again raised the question about the laboratory's strategy and relationship to the brewery's needs, creating tension between the faction of the laboratory supervisory board, which wanted completely free basic research, and the more brewery-oriented part of the board. Carbohydrate research and the ongoing tomato disease research were some of the topics that were considered less relevant by several members of the board.

These conflicts and the board's uncertain line as a consequence of its internal disagreement helped create unease about the laboratory and, eventually, something of a chaotic relationship that has only recently been redressed. In particular, two members of the supervisory board, Carlsberg Foundation board members and Professors C. J. Ballhausen and Axel Michelsen, were firm about the laboratory's right to free research, while the chairman Povl Krogsgaard-Larsen made a great effort to get the laboratory on track again. He believed the chain had come off the wheel already when Johannes Schmidt in his time between the wars had been allowed to conduct studies of eels at the laboratory instead of topics relevant to the brewery. That had to be fixed, and Krogsgaard wanted a firmer line, supported by Carlsberg CFO Jørn P. Jensen, but as mentioned they were countered by others in the Foundation and on the laboratory board. Not until after the 2007 amendments to the Carlsberg Foundation's charter did the lab's board clearly establish that the operations in the Carlsberg Laboratory's research departments were to be directed toward the production of beer and other beverages.

The years after Bock's departure from the laboratory in 2007 were a difficult transition phase with many short-term management hires who were not capable of maneuvering with sufficient assurance in the difficult waters between pure research and practical use for the brewery. Organizationally, the laboratory had come to a standstill in many ways. According to the laboratory's historian, Professor Peder Olesen Larsen, the laboratory was "a shadow of itself"[45] in the decade after 2004 and actually "on the edge of becoming marginalized".[46]

It looked from the outside as if the laboratory found itself in a "pocket of time" in which very little had changed since the 1980s and 1990s. The laboratory's previous reputation as an attractive and innovative workplace was seriously eroded, and this had to be remedied. Since then, there has been an almost complete turnover of the laboratory's staff, and after another amendment of the Carlsberg Foundation's charter in 2013 with respect to the relations to the laboratory, it became an integrated part of the Carlsberg Research Center (CRC). The objective expressed was that the CRC, including the laboratory, was to be an international leader in brewery-related research. Research and development areas were designated as barley and hops, yeast, new ingredients, and nutrients as well as brewing chemistry, technology, and quality control, as well as enzymes. As to the organization itself, it was determined that the laboratory was to be led by a research director and that four additional researchers with the title of professor could be hired with specialties in plant physiology, yeast genetics, chemistry, or enzymology.

The lab's board continued to include the three scientific members from the Carlsberg Foundation board, chosen by the Royal Academy, and the laboratory continued to receive support from 8% of the Foundation's grants. At the same time, the charter maintained as a governing principle that no research results were to be kept secret. It was now worded in a more modern form: publication could occur in the form of patent applications—which was, thus, in line with Carlsberg CEO Poul J. Svanholm's desire to fulfill the publication requirement by taking out patents. New advanced research equipment was also acquired, and the laboratory's portfolio of issued and pending patents in recent years shows how the laboratory's researchers have achieved results and made inventions of great industrial relevance.

In 2015, the charter provisions regarding the Carlsberg Research Laboratory were again changed to adapt to conditions around the laboratory and the brewery and to the reality that it was fundamentally Carlsberg A/S that paid for its operations. The laboratory's task was still formulated to "procure

[45]Loc. cit., p. 239.

[46]Loc. cit., p. 241.

as complete a scientific foundation for malting, brewing, and fermentation operations as possible", and reference was made to the so-called quality clause, still the only passage left written in the Brewer's orthography with its phrasing from 1882.[47] This was considered such a strong expression of the founder's will that the "Carlsberg Research Laboratory's purpose, cf. clause 8.1, must in no way (*ingensinde)* be abandoned. Nor may the laboratory ever be merged into another institute".[48] The requirement that research results were not to be kept secret was observed but still in the adapted form that their publication could occur in scientific works and patent applications. The previous supervisory board was replaced by a supervisory committee with three representatives of the Carlsberg Foundation and two members selected by the Royal Academy on recommendation by the brewery. This committee did not have management authority but solely conducted supervision, as the name implies.

The Carlsberg Laboratory as one of the institutions in the so-called Carlsberg family has also felt new winds after the 2012 shift in the Carlsberg Foundation chairmanship and an ever stronger consciousness at Carlsberg of its historical heritage. Over the course of time, the laboratory has played a varying role in the history of the brewery and Danish research. We have heard about its establishment and its research, the prestige that, for many years, came from working at the laboratory, and the debate on the relevance of this research to the brewery, which led to the laboratory being taken over in 1972 by the brewery. The extent to which and how the laboratory in recent years has tried and succeeded in living up to the Brewer's expectations is, in itself, a good story.

Since 2014, geneticist and biochemist Birgitte Skadhauge, who has been affiliated with the laboratory since 1987, has been its research director with the title of Vice President at Carlsberg A/S. The laboratory is now a world-leading institution with regard to the study of barley malt and on the cutting edge when it comes to the exploitation of raw materials, the recycling of products, and the general development of the so-called circular economy. Fermentation processes are still an important part of research, and the laboratory's staff publishes in leading scientific journals. Plant breeding projects in Russia, taking into consideration the cultivation conditions there, are also among the laboratory's key issues right now.

---

[47]Art. 8.1.1.

[48]Art. 8.5.2.

As chairperson for the Carlsberg Foundation and the board (now the supervisory council) for the laboratory, the Foundation chairperson, Flemming Besenbacher, and the laboratory research director have been the driving force in recent years behind the regeneration of the laboratory, helping it to regain its position as a leading international research center. This goal now seems to have been reached in plant breeding (including, of course, barley in particular), which is a focal point of the laboratory's research. The projects worked on in plant breeding, yeast strain research, and new technology, which can streamline the brewing process, are so advanced as to be revolutionary. At the same time, it is interesting to observe that, in the laboratory as well as in the brewery, there is growing consciousness in these years about the heritage of J. C. Jacobsen. He wanted a laboratory that could contribute at a high level to disciplines within the natural sciences that had significance for the brewery industry, and it is for this objective that the laboratory works today.

The laboratory has been wide-ranging in its research. At times, it was difficult to maintain the course, but much indicates that they are now back on the track that was marked out in 1876, taking appropriate consideration of the fact that several revolutions have happened in science since the foundation of the laboratory. The lab lived long in the shadow of the great results from the first decades of its history, and regaining the attention the laboratory once garnered is today one of the objectives of the research. It was part of J. C. Jacobsen's basic teaching that the brewer who wanted to make progress had to understand science, and this point of view is an essential component of the cooperation between brewery and laboratory.

Today, a great effort is being made to maintain the laboratory's identity, to live up to J. C. Jacobsen's intentions, and to integrate the laboratory as a part of the "Carlsberg family", which the foundation and the brewery use in a common "branding". Therefore, today, the connection between laboratory and brewery goes through the brewery's marketing department and not its production department. At the same time, it is important for the laboratory not to close in on itself but to be an active part of a number of projects in collaboration with universities or industrial enterprises.

It was almost symbolic for the laboratory's new line, which actually stands firmly on the Brewer's ideas, that, in 2015, during cellar restoration work a couple of old bottles of beer were found which appeared to be produced with the "pure" yeast that Emil Christian Hansen had cultivated in 1883. The laboratory succeeded in isolating living yeast cells in the old bottles, and the brewery was then able to produce beer—naturally, called 1883—with the unique taste from that time. It has already become a great success in Denmark, Norway, and England, and will also be launched in China.

However, even more important than reconstructing beer from the past is creating an active research environment that contributes to both the brewery and society with trailblazing new research within the laboratory's research fields. The history of the Carlsberg Research Laboratory, therefore, is not a side story in relation to the foundation and the brewery. It is the story of a central research institution, which was an innovation in its time, whose survival for the benefit of the brewery and society was a primary reason the Brewer established the Carlsberg Foundation. Today, with its most recent results, both its own and those achieved in collaboration with others, it helps to create prestige around the name of Carlsberg and to enhance the quality of its products.

5.12 The Carlsberg Foundation and Other Commercial Foundations

The Carlsberg Foundation was unique in its time as a large foundation to support science and later, after taking over the Carlsberg Breweries in 1888, as the first commercial foundation. Today, it is far from alone in supporting Danish science or being a large and well-known foundation in Denmark. A series of other and significantly larger private foundations based on business also distribute substantial research funding. The largest foundations today in Denmark with annual disbursements of more than a billion Danish crowns are the Novo Nordisk Foundation,[49] the Realdania Foundation, and the A. P. Møller og Hustru Chastine MC-Kinney Møllers Fond til Almene Formålfonden. They are followed by an intermediate group with disbursements between one half and a billion Danish crowns (the Villum Foundation, Tryg Foundation, Lundbeck Foundation, and Nordea Foundation). In terms of size, the Carlsberg Foundation is in a third group, together with the Augustinus Foundation and the Velux Foundation with disbursements of around DKK 3–400 million. Measured in disbursements, the Carlsberg Foundation is the eighth-largest with overall payouts in 2017 of around DKK 400 million. Most of these foundations are closely connected to great business enterprises but have chosen a different model for the exercise of their influence than the Carlsberg Foundation.

A difficulty in connection with the designation of board members of the Carlsberg Foundation is its dual function of distributing the Foundation's

[49]On this, see Den danske fondsanalyse 2017.

means for science-related purposes while, at the same time, participating in the management of Carlsberg A/S from which the money comes. The Foundation's former chairman Povl Krogsgaard-Larsen saw his service on the Foundation's executive board not in its own right but as "a mandate from the Danish Royal Academy...." Therefore, he spoke and acted on the Academy's behalf.[50] There is, however, no consensus or clear practice as to whether there is such a mandate.

Of the important part of the Foundation's duties, which have to do with disbursements for scientific purposes, a former chairman P. Brandt Rehberg said that, "of course, they cannot—five men—cover all the sciences .... They have to ask ...." At the same time, he pointed out that the board's members had "a very broad familiarity with what happened in Danish science...." Just as important for Brandt Rehberg, who—as mentioned above—was in his time a key person in connection with the consolidation of Carlsberg and DFB, was that "they were to be a board for a big commercial business and earn money .... They were the ones who were to earn money with the help of the breweries". This was said in 1975, when Brandt Rehberg had stepped down from the Foundation's executive board. He talked about the old days and had not himself experienced the new era in which the Foundation board was part of a professional board of the merged Carlsberg and Tuborg.[51]

Rehberg's considerations are now more than forty years old. Even though the Foundation today is no longer the economic sole owner of Carlsberg A/S, the Foundation, due to its possession of a majority of votes, still has the controlling influence of the Carlsberg brewery concern. Therefore, the Foundation board ultimately bears the responsibility for administration and must ensure there is a forceful CEO and a competent executive board in the brewery.

Since 1977, when for the first time the chairmanship of the Carlsberg Foundation was combined with the presidency of the Carlsberg A/S board, the Foundation's chairperson has been the key figure of the board and the main contact to the brewery's management. The viability of this construction in which the chairperson of the Carlsberg Foundation is also the chairperson for and, thus, a driving force in the brewery's board presumes that the Danish Royal Academy can provide a member with the rare combination of a high level of scientific knowledge and insight into business and corporate management. This construction is unusual. Most Danish foundations that control

---

[50]Loc. cit., p. 222.

[51]He also express the truth with reference to the rules at that time, that, when you "are first elected into the Carlsberg Foundation, you remain there until you step down yourself, possibly far too long".

a big company opt for a solution in which the company board is completely separate from the foundation board with an independent chairman and no or only a limited representation of members from the foundation board. This is also the normal "good governance" recommendation.

While most other commercial foundations have changed their practice, the Carlsberg Foundation since 1970 maintains an arrangement in which members of the Carlsberg Foundation are on the board of both the foundation and Carlsberg A/S.[52]

It has been observed that this Carlsberg Foundation model is not in complete compliance with modern recommendations for good foundation management, and the Foundation, therefore, has had to justify this choice to the supervisory authorities. The justification is brief and goes like this: "It is of crucial significance for the Foundation's board to have an exhaustive familiarity with the operations of Carlsberg A/S. Therefore, all board members in the Foundation are current members of the board for Carlsberg A/S". This argumentation has historical reasons, and the present construction also secures—the board argues—an equal position among the Foundation board members. It is also argued that the members of the board of the Foundation guarantee that Carlsberg A/S respects the values of J. C. Jacobsen and keeps it HQ in Denmark. It is also mentioned that the board of the Foundation is particularly observant in maintaining the values of J. C. Jacobsen, which may seem more distant to board members of Carlsberg A/S with a foreign background. Additional advantages are that the professors can add another dimension to the board's work than the purely business one and that greater clarity as to responsibility is thus achieved.

A disadvantage for the board of an international firm like Carlsberg A/S, on the other hand, is that representation consisting of five members of the same nationality and uniform academic skills and university background does not provide the variation necessary to add professional knowledge to the board. This means that the board must supply itself with a corresponding number of members with international management experience. Thus, the board of Carlsberg A/S, which must include a similar number of employee representatives, is very large in relation to what is otherwise considered expedient. In weighing the advantages and disadvantages of the Carlsberg Foundation's mode of representation on the company board, opinions are divided. There are the positive arguments of the Foundation board, on one hand, as against modern practices of "good governance", the actual practice

---

[52]Serving on the board of the Carlsberg Foundation is thus a time consuming job with a total remuneration (including fee as member of the board of the Carlsberg A/S significantly above (and normally in addition to) a professor's salary.

of most commercial foundations, and also the skepticism expressed by former Carlsberg CEOs, other business members or executives from the Carlsberg A/S board, who are less convinced of the importance for the business of the input from the "professors".[53]

In October 2007, when the rumors about the takeover of S&N surfaced, the newspaper *Financial Times* rewrote one of Carlsberg's slogans and described Carlsberg A/S's board as "the weirdest board in the world". This may be a more or less charming way of indicating unprofessionalism in and of itself, but it should also give rise to reflection.

On the other hand, professionalism also has its limits. It is worth remembering how Robert H. Jackson, US Supreme Court Justice and later the American chief prosecutor at the Nuremberg trials, is quoted as having said during a debate on US business policy in 1940: "In fact, I don't know which brand of wisdom I distrust the most: That of the theorists who have studied a business but never run one, or that of the executives who have run a business but who have never studied it".[54]

Behind the desire to maintain the Foundation's current full representation may be traced a creditable endeavor to live up to the responsibility of upholding Jacobsenian values, accompanied by a certain mistrust of the predominantly foreign board members' understanding of the Brewer's unique spirit and the brewery's national significance. Flemming Besenbacher expressed something similar as a justification for "the dominion of professors as we a little sarcastically and also condescendingly call it". More generally, he stated as a defense of the very foundation construction in 2011:

"The recent financial crises have shown that we do not need to be so completely blinded by those who come from business schools and boards that have been a part of an old-boys network.... I think we can say that, here, too, the Brewer was ahead of his time. When he had to admit that his son Carl could not take over the firm and run it in Brewer Jacobsen's spirit, he established the world's first commercial foundation. It was not populated with bankers and lawyers—the danger would be too much focus on short-term profit. Instead, he went to science at the universities in order to find people for the Foundation board, and, as far as I can see, it is evidence that,

[53]Former vice-president of the Carlsberg A/S board, Mollerup (1992), p. 79 f, said of the "professors" on the board that, regardless of the fact that they do not have experience from business life, they "often [had] with their academic schooling and background points of view and assessments that attacked problems in a refreshing and untraditional way that, every so often, might give the rest of us occasion to take a more grounded position into consideration.".

[54]Quoted by Robert S. Weinberg in Tremblay and Tremblay (2005), p. IX.

even then, Jacobsen understood the importance of broad thinking on the board".[55]

Other large Danish commercial foundations have made other choices. In particular, one may point to the huge Novo Nordisk Foundation, which has placed a holding company between the foundation and the business and has the foundation represented in the holding company but not necessarily on the corporate board.

This, however, is not the place to decide this question. It should find its solution in serious reflections on whether the best and most professional and efficient way to staff and to make decisions on a professional board of a worldwide brewing company speaks in favor of substituting the Jacobsen model from 1876 with a model that is more reminiscent of what similar and even bigger Danish foundations do.

5.13 Pursue Perfection

The management of the Carlsberg brewery and the Carlsberg Foundation leadership today seem more transparent and outgoing after the collaboration between foundation and brewery has been intensified in recent years. In 2015, a new deputy chairperson for Carlsberg's board took office. It was one of Denmark's most distinguished businessmen, CEO Lars Rebien Sørensen, who came from Novo Nordisk and, thus, had experience not only with the country's largest firm but also with a foundation-owned business, where they were familiar with insulin, fermentation processes, and other things that had significance for a brewery business. At that point, a change of management was in process that resulted in the designation in 2015 of a Dutchman, Cees t'Hart, as the new Carlsberg CEO and the brewery's first foreign head. He came from a position as CEO of a large Dutch food enterprise, had previously been employed by the international concern Unilever, and has had many international posts. The losses in Russia still had to be cleaned up and new roads to other markets found, first and foremost, in East Asia and India in order to compensate for what was lost by fostering efficiency, development, and growth in the firm. Carlsberg is still losing market shares in Russia. Since 2013, market share fell from 35% to about 31% in this very competitive market.

The appointment of Cees t'Hart was followed by a major change in management at the CFO and middle-management level. Carlsberg A/S was

[55] *Berlingske Tidende*, 28 November 2011.

still challenged by dependence on developments in the Russian market and by the need for increased earnings and growth in Asia to make up for the stagnating European market. There was a need for a reduction of the less efficient parts of the concern and a strengthening of others in order to reduce unnecessary costs.

One objective for the Carlsberg Foundation and, particularly, for the Foundation's current chairman is to exploit the Foundation's potential as a part of promoting the brewery, the Carlsberg Group. With the change of leadership in 2015, the significance of the Foundation chairmanship post for the business has come more and more into the foreground. A professionalization of the board chairperson has occurred whereby the chairperson has also grown closer to the brewery management and actively participates in any change in leadership. Today, the chairmanship needs far more operational and strategic thinking and a sense of "big business" and management, which demands special personal requirements. Not everyone can live up to them. An important but open question in the long term, therefore, is whether the Foundation is capable—and whether it is desirable for it to be capable—of nominating a chairperson who can also meet the requirements of the chairmanship post at Carlsberg A/S.

One possibility is the model from the Orkla days when the brewery chairmanship post at Carlsberg Breweries was filled by a person with business experience (the chairperson of the Carlsberg Foundation acted as deputy chairperson). This, if combined with a reduction of the representation of the Foundation, allows the corporate board to lead professionally by making business decisions with fewer representatives on the board but with the Foundation chairperson represented. However, this is in the future. Respect was created in the Orkla years for the chairmanship post. The relationship between business and foundation was turned topsy-turvy as a part of a transformation process from the Foundation's heretofore more reticent role and by overcoming a traditional distance-taking by the Foundation. Flemming Besenbacher is probably the first chairman for the Foundation with a real program for the management of Carlsberg A/S, which has clearly become the most important part of the chairman's work as a precondition that there is a yield for the Foundation at all.

A professionalization of board work, openness and transparency, communication, diversity on the board, employees with real skills, the use of the Carlsberg 'family' in the branding of the brewery all have high priority with the chairperson. Especially conspicuous just now is the idea of what people already in the first decade of the 2000s called building "a winning Carlsberg culture". This has to do with exploiting the potential in the Foundation's business as a part of Carlsberg's brand in relation to potential customers and, internally, making Carlsberg's employees conscious of belonging to a business that is something special: "Having a well-defined set of values is important. I hear that everywhere in the world. I am not CEO, and I do not tell the world how Carlsberg achieves its goals but from where and how our values and history support the way we run a business. I also see a need to relate how we imagine the world will look in the future. Here, our historical heritage has significance", says Besenbacher.[56]

One challenge in today's beer market is a growing consciousness in consumers about the quality of beer and their willingness to pay more for specialty beers. Quality is not an objective measure but has to do with hitting production specifications that the brewery itself lays down. Seen from this perspective, "ordinary" beer lives up to the standard of a quality product, and this is what Brewer Jacobsen in his time meant when he spoke of quality. He placed great demands on himself for his product, and he would not sell beer that did not live up to those demands. Quality has to do with the fulfillment of one's own objectives, and they can be different; or it may happen that consumers need variation in the form of special beers such as that so-called microbreweries deliver but which Carlsberg can also do. The desire for variation has led to a sort of revolution in the market where thousands of small breweries have popped up, and so-called "craft beer" has been a real competitor to which the major breweries must pay attention. Even in 2003, Carlsberg decided to establish a microbrewery for the production of "craft beer" and a visitor's center in the old brewery buildings in Valby with a view toward "a general elevation of beer culture in Denmark". This has continued with varying fortitude in recent years, and today quality beer, produced at a microbrewery in the old Carlsberg buildings, has broken through as an important part of Carlsberg's selection. On the other hand, Carlsberg does not provide beer for the so-called "discount market" for cheaper sorts of beer with another standard of quality, which constitutes about a fourth of Danish consumption.

It can be a management challenge to find the balance between long-term solutions and the desire to see results in the short term. Before the turn of the millennium, the management culture at Carlsberg, as we have seen, was based on long-term contracts for which it was the exception for the top managers not to remain in place for an extended period of time. Old school Carlsberg CEOs such as Kühle, Peter C. Poulsen, A. W. Nielsen, or Poul J. Svanholm were each responsible for the firm for periods of around twenty years or

[56]Interview with Flemming Besenbacher, *Evernote*, 2 January 2018.

more. That has changed. CEOs come and go and are switched out today at a completely different tempo than before. Sometimes, more short-sighted decisions are made, and often salary and bonus systems are fashioned so that short-term results are more readily apparent. All this cannot help but influence the way Carlsberg is managed, and this means that, today, the board is needed to secure continuity in the firm to just as high a degree as the day-to-day management.

Carlsberg's newest strategy plan is called SAIL'22 with the slogans: "Strengthen the core", "Position for growth", and "Create a winning culture". An important part of the strategy is to penetrate the market with more expensive craft beer, which has been in strong ascendancy in recent years. It may also help to stress how Carlsberg upholds the so-called Jacobsenian values and visions, and naming a series of special beers for Jacobsen is a direct reference to J. C. Jacobsen's quality requirements as they were expressed in the "golden words". Thus, the development of more expensive but also, in the opinion of many, more varied and delicious special beers that are coddled a bit more, all of which bear the Carlsberg name, is a part of branding the brewery. The brewer's demand for perfection is in Carlsberg's 2016 annual report with a smart and almost poetic melding of the words of the American Declaration of Independence on the right to "pursue happiness" and Jacobsen's "golden words": "We pursue perfection every day. We strive to brew better beers, beers that stand at the heart of moments that bring people together. We don't settle for immediate gain when we can create a better tomorrow for all of us. Brewing for a better today and tomorrow. Bringing our purpose to life restores the founder's mentality to our Company. This means that we enthusiastically grow our business and create value for our stakeholders while also having a compelling *raison d'être*".

It did not take CEO Cees t'Hart long to orient himself with respect to Carlsberg's long history as a brand. On the occasion of the brewery's 170th anniversary in 2017, he said:

> We would like to use our 170th anniversary to celebrate the past and toast the future. Carlsberg has engaged in brewing in order to create a better day today and tomorrow since 1847. A better day today through better beer and a better day tomorrow through investments in knowledge and sustainability. Today's revival allows even more people to experience our founder's unique mentality and how he raised the bar and shared with the world.[57]

---

[57] From *Newsroom Carlsberg* 2017.

Is Carlsberg the right size today? Carlsberg is the world's third-largest brewery but with very great distance to the world's largest brewery amalgamation (of Anheuser-Busch, Inbev, and SABMiller), which possesses since 2016 around 30% of the world market with virtually the entire US. There is less distance to the next closest competitor, Heineken, with about 9%. Carlsberg's share of the world market is estimated at about 6%. It is paradoxical and thought-provoking that breweries that were originally smaller than Carlsberg, Interbrew (which grew to become ABInbev (ABI)) or Heineken, ended up becoming larger than Carlsberg. They entered earlier into the race to buy up breweries. At that point, the charter and the Foundation board's reverence for its capital requirement became a hindrance to expansion. But the foundation construction has also had a different, positive effect on the business. It secured Carlsberg A/S's survival as a Danish firm with headquarters in Denmark, and it protects against anyone else from taking control of Carlsberg. On this point, it has pursued its great mission and demonstrated its tenacity. Foundation board members come and go, but the Foundation persists; and, now for 130 years, it has been able to preserve the brewery from buyouts and maintained Carlsberg as "our beer". That was what the Brewer wanted, and it would fail in its task if the company and the Foundation one day decided to sell Carlsberg.

As an international firm with 41,000 employees, Carlsberg is something completely different from the brewery that J. C. Jacobsen turned over to the Carlsberg Foundation to ensure the quality of the beer. A sale of the Foundation's assets in Carlsberg would create a very rich foundation, and it would get rid of any business concerns, but it would also be a prioritization of the Foundation over the brewery. This cannot happen without an extensive discussion of whether the Foundation and the Academy would betray the Brewer's confidence in the Royal Academy as an institution, whose independence and judgment he respected to such a degree that he gave the Academy the overall responsibility for the Foundation and the designation of its board. On the other hand, it may be contemplated whether it makes sense to pretend one is heading a brewery that, in reality, is a completely different place than Jacobsen had imagined, one that is managed in a completely different way and according to completely different principles than his. It may also happen that the market is developing internationally in a way that favors very large concerns, so that Carlsberg cannot win and must resign itself to a reduction of its position to a regional brewery and, consequently, more limited earnings. Therefore, it is still important for the Foundation's board with the dominant influence in Carlsberg A/S to maintain the long view and secure good management of the brewery to ensure profit and to preserve the fundamental values linked to Carlsberg as a business that retains its headquarters in Denmark. Some things may change, but one thing is certain: the beer world, like its product, is "fast moving", and nothing remains the same.

References

Bjerager, A.-L., Krogsgaard-Larsen, P. (2011). *Bryggerens lærling : Povl Krogsgaard-Larsens erindringer*. Gyldendal.

Fraenkel, A. (1897). *Gamle Carlsberg. Et Bidrag til dansk Industrihistorie og industriel Udviklingshistorie*. Hagerup. Odense.

Hatch, M. J., & Schultz, M. (2017). Toward a theory of using history authentically: Historizing the Carlsberg Group. *Administrative Science Quarterly, 4*(62), 657–697.

Hatch, M. J., Schultz, M., & Skov, A.-M. (2015). Organizational identity and culture in the context of managed change: Transformation in the Carlsberg Group, 2009–2013. *Academy of Management Discoveries, 1*(1), 56–68.

Lunde, N. (2008). Hr. Møllers nye mand. Niels Smedegaards revolution på Esplanaden – og på Carlsberg. Copenhagen: Jyllands-Postens Forlag.

Mollerup, E. (1992). *Hvad formanden gør*. Copenhagen: Gyldendal.

Sogner, Berg, Espeli. (2004). *Brytningstider. Storselskapet Orkla 1654–2004*. Orion.

Swinnen, J., & Briski, D. (2017). *Beeronomics. How beer explains the world*. Oxford: Oxford University Press.

Tremblay, V. J., & Tremblay, C. H. (2005). *The U.S. brewing industry. Data and economic analysis*. Massachusetts: Massachusetts Institute of Technology.

Dramatis Personae

Admittedly, the Carlsberg story is primarily a story of men in the old-fashioned binary sense before modern gender theory considerations. That men are in the majority has probably less to do with beer as a product, even though it is certainly a fact that considerably more men than women like to drink beer. Rather, it is due to traditional Danish business practices, which are dominated by men and their networks and the still comparatively small number of women reaching the top echelons of Danish science. In both instances, male domination has been massive, and women appear in this book mostly as invisible wives behind the success. Until now, only four women have been on the executive board of the Carlsberg Foundation, and—with the exception of the present director of the Carlsberg Laboratory—no women have had top positions in the management of the brewery.

The history of Carlsberg continues to be a man's story in the sense that the leading actors, by far, are often high-profiled men who (in addition to managing, talking loudly, and bullying) backstab, conspire with or against, or run down other men. In this way, the history of Carlsberg resembles other business histories. The story plays out, for the most part, in the corridors of power in a Copenhagen suburb called Valby or in the atmospheric headquarters of the Carlsberg Foundation in the center of Copenhagen. We only rarely make excursions to the many women and men found in the engine rooms and bottling plants or other places where beer is produced, packaged, or distributed. On the other hand, it is a story about often rather talented men or, at least, men who know or knew what they wanted and only rarely

D. Tamm, *The Carlsberg Story*,
https://doi.org/10.1007/978-3-030-52670-2

doubted their own abilities even when there might be reasons to do so. This is a book that does not deal in false modesty but with beer and its masters.

Jacobsen Family

J. C. Jacobsen, brewer, patron, founder of Old Carlsberg, founder of the Carlsberg Foundation in 1876, and role model for most of those who have had anything to do with the management of Carlsberg over the years.

Carl Jacobsen, his son, passionate art collector, founder of New Carlsberg, founder of the New Carlsberg Foundation 1901–02.

Helge Jacobsen, son of Carl, director of his father's museum, New Carlsberg Glyptotek, and Chairman of the New Carlsberg Foundation.

Vagn Jacobsen, younger son of Carl, brewery director without influence, troublemaker.

The Carlsberg Foundation

Kristian Erslev, in his time, a famous Danish historian, visionary chairman of the Carlsberg Foundation 1913–1926.

Johannes Pedersen, Semitic philologist and historian of religion, long-serving Chairman of the Carlsberg Foundation 1933–1955.

Niels Bjerrum, chemist, chairman of Carlsberg's professional brewery council 1933–1953 and thereby the Foundation's *éminence gris* in relation to the brewery.

Stig Iuul, legal historian, Chairman of the Carlsberg Foundation 1963–69, tried in vain to control the brewery's almighty CEO, A. W. Nielsen. He died during preliminary negotiations on the merger of Carlsberg and Tuborg.

P. Brandt Rehberg, physiologist, old Resistance fighter during WW II. As an energetic Chairman of the Carlsberg Foundation 1969–1971, he skillfully and efficiently paved the way for the merger with Tuborg.

Kristof Glamann, historian, Chairman of the Carlsberg Foundation 1976–1993, wrote books about the founders of Carlsberg but probably had too heavy a hand with too little understanding of the need for capital, thus leading a restrictive policy that resulted in the brewery missing good business opportunities for a number of years.

Poul Christian Matthiessen, demographer, cautious Chairman of the Carlsberg Foundation 1993–2003, who helped introduce a new management style and establish a framework for cooperation with the Norwegian concern Orkla, which gave Carlsberg a decisive push forward.

Povl Krogsgaard-Larsen, pharmacist, Chairman of the Carlsberg Foundation 2003–2012, dynamic, responsive to Carlsberg's desire for expansion and active in the bold decisions to cease collaboration with Orkla and to initiate the hostile takeover of S&N.

Flemming Besenbacher, nanophysicist, chairman of the Carlsberg Foundation since 2012, driving force in the work today to strengthen Carlsberg's international status and Carlsberg's branding with the help of the Foundation.

Carlsberg

S. A. van der Aa Kühle, J. C. Jacobsen's man, legendary CEO of Carlsberg until his death in 1906, initiator of the agreement of 1903, which eliminated competition between Carlsberg and Tuborg.

Poul C. Poulsen, Carl Jacobsen's man, who succeeded him as a talented and dependable CEO of Carlsberg until 1934.

Frederik Sander, talented but controversial CEO of Carlsberg 1934–1945 with strong opinions that, presented in an unfortunate form, led to his resignation after the Occupation.

Halfdan Hendriksen, well-known Danish businessman with a flair for politics who, as CEO of Carlsberg 1945–1953, became an enduring but reliable transitional figure.

Karsten Skat-Rørdam, correct and proper Danish civil servant who, by what came out as a mistake, became CEO of Carlsberg for two years 1953–1955.

A. W. Nielsen, incredibly talented and diligent but also hypersensitive and difficult CEO of Carlsberg who, in the years after 1956, built up Carlsberg into one of the Denmark's leading firms ready to take over Tuborg and, with Nielsen as the driving force, actually did so.

Poul J. Svanholm, CEO of Carlsberg 1972/4–1996, leading Danish businessman with a powerful personality, who was probably not given sufficient opportunities by the Carlsberg Foundation under Glamann's chairmanship to place Carlsberg internationally.

Flemming Lindeløv, director of Carlsberg 1996–2001, came from the outside with good intentions and helped shift orientation in the brewery toward international expansion and concentration on the sale of beer, amiable and accommodating but not quite suited for the job nor sufficiently confidence-inspiring to be able to last as director over the long term.

Palle Marcus, important Danish business man, active and powerful vice-chairman of Carlsberg A/S 1997 and chairman of Carlsberg Breweries 2001–2002, helped implement decisive changes in Carlsberg's management and business, which were the premise for the brewery's expansion in subsequent years.

Jens Bigum, known as a tough and talented businessman, also a very active and skilled vice-chairman of Carlsberg A/S 2002–2008. With a firm hand, he guided Carlsberg out of its relationship with the Norwegian company Orkla and later helped orchestrate the attack on the Scottish & Newcastle brewery.

Nils Smedegaard Andersen, veteran of Carlsberg. As a very talented CEO 2001–2007, he led Carlsberg with his good contacts and firm, skilled leadership into the international super-league of breweries.

Jørn P. Jensen, CFO of Carlsberg from 2000–2015, who got a key position in connection with the many and (in the opinion of some) occasionally bold investments and purchases in those years.

Jørgen Buhl Rasmussen, CEO of Carlsberg 2007–2015 and thus the person with the responsibility for constructing Carlsberg's organization after the acquisition of the Russian company Baltika.

Others

H. C. Ørsted, world-famous Danish physicist, J. C. Jacobsen's idol as a scientist and as a citizen.

J. N. Madvig, classical philologist, president of the Danish Royal Academy in 1876.

Louis Pasteur, world-renowned chemist and microbiologist, whose yeast studies were trailblazing for beer production, J. C. Jacobsen's international hero.

Emil Christian Hansen, outstanding Danish microbiologist who, in 1883, discovered how to isolate yeast cells, so yeast could be cultivated for use in beer production.

Benny Dessau, CEO at Tuborg 1894–1937. With respect to Carlsberg, he was a sometimes worrying but talented businessman and the dynamic leader of Tuborg.

Herbert Jerichow, son-in-law of Benny Dessau who succeeded Dessau as CEO of Tuborg. He endorsed countless complaints about alleged breaches of the principle of equality between the breweries but, at the same time, was an enterprising brewery manager who, in the years up to 1959, tried to modernize and make efficient Tuborg's production apparatus.

Bernt Hjejle, barrister, excellent jurist and chairman of Tuborg (DFB) and, thus, the head negotiator for that side on the merger of the breweries in 1970.

Archives

For anyone who would write the history of the Carlsberg Foundation and the Foundation's management of Carlsberg, the primary source of knowledge is the Foundation's archives, which contain unique material that illuminates the relationship between the Foundation and the brewery over the years. It is all found in boxes but not everything is exactly where you might think it is. It is a little like what they said about English military supplies during the Crimean War: everything was there, just not where one would expect to find it. But once one has found one's way around the files, it appears clearly from the comprehensive minutes of meetings that the 'academics' made decisions after thorough consideration. As a rule and especially in the older period, the minutes are very thorough and attempt to repeat exactly the words and style of the speaker. The correspondence is also very rich, so the archives provide an opportunity to an extent that is unusual for business concerns to understand and analyze the decisions made.

This account is based to a wide extent on records in the Carlsberg Foundation's (CF) archives. Here may be found the minutes from the Foundation's meetings since 1876 in consecutive sequence, cited as CFP. The minutes of the brewery council 1922–1969 are cited as BRP. Other materials in the archives are marked as A: general archives and B: personal archives. Records from the Danish Ministry of Justice and the Department of Civil Affairs have only to an insignificant extent been accessible or contained material of significance. The author also has had access to some case material at the Danish Business Authority.

D. Tamm, *The Carlsberg Story*,
https://doi.org/10.1007/978-3-030-52670-2

Bibliography

Almind, G., & Lindsten, J. (2011). *Novo nordisk fondens historie: Funderinger* [Eng. trans. Novo Nordisk Foundation, 2012]. Hellerup: Novo Nordisk Fonden.

Bergh, T., Espeli, H., & Sogner, K. (2004). *Brytningstider: Storselskabet Orkla 1654–2004*. Oslo: Orion Forlag.

Bjerager, A.-L. (2011). *Brygger for folket* [Eng. trans. The People's Brewer, 2011]. Copenhagen: Gyldendal.

Bjerager, A.-L., & Krogsgaard-Larsen, P. (2011). *Bryggerens lærling: Povl Krogsgaard-Larsens erindringer*. Copenhagen: Gyldendal.

Brøndum, C. (1978). *Grundsætningerne for Ølbryggeriet tilligemed Beskrivelse over den i Kjøbenhavn meest brugelige Brygningsmaade* (Facsimile ed.). Copenhagen: Scoop.

Carlsbergfondet. (1930). *Carlsbergfondet 1876–1926: Et Jubilæumsskrift udgivet af Carlsbergfondets Direktion* (Vol. 1–2). Copenhagen: Carlsbergfondet.

Chakravarty, D. (2016). *Jo–Carlsbergfruen, der gik sine gene vegne*. Copenhagen: Gyldendal.

Christiansen Svenn Eske. (1976/77). … et liv i byggeriets tjeneste. Strejftog, n.d.

Christensen, P. T., Schoop, K., & Lindhe, J. M. (2018). *Svenn Eske Christensen-Velfærdsarkitekten*. Copenhagen: Aristo.

Dahlberg, R., Iversen, M., & Lindén, T. (Eds.). (1999). *Bryggerne og de tre store udfordringer. Bryggeriforeningen i 100 år*. Copenhagen: Bryggeriforeningen.

Drachmann, E. ([1882] 2011). Jørgensen, L. D. (Ed.). *Den der elsker mest. Dagbogsblade skrevet af Ellen Drachmann f. Bentzon, April 1882 til April 1945*. Copenhagen: Høst.

Erichsen, J., & Tamm, D. (2015). *Grever, baroner og husmænd. Opgøret med de store danske godser*. Copenhagen: Gylendal.

D. Tamm, *The Carlsberg Story*,
https://doi.org/10.1007/978-3-030-52670-2

Fraenkel, A. (1907). *Gamle Carlsberg: Et bidrag til dansk Industrihistorie og industriel Udviklingshistorie*. Odense: Hagerup.
Glamann, K. (1993). *Carlsbergfondet siden 1970* [Eng. trans. The Carlsberg Foundation since 1970, 1994]. Copenhagen: Carlsbergfondet.
Glamann, K. (1997). *Vores øl og hele verdens: Carlsberggruppen siden 1970*. Copenhagen: Gyldendal.
Glamann, K. (2002). *En blandet landhandel*. Copenhagen: Gyldendal.
Jacobsen, J. C. (1911). *Et Mindeskrift*. Copenhagen.
Jacobsen, K. (1997). *Svanholm*. Copenhagen: Gyldendal.
Jacobsen, Kirsten. (2000). *Den brutale redelighed–en bog om Ole Scherfig*. Copenhagen: Gyldendal.
Johansen, H. C., & Møller, A. M. (2005). *Fonde som fundament for dansk industri*. Odense: Syddansk Universitetsforlag.
Kerte, J. (2017). *"Tuborgrøveriet" in Forbryderjagt: På sporet af morderne med vor tids dansk kriminalteknikere*. Copenhagen: Lindhardt og Ringhof.
Knudsen, M. (2010). *Videnskabens mand: Formidleren, fysiologen og forskningsaktivisten Poul Brandt Rehberg*. Århus: Aarhus Universitets forlag.
Matthiessen, P. C. (2017). *Følg med tiden: Ikke med strømmen*. Copenhagen: Gads Forlag.
Nielsen, I. K. (1990). *En Bryggeriarbejders Liv: Erindringer*. Copenhagen: Nyt Nordiske Forlag.
Nielsen, N. J. (1997). *Tuborg. Arbejdsliv og dagligdag 1955–95: Dissertation*. Copenhagen: Det Samfundsvidenskabelige Fakultet, Københavns Universitet.
Pedersen, J. (1942). *Carlsbergfondet* [Eng. trans. The Carlsberg Foundation, 1956]. Copenhagen: Munksgaard.
Poltisk revy (1978). *Politisk revys bryggerigruppe: Bryggeriarbejderne og ølkapitalen. Elefanterne drager vestpå*. Copenhagen: Politisk Revy.
Steenstrup, J. (1921). *Carl Jacobsen og hans Fader: en Skildring af to danske Borgeres Udvikling: Efter Breve og Erindring*. M.P. Madsens Boghandel.
Stemann, H. (1930). *F. Mehldal og hans Venner (117 ff.)* (Vol. 4) Odense: Hagerup.
Tamm, D. (1984). *Retsopgøret efter besættelsen*. Copenhagen: Jurist- og Økonomforbundets Forlag.
Thomsen, S. (2011). *"De gyldne ord og moderne governanceprincipper" in Carlsbergfondet 2011* (pp. 108–115). Copenhagen: Carlsberg.
Tremblay, V. J., & Tremblay, C. H. (2005). *The U.S. brewing industry: Data and economic analysis*. Massachusetts: Massachusetts Institute of Technology.
Verstl, I., & Faltermeier, E. (2016). *The beer monopoly: How brewers bought and built for world domination*. Nuremberg: Brauwelt.
Wilson, R. G., & Gourvisch, T. R. (2005). *The dynamics of the international brewing industry since 1800*. London and NY: Routledge.
Zanker-von Meyer, D. (1982). *Die Bauten von J. C. und Carl Jacobsen*. Munich and Berlin: Deutscher Kunstverlag.

The manufacturer's authorised representative in the EU is Springer Nature Customer Service Centre GmbH, Europaplatz 3, 69115 Heidelberg, Germany. If you have any concerns regarding our products, please contact ProductSafety@springernature.com

Printed and bound by CPI Group (UK) Ltd, Croydon, CR0 4YY
22/09/2026
02220945-0003